TALES FROM THE
GREEK DRAMA

"The voluminous learning of past ages (has) to be recast in easier and more manageable forms. And if Greek literature is not to pass away, it seems to be necessary that in every age some one who has drunk deeply from the original fountain should renew the love of it in the world, and once more present that old life, with its great ideas and great actions, its creations in politics and in art, like the distant remembrances of youth, before the delighted eyes of mankind."

BENJAMIN JOWETT
Introduction to his translation of
Thucydides, Oxford-Clarendon Press, 1881

TALES FROM THE GREEK DRAMA

By H. R. JOLLIFFE

BOLCHAZY-CARDUCCI Publishers, Inc.
Wauconda, Illinois

©1981 Bolchazy-Carducci Publishers, Inc.

Reprint of the 1962 Chilton Books edition
Third Printing, 1998

Published by
Bolchazy-Carducci Publishers, Inc.
1000 Brown Street, Wauconda, Illinois 60084

Printed in the United States of America
1998
by United Graphics

ISBN 0-86516-013-9

```
          Library of Congress Cataloging-in-Publication
Jolliffe, H. R. (Harold Richard).  1090-
     Tales from the Greek drama / by H.R. Jolliffe.
        p.    cm.
     ISBN 0-86516-013-9 (alk. paper)
     1. Greek drama--Adaptations.  2. Mythology, Greek--Fiction.
  I. Title.
  PA3628.J65   1998
  813'.54--dc21                                         98-34040
                                                            CIP
```

To PEGGY

ACKNOWLEDGMENTS

I am deeply grateful to my friend Irwin R. Blacker, a novelist of many talents, for his long insistence that his old professor should undertake such a book as this. I also want to express my sincerest thanks to Dr. Clyde W. Wilkinson, of the University of Florida, and to Mrs. W. Cameron Meyers, the wife of one of my colleagues at Michigan State University, for reading most of the manuscript and making many helpful comments and suggestions.

AUTHOR'S PREFACE

The ancient drama was a fusion of all the arts. Unfortunately its music, dance, scenery, masks, and costumes have all been lost beyond recall. Even its poetry disappears, as all poetry must, in translation. Yet if we could recreate the drama exactly as it was—and we can't—its ancient form would seem strange and alien to the modern theater-goer. The conventions of the Greek drama would obscure the story and confuse the viewer. But the story is the thing, and its force lies not on the printed page or what happens on the stage but in the effect it has on the hearts and minds of men.

Audiences, according to Victor Hugo, are made up of thinkers who demand character, women who demand passion, and the mob which demands action. The Greek drama offers all these and more. But the thrill it offers is not to be found in the dead synopses of a handbook of mythology. These are just little cultural pills that some take without pleasure for the good they are supposed to do. The student of Greek gets a great deal more from the plays, but when he is toiling through grammar and syntax, the stories come too slowly to explode full force. However much he comes to appreciate them later, he misses the excitement of fast discovery.

Most people approach Greek drama through its many translations—most of which add some "stage directions" to compensate for the missing action. Unfortunately, such readers are sometimes frustrated by trying to view things through a stained-glass window of many obscure allusions. I have tried to solve this problem and bring to my readers more of the instant impact of a modern play or novel. For that was what these plays had 2,400 years ago—immediate impact. Greek audiences did not have to consult handbooks or footnotes or solve literary mysteries. They came, they saw, and they reacted to the play as it unfolded before them.

To illustrate part of the problem I might cite an example in reverse. The satirist Bob Newhart has an amusing sketch in which he plays a public relations man telephoning President Lincoln about what to say at Gettysburg. Why do we laugh? Only because we can put into the pot of total comprehension *our own* knowledge of Lincoln, the Address, and the foibles of Madison Avenue. Otherwise the sketch would be meaningless. A more sombre illustration might be a scene in an old movie where a couple stand by a steamer rail in the moonlight. As they move away, a life-preserver is revealed marked "S.S. Titanic."

By the same token, the literal translation of a Greek reference to the "nightingale" or the "riddling songstress" is no translation at all except for the person who already knows the legend of Itys or the story of the Sphinx. To give the reader more of the original feeling and impact of these plays, then, I have written what might be called "semantic translations."

They come mostly from the lines of the Greek, whose thought and feeling I have tried to translate faithfully. But I have edited out some minor points of purely ancient interest and sometimes condensed the material into what seems a more modern reading tempo. Most of what does not come

Author's Preface

from the written lines would have been expressed by setting, voice, gesture and action. For a play is far more than its mere written dialog; otherwise the whole production would have been superfluous. There remain, as I mentioned above, some things the ancient playwrights neglected to say simply because everyone in those days knew them. Rather than clutter these stories with footnotes for the modern reader, I have woven these ideas into the story wherever I could.

But I have not been creative—merely interpretive, striving like a conscientious actor to bring out the full flavor of meaning. Even so, no two actors present precisely the same Hamlet. Some interpretations have to be made. So where several interpretations are possible I sometimes make a choice rather than leave a puzzle.

If some deplore this as "instant drama," I can only say that the impact of drama should be immediate. Otherwise it becomes not an experience, but a study. All translations are substitutes of a kind for the original. But I hope these stories will be more than substitutes and will serve as a pleasant introduction, not only to the more traditional translations, but also to further exploration of some of the wonders of ancient Greece.

H. R. JOLLIFFE

East Lansing, Michigan

CONTENTS

INTRODUCTION
Page 1

Euripides
MEDEA
Page 11

Euripides
ALCESTIS
Page 45

Sophocles
OEDIPUS THE KING
Page 71

Sophocles
OEDIPUS AT COLONUS
Page 95

Sophocles
ANTIGONE
Page 121

Euripides
HIPPOLYTUS
Page 151

Euripides and *Euripides the Younger*
IPHIGENIA IN AULIS
Page 183

Sophocles
AJAX
Page 213

Aeschylus
AGAMEMNON
Page 239

Sophocles and *Aeschylus*
ELECTRA
Page 271

THE THEATER OF THE GREEKS
Page 305

TALES FROM THE
GREEK DRAMA

INTRODUCTION

No spot in history ever shone with more concentrated brilliance than the Athens of 2,400 years ago. It was almost as if men like Lincoln, Einstein, Freud, Shakespeare, and Michelangelo had all been fellow townsmen. New ideas were exploding everywhere. Democracy had ousted tyranny; the poorest citizens enjoyed a new equality under the law. As freemen, they had beaten back the might of Persia. Athens had become the school and jewel of Hellas, her glories symbolized in the building of the Parthenon.

This was the golden age, though it had a few shadows. Women had little share in this brave new life. Democracy also excluded slaves and developed a weakness for rabblerousers. Some taint was attached to Athens' new-found wealth, and her allies, freed from the Persian threat, soon began to chafe at her arrogant yoke. Her glory and honor were further diminished during the Peloponnesian War.

THE BIRTH OF DRAMA

It was in this brief golden age that drama was born and reached such heights as were never equaled in the next two thousand years. *Drama* means "action," but the Greek drama grew out of what had been purely lyric poetry sung by a dancing chorus. Some sort of dialog had been created earlier by adding a single "actor," but a living story was hardly possible, since this actor had no one to contend with except the chorus.

Aeschylus broke this static pattern by adding a second "contender" (a *deuteragonist* to the *protagonist*) and later adopted Sophocles' innovation of a third (*tritagonist*). With these three actors wearing masks and each playing several roles, many lines of action became possible, and the drama began to move.

THE GREAT TRIO

Aeschylus, Sophocles, Euripides—these were the men who developed the drama and shaped the course of Western literature.

Aeschylus wrote his tragedies in groups of threes, and we now have one play each from four of his trilogies. However, they are too strange and plotless for most modern tastes, too thunderous in their poetic imagery. But we also have his final trilogy complete, beginning with *Agamemnon*. It thunders, too, but with a more dramatic story.

Sophocles worked on a less grand scale. He broke up the massive trilogies into single, independent plays, each a masterpiece of unity and deft construction. In every play he exalted some heroic figure battling the forces of fate. "I picture men as they ought to be," he is supposed to have said. "Euripides paints them as they are."

And this was true. What Euripides lost in tragic grandeur he gained in psychological realism. He focused on real people with all their pretensions, weaknesses, and conflicts, and found a new nobility in such "inferior" beings as women, foreigners, and slaves. At times his plots and structures seem confused or strangely archaic. But his realism makes him seem most modern of all.

We now have seven plays each from Aeschylus and Sophocles, and nineteen ascribed to Euripides. Some are still staged today—even filmed and televised. And all of them, with many twists and disguises, live on in thousands of other stories, for no author today is wholly free from their influence.

AN AGE OF FERMENT

The exciting world in which these three men lived was strangely like our own. For in many ideas and institutions, Athens was almost a test tube or pilot study for the modern world.

It was an age of question, discovery, and punctured beliefs. For one thing, men were learning the difference between *custom* and *nature*. Nature, they found, had unchangeable laws regardless of place or time. And these were to be learned by observation rather than by myth or priestcraft. But custom was full of man-made laws, beliefs, traditions, and values that varied strangely the farther men traveled.

Today the early science seems crude, but it broke the shackles of superstition. Men were mapping the earth and predicting eclipses of the moon. One of Euripides' teachers dared to say the sun was no god but a ball of fire, bigger, at least, than the Peloponnesus. Others said matter was indestructible, and went on to outline a sort of atomic theory. Still others were tracing the natural course and cause of many diseases. How much faster the world might have moved if such inquiring men had never been banished by mobs who proceeded to burn their books.

THE FADING GODS

The Greek dramas dealt mostly with the woes of more ancient kings who belonged to an age of gods and heroes. But the enlightened Athenian was tending to lose any literal belief in the immoral, capricious Olympian gods of that earlier day. Even Aeschylus seems monotheistically inclined, often speaking of God in the singular or exalting Zeus in a class by himself.

Sophocles may have been more agnostic than most men think, for he seldom made the traditional gods a motivating force in his plays. He focused more on the divinity of the uncompromising hero. The greatest wonder on earth is man, his chorus sings, for he has conquered all but death. Sophocles' heaven on earth was the well-tempered state where "justice of the gods" prevailed.

When the Olympian gods reappear full force in the plays of Euripides, they are not to be taken too literally. In fact, Euripides often debunks them with subtle irony. Sophisticated members of his audience, at least, must have taken his gods as symbols which were no more real than the Devil himself in a modern play. If the fundamentalists wanted to believe in them, well, there they were, acting as badly as they did in Homer.

FROM RITUAL TO MORALITY

While the Greek dramas are moral and do carry traces of myth and ritual it would be misleading to call them "religious" or to say that the Greeks went to the theater as we go to church. They were performed at a spring festival for Dionysus, and according to modern theory they grew from rites for the vegetation god, who waxes too strong and is destroyed, but rises again each spring. But holy days easily grow into holidays. And it is hard to think of audiences as "worshipers" when they shout for encores or hiss and pelt what they don't like off the stage.

These plays, though moral, deal with crimes. Like modern psychology, they probe the abnormal to learn about the normal. Most of these crimes still occur today, as every newsman knows. Greek tragedy magnifies them, yet holds them at a distance. Family murders, adultery, incest, and revenge are portrayed as the deeds of far-off kings and heroes, the sons or scions of the gods. They struggle with fate and fall with a mighty crash that rocks lesser mortals with horror and pity. It was only Euripides who brought them closer. His heroes were made of more common cloth—his fellow Athenians in ancient disguise—hating, loving, and reacting in ways all men could recognize. And the recognition must have been painful at times.

Drama was immoral in the eyes of the philosopher Plato. He would have banished poets from his ideal state. But Aristotle thought tragedy somehow purified the minds and the emotions of spectators and made them more serene. He called this purification a *katharsis*.

MAN, FATE, AND THE GODS

Man's agonized question in every crisis is "Why?" What are these hidden forces that push him around, impel his acts, bring on his doom? Are they blind or knowing, unfair or just? To this vast area of unknown causation the Greeks gave such names as Fate or Necessity. Not that they really believed the Fates were three old sisters spinning the thread of life —that was obviously just a poetic figure. The Greeks were as much puzzled as we are.

Any Greek who believed in an over-all scheme of Divine Justice had to find the evidence for such a system here on earth; he had no belief in the kind of afterlife where accounts are squared. One or two mortals in mythology might have become gods, but most of the dead wandered in Hades, beneath the earth. There, with nothing but memories, they lingered as cheerless, colorless shadows—exactly as we meet them in our dreams. "I would rather be the lowest serf of the meanest man on earth than king among the dead," the ghost of Achilles tells Odysseus in the *Odyssey*.

Aeschylus struggles most with the riddle of Divine Justice. He seems to represent Fate and the gods as one, working their will through men. This view leaves man with little will of his own. He does not commit sin so much as he is driven to it—usually to avenge or pay for other sins. And these other sins may not be his at all. As in the old blood-feud days, when families took vengeance on each other regardless of who was responsible for the original wrong, the gods seemed to keep family accounts, and children had to pay for the sins of their fathers.

This idea of ancestral sin, however, is not as basic a theme in Greek drama as is commonly supposed. In *Agamemnon*, where it seems most prominent, the question is raised: if evils are needed to purge other evils where will the chain of evil end? And it ends, symbolically, in the third play of the trilogy when justice is turned over to the courts of men, and the divine avengers (the Furies) are retired from active service to a shrine and called "The Kindly Ones."

Sophocles clearly gives man a will (though Freudians have taken it away again). The idea of hereditary guilt exists in the *Oedipus* plays by legendary necessity, but if we compare these plays with the older legends, we find that Sophocles actually played down the theme. Euripides ridicules the whole idea. True, a character may wonder what sins of his ancestors the gods are making him pay for in misery. But he is just a character making a traditional rationalization rather than a mouthpiece of the author's ideas. Beneath the surface, Euripides seems to say that fate lies less in our stars than in ourselves.

It was generally believed, however, that the future in its entirety was already determined as surely as the past. The Greeks thought of fate in terms of a hidden script that life must follow rigidly. The script was known by the gods, and occasionally bits of it were revealed to man. It is interesting to note that while the gods knew what would happen in the future, in most cases they were powerless to change the course of events. They were omniscient but not omnipotent.

THE ORACLE AT DELPHI

When the gods chose to reveal part of the script, it was Apollo and his priests who communicated with man. Apollo's great center of revelation was the oracle at Delphi. And this institution was no mere legend. It was a real and powerful organization, with a multi-million-dollar endowment, which lasted down to the Christian era.

For many centuries, men from all parts of Greece journeyed to Delphi with their questions and submitted them at the temple. The Pythian priestess would mount a tripod over some vapors and go into a trance, crying out her answers. A temple priest would promptly translate her inspired utterances into poetry—often so obscured by metaphor that the answer might fit almost any eventuality.

The Delphic oracle was a potent unifying force in a disunited Greece. It probably had a widespread secret-service network, for its wisdom was highly regarded. Nevertheless, it was fairly common knowledge that kings and politicians could bribe the oracle and rig the answers. Perhaps only Euripides dared to say that Apollo himself might be evil, but the integrity of his priests and soothsayers was freely suspected.

THE GOLDEN MEAN

The basic plot of almost every story ever written can be boiled down to a single phrase—"man up against it." And "it" can be any combination of forces—inner drives and complexes or outside pressures from nature, the gods, blind fate, men, or society as a whole. In the face of these pressures—and the Greeks did not differentiate between them as much as we—a man's best defense was *sophrosyne*. We can't quite translate that word (though we sometimes try with "wisdom," "moderation" or "restraint") because we don't have quite the same idea. But it was an all-pervasive one with the Greeks, as "adjustment" is with some psychologists today.

Our big difficulty lies in our unfortunate tendency toward black-and-white thinking. We have two mental bins labeled "good" and "bad" into which we sort almost everything. And we pride ourselves on our wisdom if we have a third bin labeled "shades of gray."

The Greeks had a different, more flexible pattern. They thought of possible modes of conduct as lying along lines of many gradations. Both ends were bad; the midpoint or "golden mean" was good—hence wise. They believed that hidden forces in general, just like nature, tended to punish any excess. Starvation and gluttony could both prove fatal. To be a spendthrift was to "miss the mark" (the Greek verb for "sin") as badly on one side as to be a miser was to miss it on the other. The meek deserved to be trampled as much as tyrants deserved to be toppled.

HYBRIS AND *NEMESIS*

Society, nature, fate, and the gods—or, if you like, the whole scheme of things—tended to punish excess of any kind. Thus we get the principle of *hybris* and *nemesis*. *Hybris* is getting too far out of line or "too big for one's britches." *Nemesis* is literally a reckoning, a squaring of the account. In the Greek plays, a character whose deeds, pride, ambition, or fame are too great and godlike (*hybris*) is likely to anger "the jealous gods," who then strike him down (*nemesis*). Of course, the whole idea is a much broader one, more like the principle of equilibrium which runs through most of the sciences.

As I said before, *sophrosyne* bears some resemblance to our shibboleth of "adjustment." But great men have usually been maladjusted, and so are Sophocles' heroes. Their virtues—whether a passion for truth, humanity, or honor—are excesses which must be punished by fate. Oedipus' obsession with the truth brings his downfall. By magnifying the "tragic flaw" and trying to dig up "sins" for Oedipus, Ajax, and even Antigone, well-meaning clerical scholars have tried to make Sophocles a sort of pre-Christian who said that the Universe is just. Actually, he says quite the opposite; in each case the punishment does not fit the crime. For heroic souls, at least, the Universe seems most unjust.

It should be remembered also that these dramas were born in a democracy where every freeman was the equal of his fellows. The Athenians had the same belief in divine equality as motivated our Declaration of Independence. Thus, merely to be a king was to be out of line—a condition of *hybris* itself. In the nature of things, a king was ripe for a fall, and ancient legends offered no dearth of examples.

MEDEA

CHARACTERS

Medea (Mee-DEE-a): Daughter of the King of Colchis, and "common-law" wife of Jason.

Jason (JAY-sun): The rightful heir to Iolcus' throne, leader of the Argonauts, now an exile in Corinth.

Creon (KREE-on): King of Corinth and father of the princess (sometimes called Glauce or Creusa) who is married to Jason. Creon of Corinth is not to be confused with Creon of Thebes in later stories.

Aegeus (EE-jooss): King of Athens (later to become father of Theseus), a traveler through Corinth.

An old nurse of Medea's.

An old servant (*paedagogus*) in charge of the two little sons of Medea and Jason.

Messenger: A servant of Jason's who is still friendly to Medea.

Corinthian women neighbors of Medea.

Medea is a world-famous tale of a woman's revenge. Medea had saved the life of Jason, the *Argo*'s captain. He brought her back to Greece as his foreign mistress, but there ambition lured him to another woman. . . .

Jason was the son of Aeson, the rightful king of Iolcus. Aeson's half brother, Pelias, had seized the throne, imprisoned Aeson, and tried to murder Jason as a boy. Jason escaped and returned as a man to claim his rights. Pelias promised to abdicate if Jason would first bring back the Golden Fleece. The Fleece symbolized the rich merchandise of the East awaiting the first bold ship of legend to venture there. It is interesting to note that the *Argo* later developed the prestige of a legendary *Mayflower*, and every city claimed that its earliest hero was one of the *Argo*'s crew.

In Jason's absence, Pelias murdered Aeson, whom he had held in prison all those years. Pelias expected Jason to meet his death on the dangerous voyage. But Jason met Medea. . . .

MEDEA

(EURIPIDES)

From the house came a moan—then the hoarse, bitter cry of a woman's despair:

"O would to the gods I were dead!"

The two little boys looked up at each other and trembled. Their mother was acting most strangely of late, and they feared her moods. But soon they went on with their play. For grief touches young hearts lightly; they quickly forget.

Not so the old nurse, who sat on a bench before Jason's house—the home he had left for the bed of that wench in the palace! "O my poor mistress!" the old woman sighed. And her heart was filled with foreboding.

She feared where Medea's dark madness might lead. The Furies themselves had no wrath like this woman scorned. For Medea's fierce love for her Jason had burned with a wild, barbaric flame. She had woven her spells and fought like a tigress—yes, even murdered—to save his life. She had borne him these children. And now, forgetful of all his oaths, he had cast her aside. By Corinthian law, it was true, she was only his foreign mistress, since none but the Greek-born held rights as wives. But surely some higher law had been broken when Jason was wheedled by Corinth's king to leave her and marry his fair-skinned daughter.

Yet the dark-browed Medea herself had blood as regal as any that flowed in Corinthian veins, for in faraway Colchis she, too, had been born the child of a king.

How happy her lot might have been, thought the nurse, had the stout ship *Argo* been crushed by the blue Clashing Rocks and never sailed on to Colchis in quest of the Golden Fleece! Would that the pines of Pelion had never been felled to make oars for her hero crew. Or that Jason's uncle, the crafty old Pelias, had never sent Jason forth from Iolcus, hoping the voyage would mean his death and the end of his claim to the throne of his murdered father.

But the *Argo* sailed on toward the rising sun. And there at the Black Sea's end they had met. Medea's eyes shone almost as black as her glistening hair. She was dark of skin, and dark in the ways of her mind. A witch, some said as they whispered of spells and sorceries. But to Jason that day she seemed fairer than all the daughters of Greece. For Aphrodite had smitten her heart with love for this blond-bearded stranger, this man from the West, whose eyes were as blue—and as cold—as the seas of his native Hellas.

And thanks to Medea's magic charms, Jason had gained the Fleece and eluded each snare of her father, the king. She even contrived the death of her brother who tried to block their escape. Then back to the towers of Iolcus they sailed, and anon she bore Jason two children. But Pelias, false to his promise, refused to give over his blood-won throne. So Medea laid plans for revenge.

She offered to teach old Pelias' daughters her secret arts. And before their eyes she slew an old ram and cut it to pieces, and tossed all the flesh in a cauldron. Then, with incantations and magic herbs—or perhaps by some trick that deceived their eyes—she caused a young ram to leap forth quite whole and alive.

"Your father, Pelias, is old and impotent," she told them, "but these same arts can restore him once more to a lusty youth." And thus beguiled, the witless daughters seized the old man in his sleep and hacked him to death. Such was his end, but Medea's guile won Jason no throne, but only the people's fury. So the pair had to flee with their babes from Iolcus to save their lives. When they sought asylum in Corinth, Medea foreswore all her black magic arts and vowed thereafter to live in peace.

With the people of Corinth they found much favor. Their home seemed a home of love to be envied. But Jason's wisdom and valor in time caught the eye of the king. King Creon [1] was growing old and bemoaning the lack of a son to succeed him. So he offered Jason his daughter's hand and the promise of his kingdom. Thus Jason was lured away from Medea, leaving her love to sicken in poisonous hate. She bewailed the day she had fled from her home and her people. She hated even the sight of her children. Where could this fury lead? The aged nurse had known her of old and feared the worst.

And now, as the nurse looked up, she saw that the graybeard who cared for the boys had come home from the marketplace.

"How is she?" the old man asked. "Has she ceased her mourning yet?"

"Ceased?" said the nurse. "How I envy your simple hopes, old man. She has only begun. We have heard but the rumblings of distant thunder. May Zeus help us all when the full storm breaks!"

"Poor, foolish woman," he said, "if a slave may speak of his mistress so. And still she knows not all of her woes."

"Why, what do you mean?" the nurse asked sharply. "Be not a miser with news."

[1] Not to be confused with Creon of Thebes (*Oedipus, Antigone*).

The old man faltered. "It is nothing, perhaps. I should not have spoken."

"No—by your beard—let me know," she pleaded. "We servants must trust one another."

"Well, to tell the truth," he said, "I was looking around, pretending not to listen. But down where the older townsmen play draughts near the sacred fountain, I heard someone say that Creon would banish these boys and their mother from Corinth. Mind you, it is only a rumor. I hope it is false."

"Surely Jason would keep his sons safe from harm, however much he may shun their mother."

"His new love burns brightly. The old ones grow dim."

"Oh, how can she bear another harsh blow? The first one has left her reeling."

"It is best not to tell her," the old man said.

"However," the nurse exclaimed, "these children should know what kind of a father they have. I could well wish him dead—were he not my master—so false and fickle he is to his friends."

"Is any man different?" the old man asked. "Surely everyone loves himself far more than his neighbors. By now you should know this. What are children or honor compared to a throne and a tender young princess?" With that, he called the boys from their play to lead them indoors.

"Keep them out of their mother's sight," the old nurse warned, "as you would from an angry bull. I like not the look in her eyes. Her fury will never sleep until someone is gored. Zeus grant that it may be her foes, not her friends!"

It was no idle warning. For almost at once she heard Medea cry:

"Out of my sight, damned children—bastard-spawn of a hateful sire and a hated mother! Curse you all! May this house fall in ruins!"

The old nurse frowned. Why did her mistress so hate her children? Poor dears, what had they to do with their father's crimes? Fierce indeed, she thought, were the moods of the mighty. Alas! they had never been taught to obey, but only command. Thus all untempered they came to the anvil of fate. How much better to learn to live among equals, with no pomp or pride, and to reach one's old age in security! Life's middle road, after all, was best. For the humbled and chastened could never fall from such cruel heights as the palace-born.

And now, some neighbor women had come to the gate. "We have heard her cries and are sad," said one, "for we loved this home."

"A home it was once but it is no more," said the nurse. "My mistress mourns and will not be comforted."

And within, they could hear Medea imploring Zeus to cleave her head with his thunderbolts.

"O foolish woman," said one, "to yearn so hard for the bed she has lost. No man is worth it. And death comes quickly enough—never pray for it. What if her husband does crave another's arms? She should not rage, but rather let Zeus be the judge of it."

And now, they could hear Medea turning her prayers to Themis, the ancient goddess of oaths. "Let my traitorous lord and his bride be destroyed," she cried and went on moaning, "O my father—the land that I left in shame—O my poor brother!"

"We really should see her," one said. "If I can help, I am not a woman to shirk my duty. Go, tell her our kindly thoughts at least."

"I will," said the nurse, "though I doubt it will do any good. She glares like a lioness with whelps at anyone who comes near her. No incantations could soothe her savage mood. Indeed they lacked wit, those men of old who invented music to charm our banquets and revels. Why waste such cheer where joy reigns already? Alas, no one yet has devised a song that will heal a broken heart."

Yet Medea, as though she had drained her soul of its curses, almost welcomed the news of her visitors.

"We must be kind to our friends," she told the nurse, "and doubly so since I came as a stranger to Corinth. It is only human to loathe a stranger at sight, to suspect him of malice before we know him. And folk would be quick to take offense if I seemed proud or aloof. No, I will greet them. A stranger to Corinth should do as Corinthians do."

So she spoke. For Iolcus had taught her one lesson: he who seeks vengeance should first win friends.

They were filled with pity to see her unkempt and distraught—an ashen hue to her olive cheeks and a reddish fire in her wide, black eyes.

"This sudden blow has crushed my soul," she told them. "There is no joy in life, my friends, and I want to die. The one who was all the world to me has proved the vilest of men—my husband."

"A woman's lot can be hard," one sighed.

"Hard, indeed," said Medea, "for nothing on earth with mind or soul can be more wretched than womankind. First we must buy our husbands in the marketplace, outbidding each other with our dowries. And what do we get? A tyrant who rules us body and soul. True, one may be better, another worse, but the gamble is still a cruel one. For no decent woman may seek a divorce. No wife may refuse what her lord demands.

"And the poor bride coming to ways that are strange must needs have the wit of a seer to know how to please her husband. Then, if by toil and by tact we do succeed and our men do not chafe at the yoke, we are counted happy. If not, we had better be dead. For a husband, if vexed in his home, can always escape and purge his soul of its sickness among his friends. But we are trapped. We have to look to one man for everything. Oh, some may say that at least we are safe from the dangers men face. How little they know! Three times would I rather stand up in line of battle than once face the birth of a child."

They all agreed.

"Even so," said Medea, "you are all better off than I. You still have your fathers' homes near at hand. You have joy in life and good friends to share it. But I am alone in an alien land, scorned by my husband, a helpless captive, without a mother or brother or kinsman to turn to."

They murmured in sympathy.

"Just one thing I ask, then," Medea said, fixing her dark eyes upon them sharply. "That is your silence—if ever I find the means to avenge these wrongs, on my husband, his bride, and her father. A woman is weak and may quail at the sight of a sword. But betray her in love, and no foe can be deadlier."

They flinched at her words and the fire in her eyes, but they had to agree that Jason had wronged her deeply. They swore that no word would escape them. Then they heard the creaking of chariot wheels that came to a halt at the gate. Some soldiers came in and posted themselves, followed by Creon the King. He was old and trembling. His beard was white. And his face, though pale and gentle by nature, was flushed with anger now.

"You, there, Medea!" he said in a high-pitched, tremulous voice. "Take away those dark looks and black thoughts. Take your children and go—straight from this land into exile."

Medea said nothing, but gazed at him sullenly.

"This is my decree," he cried, "and I shall enforce it. I will not return to the palace until you are thrust from my borders."

"Now I am ruined, indeed," said Medea. "My enemies swoop down upon me full sail. Just one thing I ask, Creon. Why?"

Then Creon spoke in a voice more his own.

"I fear you," he said. "Why should I hide it? I fear you will brew some incurable ill for my daughter. For you are a witch at heart. You possess a witch's skill and are goaded to hate by your thwarted love."

Medea opened her eyes with a look of surprise.

"Oh, yes," he went on, "I was told all about the threats you have uttered against my child, the bridegroom, and me. I cannot delay. So hate me now as you please. I could bear your hatred far better than later remorse."

"O Creon," Medea said sadly, with downcast eyes, "my reputation has been my ruin. It shows that no parent should teach his child to be wise, for wisdom is always distrusted. Alas, some think I am clever and hate me. Some think me too bold, and some fear my silence. And now, it seems, you really believe I might harm your home. Do not fear me, Creon," she went on softly. "What power have I to harm a king? And why should I hate you? You did me no wrong. You simply betrothed your daughter—as any good father would—to the man of your fancy. It is only my husband I hate, if anyone. True, I might pity your choice, but I grudge you nothing—just wish you luck. So please let me stay—for I know my place. I will cause you no trouble."

"Your words are gentle," Creon admitted. "Yet for that very reason I fear what lurks in your mind. A hot-tempered foe is more to be trusted." He raised his voice. "No. Go at once, and no more speeches! Not all of your arts could change my decree, for I feel the hate in your eyes."

Then Medea threw herself down on the earth before him and cried:

"By your knees—by your daughter—I plead."

"You are wasting your words," said Creon, drawing away.

"Can you feel no pity?"

"No pity so great as my love for my child."

"Oh, love can be so cruel!" Medea cried.

"That depends how it strikes," said Creon.

"O Zeus," cried Medea, "mark well the cause of my woes!"

"Enough of that!" said Creon sternly. "Begone, and take my troubles away with you."

"*Your* troubles?" Medea exclaimed.

"Must I have my soldiers throw you out?"

"No, Creon, not that! But please hear me . . ."

"Oh, woman, why do you keep on besieging me?"

"I will leave this land," Medea said. "That is no longer my plea."

"Then, why persist? Why not leave without trouble?"

"All I ask is that you grant me just one more day—a day to prepare for my exile and to care for these children whose father neglects them." She seized his hand. "Oh, at least pity *them!* You, too, have a child, so you must have some feeling. I care no longer what happens to me, but I weep for these babes who have yet to learn the meaning of sorrow."

"I was never a tyrant at heart," said Creon, wavering, "and my weakness has often proved my undoing. I feel I am wrong to grant your request—and I warn you!" His voice rose again. "If tomorrow's sun finds you and your children still in my land, you will die. But stay, if you must, for this one day alone."

Surely one day was too short for the mischief he feared. Even so, he was cursing his folly all the way home to his palace. And well he might, for Medea was telling her friends:

"Do you think I could ever have fawned on that man except to gain something by guile? Not I. The witless old fool! He had me right in his hands, and he let me escape. Now may all three of them rue it!" And laughing wildly, she went in the house.

The women began to muse on the strangeness of things. Was the world so awry that waters were running uphill? Was the vaunted justice of Greece all unjust? Was their faith in the gods a delusion? Were men just a weak and faithless race, and their own the more glorious sex?

Not so had the ancient poets taught—but the poets were men. What if Phoebus Apollo had given his gift of song to women? How different their themes might have been! In Medea's plight they could see their own, for each was enchained to the whim of one man. Was not her betrayal the shame of all Greece? Surely her wish for revenge was just.

Meanwhile Medea's mind was a seething cauldron of vengeful thoughts, but she had no plan. She must find one quickly; it must not fail. First she pictured herself setting fire to the palace and smiled at the thought of the two of them writhing in flames. Then she dreamed of silently stealing up to their bed and plunging a well-whetted blade in their bodies. But if she were caught with a torch or a sword, she reflected, she would surely be slain and her foes would mock her.

Better then, perhaps, that shortest and surest way in which women excelled—some deadly poison. She knew drugs that would eat away human flesh. And some gift could be dipped in these. But suppose she succeeded, what then? Who would protect her? Where could she flee? She would not have a husband's aid as she had in Iolcus. So first she must plan for some haven of refuge, some place to live and enjoy the sweet taste of revenge. Yet, if all else failed she would seize her sword and let death overtake her if need be.

She called on dark Hecate's aid for her schemes. Her tormentors must pay in full measure. Bitter would be their wedding and wooing, bitter their plot for her exile. Medea would not be their laughingstock—not she, a child of the Sun-god's race. Let weaker women seek praise for their virtue. The name of Medea would ring through the ages for cunning and courage.

Outside, all the voices had suddenly ceased, and Medea went to the door. She froze on the threshold and drew in her breath with a hiss. For Jason was standing beside the gate. How she hated that godlike, blond-bearded face—that look of injured innocence! His eyes were cold and aloof as he said:

"How many times have I told you, my dear, that your vicious temper would bring you to ruin? Had you only bowed to our ruler's wisdom, you might have remained here. But no, you could not restrain your lawless tongue and those threats that have brought on your exile. I do not care how you slander me. Keep on crying forever that Jason is vilest of men. But threatening our king! Count it merciful luck that you suffer no more than banishment. I was doing the best that I could for you. I tried to soften our ruler's wrath—but you raged right on.

"Even so, I would not have you face all the ills of your exile in want. I shall make some provision for you and your sons. For, much as you hate me, I still cannot harbor a grudge."

"You loathsome excuse for a man," snarled Medea. "Do you think it is boldness to face me, the woman you wronged? No, it marks you as having that worst of all human diseases—complete loss of shame. Even so, it is well you are here. I can ease my soul as I watch you cringe.

"To start with, I saved your life. And every Greek who sailed on the *Argo* knows it. It was I who taught you to tame the fire-breathing bulls. I slew the dragon that guarded the Golden Fleece. To me alone do you owe your escape. I deserted my home and—with more love than wits—I sailed with you back to Iolcus. There, again for your sake, I encompassed the death of Pelias. And now, heartless ingrate, you toss me aside for another woman.

"Had I been barren, such lust might have had some color of right, but I gave you two children. You have shattered my faith in the holiest oaths. And if you still believed there were gods in heaven, your very soul would cry out in shame. How often you clasped my knees as a suppliant, held my hand in a pledge of faith—how I shudder to think of such traitorous flesh touching mine!

"But still let me ask you, like an old friend—and *that* is a bitter jest—just where can I turn for help? To the home and the land I deserted for you? To Pelias' daughters? A kindly welcome they would give me! Then where? Alas, for your sake, the world is full of my foes. How grateful you are! To prove your devotion and make me the most envied wife in all Hellas, you throw me out—alone with my babes—into this world I have stripped of my friends. What a fine adornment it is for a royal bridegroom to have his sons and the wife to whom he owes his life go forth as vagrants, begging their bread! O Zeus, why do men not carry some outward sign of their worth like coins? Then we could recognize the villainous soul in time."

Jason replied with icy derision:

"It would take a good sailor to weather the storm of your words. But since you have heaped up the score of my debts, let me tell you one thing. To Aphrodite alone do I owe my safe voyage. It is harsh to say it, perhaps, but whatever you did was only because you were smitten with love for me. So you could not help it, my dear. Still, let me be generous and say it was kindly done for whatever cause. Even so, you have gained far more than you gave.

"Consider this. You are living in glorious Greece instead of your backward, barbaric land. You have learned our civilized ways and the meaning of justice. The Greeks are aware of your wit and skill. What fame could you ever have won at the ends of the earth? And as for my marriage—that was a decent and prudent way to help you and your children. . . ."

Medea gave a bitter laugh.

"No, hear me out," said Jason. "After all the trouble you caused in Iolcus, what better bulwark could I, as an exile, find than wedding the daughter of Corinth's king? It was not that I loathed you—much as you fume at the thought—nor did I lust for another bride. As for children, our two are enough —I had no complaint. It behooved me, however, to try to ensure that all of us would live on in ease, not shunned by our friends for our poverty. I wanted to rear my sons as befitted my ancient line. So I sought to beget them brothers of royal rank that we all might live in happiness and prosperity. You have no more need for children, yourself, but such royal children could profit us all.

"Was I wrong? Even you would not say so except that the princess' charms are goading your jealousy. You women are all alike. You think that the whole world depends on how well you can hold your men to your beds. Let a rival appear, and you blindly fight even your own best interests, hating all that is fair and good. Too bad you are needed to give us children. For women are surely the plague of mankind."

Medea could scarcely hold back her hands from that mocking face.

"You weave such clever speeches," she said, "but one single fact will destroy you. If your reasons were all so noble and pure, then why did you fear to tell me?"

"And win your blessing beyond a doubt," sneered Jason. "Even now your wrath is beyond all reason."

"The truth is," Medea said, "that you felt ashamed to grow old with a foreign wife."

"No, it is not," Jason said. "Must I tell you again? I do not love her. I wed her to strengthen our house, to help my two sons—and you."

"May I never seek wealth at such pain to another," Medea sighed.

"I could teach you a better prayer than that," said Jason. "Pray for the wisdom to know good fortune from bad."

"Go on adding insult to outrage," Medea said bitterly. "You have a refuge. I have none."

"And who is to blame?"

"I was not the one who betrayed our marriage."

"I refuse to argue it further," said Jason. "But I want to provide for you and your children unstintingly. Let me give you some part of my fortune to help you along your way, as well as some letters to friends who will treat you kindly. It would be very foolish to spurn my offer. For anger will bring you no gain."

"Keep your gold and your friends," said Medea. "I want them not. No good can come from a traitor's gifts."

"Then I call on the gods to witness," said Jason, rolling his eyes to the heavens, "I have done all I could for you, and you have rejected my aid. On your own head lie all your misery!"

"Oh, go away!" said Medea. "Go back to your virgin bride. You have lingered too long from her pale, white limbs. May the gods bless your marriage—with bitter regrets!"

Jason left with a helpless shrug. It was idle to argue with such a woman. Or any woman, perhaps. He had failed to sway that silent jury of neighbors. All the women condemned him now. Love, they felt, was the dearest gift of the gods—

but lust was the direst curse. It led to hatred and death, or worse. It had doomed Medea to wander unpitied in friendless lands. No wonder she groaned in despair. They knew of no fate more bitter than exile—no kindly thoughts that could comfort her.

Meanwhile, a stranger was traveling through the streets—a king, though he wore the garb of a pilgrim. A grievous woe had sent him to Delphi seeking an answer. But now he was filled with dismay, for the oracle's answer itself was a riddle he could not unravel. Perhaps his good friend in Troezen might solve it. If not. . . . He was struck with a sudden thought! Why, right here in Corinth a woman lived—a clever woman, he knew. If the oracle failed him, perhaps her herbs and charms might prove a remedy for his plight.

Thus it was that Aegeus, King of Athens, had turned aside his chariot to seek out the house of Jason.

"Rejoice, Medea!" he hailed her, on seeing her from the gate. The women looked up. His familiar greeting, here on the threshold of sorrow, had struck their ears with a strange sort of irony. They did not recognize this tall, handsome stranger whose beard was flecked with the gray of approaching age. But Medea knew him at once. Here, she thought, might be her deliverance.

"Rejoice, O Aegeus, son of wise Pandion," she hailed him. "What brings you here?"

And he told her. One thing alone had marred his marriage. Although he had never shunned the bed of his wife, he had failed all these years to beget a child. Thus, sure that some god must have cursed his loins, he had gone to consult the oracle.

"And what were Apollo's words?" asked Medea.

"Most simple and clear, yet too deep for my wit, that I was not to unfasten the wineskin until I reached home."

Forsooth, he must bed with no virgins along the way,

thought Medea, but did not tell him. Instead she asked, "But what leads you now so far astray from the road back to Athens?"

"I was going to Troezen to see King Pittheus," said Aegeus. "He is old and wise—and was once my dearest companion in arms."

"Yes, he might know the answer," Medea said with hidden guile. "For he is a pious man and skilled in such matters. I wish you luck." But with that, she began to weep.

"What is wrong?" asked Aegeus.

"My husband," Medea replied, "is the basest of men. O Aegeus, despite all I suffered for him, he has wronged me by taking another wife."

"Surely he would not dare . . ."

"But he has—and to my disgrace."

"Did you give him some reason to hate your bed?"

"No! Nothing but lust has made him unfaithful."

"Then may he perish for a scoundrel!" Aegeus exclaimed. "Who is the woman?"

"The princess," Medea said. "But that is not all. Now her father, King Creon, is banishing me and my children from Corinth."

"Does Jason allow this? For shame, if he does!"

"He pretends to be pained, but his heart is glad."

Anger and pity were rising in Aegeus' face. Here were woes just as great as his own. Now, thought Medea, the time had come to strike. She knelt down before him, clasping his beard and his knees in a suppliant gesture, and cried:

"O Aegeus, I am so wretched! Save me! Let me not suffer, but give me your city, your home, and your hearth as a refuge. The gods will reward you—with children. For I know the drugs and the charms that will cure your affliction."

For many reasons Aegeus was fain to grant her request.

Humanity, yes, and the promise of children sent his heart bounding to joy from despair. Yet he faltered. The oracle's cryptic words had forbidden *something* before he reached home.

"I cannot take you with me now from this land," he said. "But if you can reach Athens without my help, my home will be your refuge forever."

"So be it," Medea agreed, "but will you give me your kingly oath?"

"Are my words not enough?" asked Aegeus.

"I trust your intent," said Medea. "Yet better the gods should mark down your words. For the houses of Pelias and Creon are powerful foes and bitter against me. If you gave me your oath, then fear of the gods would never allow you to let them drag me away. Otherwise you might some day be tempted by gifts or threats to yield me up. For my foes have great riches and power, while I have nothing."

"You are, indeed, a clever woman," said Aegeus. "But such an oath will protect me, too. For I can cite it if ever I have to resist their demands or blandishments. What gods, then, should I invoke?"

"Swear by the Earth and my own father's father, the Sun —by the whole race of gods—you will never cast me out nor yield me up to my foes."

Aegeus repeated the oath as she gave it, calling down on his head every punishment meet for the wicked if ever he broke his word.

"Now go with blessings," Medea said, "and when I have done what I must and achieved my desires, I shall come to aid you in Athens."

"And may Hermes guide you safely home," one of the women added. "May you gain all you seek, for to us you seem noble and righteous."

When he had left them, Medea exclaimed: "O Zeus and

Justice and Light of the Sun, I shall triumph at last. My hated foes shall fall to my vengeance, for now a safe harbor awaits me."

She told the old nurse to hurry to Jason and say she relented and begged to see him once more. Then she said to her friends:

"My words will be oh so soft when he comes, with a 'Yes, my lord, you were right, my lord.' I shall even praise that scoundrel's marriage as nobly conceived and a boon to us all. I shall beg him to let his sons stay in Corinth though I go away. But not for their foes to mock—oh, no! I shall use them to slay the princess by guile. For I have a robe of finest weave and a coronet carved in gold, which I have dipped in poison. These will my sons bear to her as gifts when they plead to be spared from exile. And when she puts on those deadly gifts she will die in agony."

No one demurred very strongly at such a fate for a husband stealer.

"But what," they asked, "will become of your children?"

Her answer froze them with horror.

"I gave them birth," she said, as she narrowed her eyes—"and I will slay them."

They could not believe her. Fathers might leave their infant daughters to die. But a mother to slay her sons in cold blood! It defied all the laws of nature. Yet Aegeus' yearning for sons unborn had planted a seed in Medea's dark mind. How much greater a father's anguish to lose the sons he had reared!

"I shall tear down the house of Jason," Medea said. "And I care not what fate awaits me. I have nothing further to live for. I was cursed from the day I let that guileful Greek lure me away from my father's halls. But, by the gods, he will pay for all he has done to me since. He shall mourn for the sons I bore him—and for those he will never beget from his bride. Never think of me as a poor, weak, defenseless wife, for I am a different breed of woman—kind to my friends, but a vengeful fury to those who wrong me. Only such a woman is worthy of glory."

They begged her to have regard for the laws of gods and men.

"I forgive your weakness," she said, "for you have not suffered my woes. But you cannot stay my hand."

"Could you really slay your own children?" they asked.

"Yes," she said fiercely, "for thus I should make his heart bleed the most."

"And leave you the saddest mother on earth."

"Enough!" said Medea. "Every word you utter will be in vain until I achieve my revenge."

Had she not heard of ancient Athens, they asked, or its happy people, the seed of the blessed gods? A sacred land unravaged by war, where the folk all danced in the warm, bright air and drank from the fountains of wisdom. The land where the Muses were born and where Aphrodite dwelt in beauty. How could this land of sacred streams, this kindly land, ever welcome the mother stained with her children's blood? Still they doubted a mother could do such a deed. In the end, they felt, when her children fell weeping and clasping her knees, her eyes would be blinded by tears, and she could not strike.

So they held to their oath of silence when Jason came.

"I am here at your bidding," he told Medea, "for, rant as you will, my wish to serve you will never fail."

But Medea seemed all contrition now.

"O Jason, forgive me," she pleaded, "and bear with my temper for old time's sake and for all we once meant to each other. At last I have yielded to reason, rebuking my former folly. How blind I was to rage against those who wished me no ill! Why, indeed, should I rail at our rulers or carp at a marriage that links my own children to Corinth's throne? And with you and the gods to care for me, what have I to suffer, even in exile? Oh, you were so right and I was so wrong!

"Had I only been wiser, I should have aided your plans from the first. I should have been there to adorn the couch of your bride, rejoicing that you had won such a prize—and such a protector for all of us. But, alas, we women are what we are—just women, to use no unkinder name. Never try to match us in malice nor sink to our level in folly. For you have been wise, and I yield to your wisdom."

Then she bade the old servant bring out the two boys.

"Come, children," she said. "We are friends again. We must all bid your father good-by. So go to him, take his hands in yours—though I have to weep." Jason was too overjoyed and relieved to heed her next words. "I tremble at dangers still lurking ahead," she said. "How long will these children remain alive to stretch loving hands to their father?"

The women shuddered. But Jason, his arms about his sons, replied, "Woman, I praise this new mood of yours and forgive all the past. It was natural, of course, that a wife should rage when her husband trafficked in other women. But you have proved clever beyond your sex. So now I rejoice that you see these things in their proper light." Then he spoke to his children:

"Your father was thinking of you above all. Now, thanks to me and the gods, you will both be honored in Corinth. May you grow in strength beside your new brothers and triumph in manhood over your father's foes."

Medea gave his happiness rein for a time, but at last she forced his attention by moaning deeply.

"Why do you weep so and hide your pallid cheeks?" he asked. "Have my words displeased you?"

"It is nothing," Medea said, with a fresh burst of tears, "but I cannot forget the fate of these children."

"Do not worry," said Jason, "for I will protect them."

"Oh, I trust you," Medea said. "But we women are weak, easily given to tears. I bore these children. And when you prayed for their happy life, compassion and fear overwhelmed me. For surely you have not forgotten that Creon has ordered their exile."

She saw the shadow cross Jason's face.

"Oh, I know that *I* must be banished," she added hastily. "I should be in the way. No one could trust me. But these poor little sons need a father's hand to guide and protect them. So plead with Creon that they, alone, may stay and grow up by your side."

"I am not sure that I can persuade him," said Jason. "But you are right, I must try."

"Then ask your bride to plead with her father."

"That I will, and, she should persuade him—if she is, indeed, a woman."

"And if she is like most other women," Medea said, "I can help you persuade her. For I will send gifts beyond any beheld by men—a fabulous gown of gossamer weave and a golden wreath. Our two boys will take them to her." She bade a servant bring forth two bundles and gave them to her children. "Oh, she will be blest a thousandfold," Medea went on, "with you as her husband and having these glorious gifts from the Sun-god himself. Take them, my children, straight to the royal bride."

"Fond woman, why rob yourself of your store?" protested Jason. "Do you think the palace lacks robes of gold? Her desire to please me alone is enough. She will need no gifts."

"No, let me do it," Medea said. "Even the gods are persuaded by gifts, they say, and gold can outweigh ten thousand words. She is like the gods—she has everything—a husband and power and beauty and youth. And yet I would give her not gold alone, but my life itself, to ransom my children from banishment. So go to the palace, my dear ones; go to your father's new wife and plead that you may not be exiled. Give her these priceless gifts. And be sure, very sure, that her own hands receive them. Then hasten home to your mother and bring her the happy news."

And the children, their servant, and Jason left with her poisoned gifts.

"The fool, the wretched fool!" Medea exclaimed. "Now he thinks he has everything—his bride, his sons, and no more trouble from me. How soon he will wish he had never been born!"

Now that her hour of revenge was near, she must conjure up some means of escape. She went to her hearth and sprinkled its embers with strange and mystic scents from the East. She prayed to the Sun and to Hecate, goddess of witches—to every dark power her spells could invoke.

When the children returned, their old attendant was full of joy. "Good news, my mistress!" he cried, as Medea came forth. "Your children will surely be free from banishment. The royal bride took your gifts in her hands and gladly heeded their plea . . ."

He was startled to see Medea turn pale and utter a moan that seemed far out of tune with his tidings.

"Have I said something wrong?" he asked.

"No," said Medea, "you told your tale, and I do not blame you."

"Then why these tears?"

"Old man," she said, "I am trapped in woes of my own devising."

He thought she meant only her banishment, and he tried

to cheer her. "Take heart," he said, "for the day will come when your sons will be calling their mother home."

To their home in Hades, she thought.

"You should not grieve so much at this parting," he said. "Many other parents have had to bear it."

"And so shall I," said Medea grimly. Then she turned to her sons. "O my children," she said, "we must soon be parted. A new home awaits you—a different world from the one I will tread in sorrow. No more can we share our joys. Alas, I shall never adorn the beds of your brides nor stand with my torch at your weddings. A curse is upon me. In vain did I suffer to give you birth. In vain were my hopes to be envied by all, to have your tender care through the years till the day I should die in your arms. Now all those sweet dreams have perished. My life will be lonely and bitter instead. Nevermore shall I see the love in your eyes . . ."

Oh, why do they smile at me so, she thought. No—I cannot do it! My heart grows faint as I see their radiant faces. I must take them with me. Good-by to my schemes! What profit to torture my husband and suffer more anguish myself? But she checked this thought. What is wrong with me? Shall my foes go unpunished? Never!

She bade the old man take the children within. Then she turned to her friends and said, as though in a trance:

"If any be present, unclean and unfit to attend this sacrifice, let them look to themselves and depart. My hand will not falter."

They trembled. These words were the words that a priest would use at the altar before he drew the knife. Yet even as she spoke them, her mother's heart was crying, No—spare the babes! Keep them with you to gladden your heart. But she stilled that cry with a shout:

"No, by the fiends of Hades! Never shall I leave my children to glut the insolence of my enemies. The die is cast. The bride is already writhing in robes of fire. I must go my unhappy way—these children a path more unhappy still."

She went indoors and drew her frightened sons to her breast, kissing their hands and their lips. She felt their soft breath upon her and stroked their gentle young flesh, gazing with wonder afresh at their beauty, their golden hair, their eyes—like Jason's! She thrust them roughly away.

I know what I am doing, she thought. I hate and I love. No mortal could be more accursed, for my hate is the greater.

Outside, the women were talking in wonder and fear.

"Those who remain unwed and childless are happiest," said one. "For children bring little but woe. We bear them in pain, then struggle to find the means to sustain them. And all the while we are filled with fear. Will they grow up to be brave and noble or weigh down our aging hearts with shame?"

"But the greatest woe," said another, "we fear to name, though it surpasses all the rest. That is to lose them."

"Ah, yes," said another. "When the shades of Death sweep our children away, the gods have done their worst."

They hoped that Medea knew it.

And while they pondered, a slave, wild-eyed with fear, his clinging tunic drenched with sweat, ran in through the gate and pounded the door till Medea came forth.

"Flee, Medea, flee!" he cried breathlessly. "For you have wrought a ghastly, unholy deed. Flee by land or by sea, but flee for your life!"

"Why should I?" Medea asked calmly.

"The royal maiden is dead, killed by your poisonous drugs—and Creon, her father, too."

"That is glorious news," said Medea. "I shall always be in your debt."

"Have you lost your mind?" asked the servant.

"Time may answer that," said Medea. "But first, my friend, tell me how they died. If in agony, good! You will double my joy."

All were hushed as he told his tale.

A wave of joy had swept through the palace, he said, when Jason had first come back with the children. Old servants, who grieved for their former mistress, whispered with joy that her quarrel was ended. They bent down and kissed the children's hands and their golden heads as they made their way to the women's quarters.

When Jason entered, the princess looked up in eager yearning, then gasped with dismay to see his children. Her cheek went pale. She covered her eyes and turned away. But Jason tried to assuage her temper. Or was it shame?

"You must not be angry, my dear," he said softly, "nor turn your back on my children. A wife must love whom her husband loves. Moreover, they bring you gifts. For my sake, accept them and plead with your father to spare my sons from exile."

The princess was still demurring but could not resist her desire to open the bundles. And when she saw those glittering gifts, she exclaimed with delight:

"O Jason, whatever you ask, I will do."

She could hardly wait for their leaving to try on the silken robe of embroidered gold. Then she put on the golden coronet and wreathed her curls about it in front of her mirror. How beautiful she looked, she thought, as she traded many a happy smile with her lifeless image. Then she rose and walked lightly around the room, often stretching out her ivory ankle and bending her head to feast her eyes on the full sweep of elegant beauty that clung to her limbs.

But suddenly came an awful change. She turned pale and

trembled and started to reel. She was barely able to stumble back and fall in a faint on her couch. An aged handmaiden, thinking a seizure of Pan or some other god was upon her, began to pray. But when she saw the foaming lips and rolling eyes, her prayer trailed off in a shriek of terror that shook the palace roof.

Some rushed for the king and some for Jason. But Jason had left to go part way home with his children. Soon the princess broke out of her speechless trance with a cry of horrible pain as flames licked out from the twofold gifts and began to devour her fair white flesh. She tried to flee, to shake off the crown from her hair and to tear the robe from her limbs, but all in vain as the flames burst forth with redoubled fury.

At last she sank to the floor, a hideous thing past all recognition save to a father's eyes. Gone was her fair young beauty as blood and flesh oozed out in the fire like resin from burning pine. The fearful caustic drug ate away all it touched, and no one dared to go near her. But her father came in, all unknowingly, and threw himself down, embracing her body and crying:

"O my poor child, what god has so foully destroyed you? What has robbed me—ripe as I am for the grave—of all I hold dear? O my child, let me die beside you."

But when he had ceased his lament and attempted to rise, her fine-spun robe held him fast as ivy clings to the laurel tree. It was like a ghastly wrestling match, for strive as he would to free himself, that body held him down. And when he pulled away with all his might, his aged flesh was torn from his bones. At last he yielded in agony and sank down beside her in death.

Such was the servant's story. Medea exulted in triumph. The women agreed that Jason would suffer justly.

"But, O the poor king," one said, "that he and his daughter should die so cruelly for Jason's sake."

Medea now seemed a beast of prey that had tasted blood. "I shall slay my children and flee," she said. "Aegeus gave me no pledge for them. He would yield them up to my vengeful foes. Then hands less merciful than mine would slay them. They could not escape. Therefore I, who gave them their life, will take it. Be brave, my heart! Shrink not from an evil that must be done! Nor think of how dear they are. For one short hour forget they are yours—then mourn them forever. O wretched, wretched one that I am!"

They stood there, stunned. But before they could order their wits, Medea had whirled through the door, closing and bolting it fast behind her.

They prayed to the Earth, to the radiant Sun to look down on this poor, doomed mother before her hand should be dyed with blood. Could the Sun endure that these children, his own descendants, should perish by mortal hands? Let the Light of Heaven restrain her! Keep her from staining her soul with sins and sorrows forever!

But the Sun was hidden beyond the clouds, and within they could hear the fearful screams of the two little brothers seeking to escape their mother's sword. The women rushed to the door and clawed in vain at its stout oak planks. At last all was quiet. They knew it was over. No mother was this, but something of iron or stone, to take the lives of her own. Oh, how hateful the bed of woman—that bed of ecstasy and anguish—the source of all men's woes!

An angry voice cried out, "Where is the fiend?"

They turned; it was Jason. His bland, blond-bearded face was contorted now, and those eyes of steel were molten with fear and rage.

"Is Medea here," he cried, "or has she fled from her deeds

of outrage? Nowhere short of heaven or hell can she escape from the king's avengers. But I care not what happens to her; let her suffer as she deserves. I must save my children before they pay with their lives for their mother's crimes."

"Wretched man, you know not the woe that awaits you."

"Why, does she seek to slay me, too?"

"Her hands are red with your children's blood."

"My children slain? O gods, no!" cried Jason. "Then she has slain me already."

"Within you will find their bodies."

"Break down the door!" Jason roared to his men. "Let me see the twofold, unspeakable horror—my poor slain sons and the she-monster I will slay."

His men tried to reach the house, but some unseen force hurled them back. The nether demons had come to Medea's aid. No more could Jason reach her, despite his rage, when Medea flung open the door and stood there exultant, sword in hand, her disheveled robe splashed with her children's blood.

"Why seek you the dead in vain," she asked, "or me, the slayer? Cease striving. Your hands can never touch me. Neither your hands nor your spears. But hurl your words if you must. Soon my father's father's chariot—dragon-drawn—shall speed me safely beyond this land."

And Jason cried out in his anguish:

"O woman accursed, abominable—to the gods, to me, and to all mankind—your blood-red sword has slain the children you bore and pierced the heart of their childless father. Fiend incarnate, no mother, you! How can you face an earth or a sun that never beheld such evil? May you die the death of the damned!

"What a miserable fool I was to bring you to Greece from your savage land—a brother-slayer and a father-betrayer! In sin you boarded the *Argo,* and now the gods are avenging your guilt on me. No woman of Greece could have dared such a deed. Oh, why did I spurn all the gentle daughters of Hellas to lie with such a beast, more fierce than Tyrrhenian Scylla?

"But why should I speak? Ten thousand reproaches could never sting you, so brazen is your heart."

"And why should I answer?" Medea replied. "Zeus in his heaven knows all that I did for you, all that I suffered. What did you expect—a life of bliss with your princess, mocking and spurning your own true wife? Did Creon think he could pander his daughter and drive me out of his land unscathed? Call me a Scylla if you like—or a tigress. It is *your* heart I feed upon."

"And you will share my grief," said Jason. "You must."

"Aye," said Medea, "I must. But even the bitterest grief is gain when it ends your joy."

"O my children," groaned Jason, "to have such a mother!"

"And such a father!"

"My hands are clean. I did not slay them."

"Not by your hands, but by your lust. You thought it nothing to wrong your wife. Now, look!" She held up the children's bodies before him. "Look at them! Look at them!" she screamed. "They are dead!"

"Dead, but they will be avenged!" cried Jason, drawing his sword and leaping toward her. But again the unseen forces hurled him back.

"Then give me my dead," he begged, "that I may bury and mourn them."

"Never!" she said. "I shall carry them off to the temple of Hera, high on the cliffs. There my own hands will lay them in sacred ground, where no foe will dare to tear up their graves or desecrate their bodies."

"May the Furies and Justice destroy you for murdering them," cried Jason.

"Cry on," said Medea. "What gods will heed the prayers of a perjured traitor? Go home and bury your bride! Or stay here and mourn if you like till old age comes upon you."

"O my dearest sons!" cried Jason.

"Dear to me," said Medea, "but never to you."

"O let me kiss them," Jason pleaded.

"You who disowned them alive?"

"By the gods, just let me touch them once."

"Never!" Medea said. "You waste your words."

"O Zeus," Jason cried, "behold what I suffer from yonder child-devouring monster! All heaven bear witness how she slew my sons and would not let me give them burial. O would to the gods I had never begotten them!"

Thus it came to pass that Jason the Prince lost everything —even his reason. Alone and friendless, he wandered through many lands. Some folk were kind and gave him crusts, some only taunts and stones. At last he returned to Iolcus, an unknown stranger in a land where once he should have been king. Some strange desire drew his steps to the shore. And there he found the proud and glorious *Argo*, a decaying hulk, half covered by sand. He lived in its shelter for many years, begging or stealing his bread, until one night a rotting beam crashed down on his head. And his life was ended.

Athenian males of 431 B.C. could be thankful their women were barred from the drama. They must have cringed at the almost indecent exposure of Jason, as the smug, egotistical Greek, and shuddered to think of a latent Medea at home. Needless to say, the judges rated *Medea* as the year's worst play. Medea was a witch, and mad, perhaps—but a woman for all of that. And she made the men listen to things they did not want to hear. This was all very shocking in a city that held a woman's greatest glory was never to be mentioned at all—for good or bad—by men.

The audience knew, incidentally, what happened to Aegeus' wish for a son. Old King Pittheus tricked him in Troezen about the oracle's meaning. Hoping to unite Athens and Troezen, Pittheus sent his daughter Aethra to Aegeus' bed. Suspecting Aethra was pregnant when he left her, Aegeus put some tokens under a heavy stone and told her that if the child became man enough to lift the stone, he should come to him in Athens with the tokens. That son became the great Athenian hero Theseus.

But what Euripides did to the legend of Medea itself was a triumph of creative imagination. It is hard to believe, but the earlier legend was far different from this one. Medea caused the death of Creon in a struggle for the throne, then fled for her life, leaving her children *for safety* in the Temple of Hera—a holy place where they would not be touched. But Creon's relatives broke into the temple and killed the children. They then tried to conceal their sacrilege by spreading false tales that Medea had slain them herself.

So Euripides simply took the "lie" of the legend as though it were true and asked: What kind of a mother could do such a thing—and why? *Medea* is the play he wrote as an answer.

ALCESTIS

CHARACTERS

Alcestis (Al-SESS-tiss): Daughter of Pelias and wife of Admetus.
Admetus (Ad-MEET-us): Son of Pheres and King of Thessaly.
Apollo (A-POLL-o): Son of Zeus and god of light, the sun, the arts, and prophecy; for a time the slave of Admetus.
Death (or *Thanatos*): A creature of the Fates who seizes the living when their time is up.
Heracles (HEAR-a-kleez) or Hercules: The strongest of mortals; son of Alcmena and Zeus; forced to serve Eurystheus, who made him perform twelve prodigious feats or "labors."
Pheres (FER-eez): Retired king of Thessaly and father of Admetus.
People of Pherae and servants of Admetus.

"Eat, drink, and be merry, for tomorrow we die."

But when Admetus got a peek at the future and found tomorrow was almost here, he did not want to go. He thought it would be easy to find a substitute who did not enjoy life so much. . . .

Euripides turned this old folk tale into a tragi-comedy whose tender beauty is laced with biting irony.

The play presents a symphonic conflict between golden brightness and funereal gloom. And, as in many of Euripides' plays, the two themes are first announced on a superhuman plane. The god Apollo meets Death on his way to claim a victim. Apollo symbolizes light and life, and all the arts of joyful living. Death, in this play, is not the great god Pluto, but a foul and greedy body-snatcher for the Fates.

Soon our story descends to human levels, and Euripides vividly bares the hypocrisy of all the rites and cliches that man employs in the face of death. The irony is somewhat relieved by the unselfish nobility of Alcestis, though even she is much too matter-of-fact to be a romantic character. The whole play has been a Rorschach blot to critics, who have never been able to agree on how good, or deplorable, it is.

ALCESTIS

(EURIPIDES)

Admetus of Thessaly was a happy king and free from all care until the day he learned that the Fates had marked him for an early death. And who can cheat the Fates? The three old Sisters spin and measure the thread of every life and snip it where they will. And once the Fates' manservant, Death, has come to claim him, what man can say, "I will not go"?

How many could bravely face that day if they knew just when it would come? Not Admetus, surely. He did not want to leave this life so soon. For he was young and rich in flocks and friends, and wed to the fairest of Pelias' daughters. Two children played on his palace floor, and both his parents were still on earth.

Now Thessaly was a kindly land, and renowned for its hospitality. Even its poorest folk would gladly share anything —except their sorrows—with any passing stranger. And none was more gracious than King Admetus. In his palace at Pherae his heart and his hearth were open to all. Even the god Apollo had felt his kindness, and not as a guest but as a serf.

This servitude had been imposed upon Apollo for defiance of his father Zeus. For of all the gods, Apollo most hated Death, and his mortal son, Asclepius, had been a great physician. But death is the order of things, and when Asclepius became so skilled that he began to restore the dead to life, Zeus had killed him with his thunderbolts.

Bitter but helpless against his father Zeus, Apollo took his vengeance on the forgers of the bolts, and beside their anvils he slew the one-eyed blacksmiths. For this misdeed he was banished from heaven and had to serve a mortal master for a year, supping with his serfs and tending his flocks.

Luckily for Apollo, Admetus was chosen as his master. The year passed easily. Often on a hillside the god would put down his bow to pick up his pipes and play his love songs. Or he would sing in a voice so beautiful it charmed the spotted leopards from their lair, and the savage lions of Othrys would come and lie peacefully with the flocks. Even the shy and dappled deer were lured from the long-needled pines to dance to his tuneful lyre.

So passed the year, and when Apollo took leave of the kindly Admetus he promised to bless his halls with song and his fields and folds with fruitfulness. But one thing more the king requested.

"Pray, ask the Sister Fates how long I have to live this happy life." Apollo frowned. This was something no man should know. But still he asked. Alas, he found Admetus' days were numbered. Now seldom can even a god avert the Fates' decrees, yet Apollo managed to beguile the three. Some say he plied the sober Sisters with forbidden wine. They relented —but only on one condition. The score of Death must not be changed.

"But if you can find one person who is willing for Death to take him on that day reserved for you," Apollo told the king, "the Sister Fates will let you live."

"I am sure I can find such a person," Admetus said. "Many have cheerless lives and little hope. For them the gift would be slight."

Little he knew how greedily all men cling to life. He pleaded with all his friends in vain, even the father who gave him his crown and the mother who gave him birth. They all refused. They loved him, yes, but none of them loved him more than life itself—save only one, his wife Alcestis.

She agreed that Death could take her and let her husband live. Admetus grieved that she should make the sacrifice; but, fearing death still more, he resolved to bear his sorrow like a man.

Now the day had come, and the Fates' manservant Death approached the halls of Admetus. His sword was drawn to shear the lock of hair that would claim the victim as his. Invisible though he was to men, his shadowy, batlike form could not escape the eye of Phoebus Apollo, who lingered near the palace gate.

"Ah, Death, you seem too eager," Apollo said. "The day has hardly dawned."

Death drew back, shielding his small, cruel eyes from the radiance of the god, and snarled: "Why do you haunt these halls, Apollo? Was it not enough to cheat us of Admetus? Have you now come armed to protect his wife?"

"My bow means nothing," Apollo said. "It is just my habit to wear it. I am here to grieve at my good friend's sorrow. . . ."

"And rob me of this second body?"

"I did not rob you of the first."

"How then is Admetus above the earth instead of under it?"

"A fair exchange. He is letting you take his wife, and she is younger and far more beautiful."

"Then, out of my way!" said Death, "for I must seize her."

"Take her if you must," Apollo said. "I doubt if I could dissuade you."

"No," said Death. "I have my orders—and my rights."

"Still," mused Apollo, "you can take her only once. Why not be patient and wait a few more years?"

"No. People respect me more when I carry off the young."

"The old give you costlier funerals."

"Now, Phoebus, are you proposing a rich man's law?"

"How so? Your wit escapes me."

"Because you would let the wealthy alone buy longer lives."

"Then I take it you will not listen to me."

"Indeed not," said Death. "By now you should know my ways."

"That I do," said Apollo. "And they are hateful to gods as they are to men."

"Talk is useless," said Death. "The woman belongs to me!"

And with that he went to claim her. Apollo smiled. He had plans of his own. But he must not linger now. The god of light had no stomach for the nasty business of death.

As the day grew brighter—although a strange chill filled the air—the folk of Pherae gathered curiously at the palace gate.

"Why is it all so quiet?" one of them whispered. "Someone should come out and bid us start our mourning—or give us hope."

"O Healer Apollo," one woman sobbed, "why have you forsaken Pelias' daughter, the noblest of wives?"

"Apollo's son could raise the dead," another said. "Too bad he could not save himself from Zeus. Oh, if only the light still shone in Asclepius' eyes, he could have brought Alcestis back."

"We do not know she has gone yet," one man reminded her.

"Oh, I am sure she has died. What else could this silence mean?"

"It must mean that she still lives. Admetus would never bury her in silence. The least he owes his virtuous wife is a proper tribute. And as yet I hear no wailing or beating of maiden breasts."

"Yet is this not the day?"

"Indeed it is. And when the good are afflicted, all good men must mourn. But look, I see no bowl of cleansing water yet put out by the gate, no lock of hair hung up in mourning."

Still, they felt, Alcestis was doomed. No god, no sacrifice, no pilgrimage could save her.

The palace gate creaked. A pert, little handmaiden peered out.

"Is she alive or dead?" they asked her.

"You might say both," she replied. "Death is upon her, and yet still she lingers. Oh, my poor mistress!" She burst into tears.

"And how is Admetus?"

"He will not realize his loss until it is too late."

"Is everything being done for her?"

"Everything indeed," said the maiden. "Her shroud is laid out with all the other adornments, for Admetus will bury her in fitting style."

"Let her know that we praise her death and declare she is the finest woman under the sun."

As the maid went in and closed the gate behind her, voices of despair and prayer were heard.

"Where, O Zeus, can our rulers find refuge from evil?"

"Must we soon shear our hair and put on our garments of mourning?"

"It is clear—too clear—we must. Yet pray to the gods, for their power is mighty."

"Healing Apollo, find us again some way of escape! Strike down the murdering hand of Death!"

"How can Admetus live without her?"

"Today he will see his dearest one dead."
"And his life will become a living death."
"Will he not seek his own life by noose or sword?"
"Say no more that marriage is bliss."
"Marriage is full of woe."

Alcestis had risen early that morning for she had much to do. First she bathed her fair-skinned body in purest water from a stream, then chose from her cedar coffers the most befitting robes and jewels. She prayed to the goddess of her hearth:

"O Mistress of this home, before I pass beneath the earth, I kneel before you for the last time. Watch kindly over my children, I pray. Find for my son a loving wife, for my girl a noble husband. And may they not die, like me, before their time but live long and happily in their native land."

From altar to altar she went, wreathing each with myrtle boughs as she prayed. But never a sigh or a tear escaped her.

Even when Death crept up unseen to clip his lock of hair, no one else knew it or saw any sign. She seemed as unchanged as a flower cut from its roots in fullest bloom. But she felt the chill of the nearness of Death. She fled to her room and flung herself on her marriage bed.

"O dearest bed," she cried, "on you I first lay and unfastened my maiden girdle for the man I loved. Though you have destroyed me, I cannot hate you. Nor could I ever be false to you or to him. Soon—though I pray not—my husband may lie upon you with another bride. She may be as happy as I, perhaps, but never will she be more true."

Again and again she kissed the bed, bathing it with her tears. And many times she still returned to it before she could go out to bid them all good-by.

Her two little children clung to her dress as she fondled

first one and then the other. All the servants were weeping. She clasped the hand of each, however lowly, and bade them all farewell.

Admetus began to realize how soon the dead are freed from sorrow, how long the living must go on in grief. He threw his arms around Alcestis and begged, "Oh, do not leave me!" Too late! The flower was cut, and soon its head would droop. Fading and barely breathing now, Alcestis asked him to lead her outside for the last time to look upon the sun.

"Ah, the sun!" she sighed, leaning on his arm. "The sky —the drifting clouds."

"They see two unhappy souls," said Admetus, "who never wronged the gods that I should lose you." She sagged in his arms. "No," he said. "Do not give in! Pray to the gods for strength."

Her mind wandered. "I see the boat on Hades' shore," she said, "and Charon the Ferryman leaning on his pole, calling, 'Come, Alcestis. Do not linger. We are late.'"

"Oh, not that voyage yet!" Admetus groaned.

"Someone is drawing . . . drawing me down a dark path. See his wings . . . his eyes . . . no, let me go!"

Admetus shook her gently. "Think of your friends . . . your children . . . and me."

"My children, farewell," Alcestis murmured. "Your mother is nothing . . . nothing. I am tired; let me rest."

Admetus set her down on a bench and knelt beside her. "Do not forsake us—by the gods—by our children, I beg. We live in you; we will die with you. We will always worship your love."

For a moment the gathering clouds passed from Alcestis' mind and she spoke her last wish plainly:

"Admetus, I am dying, and your eyes cannot deny it. But this was my choice; I did not have to die. I might have lived on in wealth and ease, courted by every young prince in Thessaly. Yet I chose to honor you with my greatest gift—my life with all of its joy and hope—that you might live on in the light. For I could not bear to have you torn from me and see our children fatherless.

"Even your parents failed you—their only child—and never could he beget or she conceive another. At their years, death would have come easily, and to die for you would have been a glorious thing. Then you and I could have gone through life together, happy in our children. But it was not to be.

"For this I ask but a little thing—not in repayment, for life is beyond all price—but in remembrance and for the sake of these dear children."

"Anything," Admetus promised, "anything."

"Then let them be masters in my home. Never marry again and rob them of love by setting a stepmother over them. She would be cruel and strike these babes of ours. More fiercely than a viper does a new wife hate the children of the first. A father can be a tower for his son, but think of my poor girl—with a new wife spreading tales to blight her chances of young and happy marriage, and no loving mother to deck her as a bride or offer gentle comfort in the time of childbirth.

"For I must die, not tomorrow or some other day, but now. The gods be with you. Remember this and do not fail me."

"Yes, yes, I promise," Admetus cried. "In life and in death you will always be my one and only bride. No girl in Thessaly after you could ever have the birth or beauty to win me as her husband. And I have children enough. May I find in them the joy I have lost in you." He went on:

"Oh, I will do far more than you ask, dear wife. The mourning will last not just for a year, but for all my life. I shall put an end to parties, flowers, drinking bouts, and music in my halls. I shall never touch the lyre again or sing to the

Libyan flute. There shall be no pleasures when you are gone. But I shall hire the most skilled artist in all the land to carve me a likeness of you. I shall keep your statue by me in bed, clasping it often and speaking your name. A cold delight, alas—but perhaps you will come to comfort me in my dreams.

"Oh, if only I had the voice of Orpheus so that I could sing my way down to Hades! I would charm the King of Death and his Queen. Neither the Hound of Hell nor the grisly Ferryman would stop me till I brought you back to light. Ah, well, you must wait for me there and prepare a place for me. For I shall order my body laid out in the same cedar casket with yours so that not even death can part me from my own true wife."

Of all these words, Alcestis heeded only one. That all the servants at hand might hear, she said: "You have heard your father's pledge, my children, never to marry again to your discomfort or my dishonor."

"Never will I look on another woman," Admetus said.

"Then take these children from my hands to yours. You must be mother to them now." As Admetus drew the boy and girl gently from her clasp, she sobbed, "Oh, my children, just when you need me most of all, I must leave you both." Her body sank back.

"Oh, what shall I do without you?" Admetus moaned.

"Time is a gentle healer," Alcestis murmured. "The dead are nothing."

"Oh, take me with you!"

"My death for you is enough." She could barely be heard now, for darkness was creeping over her eyes.

"I am lost if you leave me," Admetus cried. "Raise your head. Look at us—do not leave your children!"

"I can . . . help you . . . no more," she gasped faintly, her limbs melting. "Good-by." The children were crying.

"Look at them! Look at them!" Admetus begged, but her voice trailed away:

"I am nothing . . . nothing . . . nothing . . ."

And she was gone.

"Oh, Mother, Mother, what is wrong?" the little boy cried. "Why are her eyes closed? Why doesn't she take my hand and speak to me? Mother, Mother, speak to your little bird."

"She cannot see you or hear you now, my son," said Admetus, drawing the boy away. "She has gone—how we will miss her!"

"Is she dead, Father?"

"Yes, my son. It is a terrible thing."

"Oh, what will Sister and I ever do?" But Admetus gave a sign to the servants and the children were led away.

Then he went out to tell the people, but they could read the tidings in his eyes before he spoke:

"Alcestis, the daughter of Pelias, is no more."

Some tried to comfort him.

"This is a blow you must bear, Admetus, as many men have done before and many will do hereafter."

"She was a noble wife," said another, "but all of us must go some day."

"I know, I know," Admetus told them. "We long knew it had to be. But now I must prepare for her burial. We must wail to the god who is never appeased.

"Let every Thessalian under my sway join in the mourning with shaven heads and robes of black. Aye, let even the manes of horses be shorn. Throughout the city let there be no sound of flute or lyre until twelve moons have passed. For no dearer body shall I ever bury—a perfect woman most worthy of all my honor, for she alone would die for me."

As he left them, all their thoughts were for the brave woman now on her lonely journey to darkness. Would the

King of Death, would the grim Ferryman of Acheron know her worth? Surely it would be known on earth. For poets across the land, even to Athens and faraway Sparta, would sing of her noble sacrifice.

Their meditations were interrupted at last by the coming of a stranger. They did not have to be told his name. His mighty, iron-muscled frame, his club, and the lion skin he wore as a tunic proclaimed him as Heracles, the strongest and bravest of mortal men.

"Tell me," the hairy, black-bearded man asked them, "will I find Admetus at home?"

"Yes, he is within," one man began to tell him, "but . . ."

Another's hand stopped him from saying more. No visitor was to be greeted with sorrow.

"What brings you to Pherae, Heracles?"

"Another task for King Eurystheus of Tiryns. I am on my way to Thrace to bring back the four horses of Diomedes."

"Don't you know they cannot be taken without a battle?"

"I am not one to stop at that," said Heracles, nor did he look it. "Surely they don't breathe fire."

"But they tear men to pieces with their ravenous jaws."

"Come, now," said Heracles. "They are horses, not mountain wolves."

"Wait till you see the blood spattered about their stalls."

"No man lives who will ever see Alcmena's son tremble at danger," laughed Heracles, slapping his huge, hairy chest.

At that moment the gate opened and Admetus came out. He had shaved off his hair and put on the black robes of mourning. But he gave Heracles the usual greeting:

"Rejoice, O son of Zeus and Alcmena."

"Joy to you, too, Admetus of Thessaly," Heracles replied.

Joy? thought Admetus. If only you knew! But a guest was a guest. Aloud he said, "Welcome, my friend!"

"But why are you in mourning?" asked Heracles.
"A burial," said Admetus, "that I am about to attend."
"Not one of your children? May the gods forbid!"
"No, they are both quite well, thank you."
"Your father? After all, his time was ripe."
"No, he and my mother are both alive," said Admetus with a twinge of bitterness.
"But surely not your wife Alcestis?"
Admetus wished neither to lie nor sadden his guest. "You knew her fate," he parried.
"That she was pledged to die for you?"
"Yes, and from the moment she made that vow she was doomed, which is the same as dead to me."
"Oh, no, my friend," said Heracles, misled. "To be and not to be are different things. But whom do you mourn at this moment?"
"A woman," said Admetus.
"Some kin by blood?" asked Heracles. Admetus was relieved that this was his question, for now he could truly say:
"No, not by blood. She came to my home from a distant land, after her father died."
"It speaks well of you to have sheltered an orphan," Heracles said. "But I must go on. A guest would be a burden to mourners."
"No, I would not think of your staying at another's house," said Admetus. "The dead are dead. But our guest hall is far from the weeping."
"Ten thousand thanks," said Heracles, "but I must not stay."
"But you must, I insist," Admetus said. He turned to a servant: "Lead him to the guest room facing away from our halls. Give him meat and drink aplenty. And shut the gates between."

Heracles shrugged his huge shoulders, but let himself be led away. After all, it was just a strange woman.

Some of the mourners waiting at the gate were shocked. Even hospitality must have some limits.

"Admetus, have you lost your mind?" one asked.

"Would you have praised me more," the king replied, "if I had driven off this guest who entertained me most lavishly in Argos? That would never bring my dear wife back. My house has lost its greatest joy, but never let it be said it has lost its welcome."

Hospitality was indeed his virtue—even to a fault—they had to admit. No wonder Apollo had blessed this house. Then why had the god deserted it now? But in truth the god had not, for it was by his doing that Heracles even now was wining and dining in its guest hall.

Admetus soon led forth from the palace those who bore the body of his wife and all the rich gifts for her tomb. He bade them all join in the mourning. But the procession had moved only a pace or two when it stopped. For Admetus' old father, Pheres, came up with attendants bearing embroidered burial robes, honey cakes, and exquisite vases and jars of spice and scented oils.

"I have come to share your sorrows, my son," the old man said. "Our loss is hard, but we must bear it. She was a fine and noble wife—a credit to her sex—who consented to be struck down instead of you by the hand of Death. So take these ornaments, my son. Let them honor the woman who died rather than let me go childless to my grave. Farewell, good woman! You pitied my gray hairs. May it go well with you! Let me tell you, my son, this is the sort of woman that makes a marriage well worthwhile."

"I never invited you to her burial," Admetus cried. "You are no friend. Away with these trinkets! She shall wear nothing of yours. Your time to mourn was when I was doomed. But no, you stayed away then and, old as you were, you let a young one die for me. Was I not your son? Did you not beget me, your wife bear me? Or was I some slave child secretly brought to her breast? You showed yourself no true father, then, but the prince of cowards. You had had everything in life—long years, riches, a crown—even a son to keep strangers from dividing your estate. Yet you neither cared nor dared to save that son, but left the task to a woman outside your kin. She alone do I regard as father and mother now."

"What kind of slave do you think you are scolding?" Pheres demanded. "I am a freeborn man of Thessaly. I begat and reared you as my heir. I know of no law in Greece that fathers must die for their sons. For good or bad, your life and your fate were your own. I gave you a kingdom to rule, and all the lands that I had from my father. What more do I owe? Neither of us was duty-bound to die for the other. Death is long and bitter; life is short, but sweet. You love the light of day. Do you think your father does not love it, too?"

"All my life," replied Admetus bitterly, "I was most respectful to you, and this is my thanks. Go away, old man, and beget some other son to take care of you. I shall not even bury you, for to you I am already dead. You old men are liars when you complain of age and pray for death. For just let Death come near you, and then you refuse to go. Suddenly old age is no burden at all."

"Cease!" begged a friend. "Your own affliction is enough. Do not enrage your father." But Pheres was already enraged.

"She died for you," he jeered. "Shame on you for cheating your own fate by killing your wife! Me a coward! Look who says so! Oh, you have hit on a clever scheme to live forever. Just keep persuading your wives to die for you. Slander me no more or you shall hear worse—the bitter truth."

Now the mourners were ashamed for the old man, too. To

think the queen's burial should be halted thus by two kings wrangling in the street!

"I shall say no more," said Admetus, "for it is you the truth hurts. Live longer than Zeus if you like."

"It was your life she lengthened, not mine."

"Because you were afraid."

"You would be laughing now if it were my old body you were carrying out. Go on, woo many women so that more may die."

"Shameless coward!" cried Admetus.

"Well, she was not shameless or a coward either," said Pheres, pointing to the body, "but lucky for you she was simple-minded."

"Be off," shouted Admetus, "and let me bury the dead."

"That is the murderer's task," said his father, "but you will still have to answer to her kin."

"Go back to your childless wife," said Admetus, "for I renounce you both. Never come under my roof again." He turned to the bearers. "Let us move on with our burden."

The old man was left standing among his attendants and rejected gifts, while the procession moved on, solemnly chanting a hymn to Hermes that Alcestis might be conducted to her rest in peace.

Meanwhile in the guest hall the servants, with orders to smile and hide their tears, were heaping the table in front of the hungry Heracles. Joint after joint of meat he would seize in his hairy paws, chew off huge chunks and wash them down with fiery wine straight from the jug; then belch and bellow for more.

"Of all the guests I ever served," one servant whispered, "he is by all odds the worst."

"More wine! More wine!" Heracles was shouting. "And stronger! This is pap."

"Look at him swill it down," said another servant peeking

through the door. "He knows the master's grief, but he has no shame."

"Nor even the decency to accept what is set before him," said another.

Soon the monstrous man had downed enough for twenty and had wreathed his head with myrtle leaves. He began to sing some bawdy love songs out of key. Behind his back the servants held their ears.

"I should be out weeping for my mistress," said one. "For she was a mother to us all, a buffer against the master's wrath. Instead, I have to fetch and carry for this brawling bandit, this cutthroat, this thief."

Though the servants tried, not all could mask their grief. At last Heracles caught sight of one whose face was downcast.

"Ho there, fellow," he shouted, "why that hang-dog look? Is that sour face and clouded brow meet for your master's guest? Come here and serve me with a broad-beamed smile."

The servant tried but only looked more doleful.

"What—brooding over a stranger's death?" asked Heracles. "Do you not know the way of all flesh? I suppose not. How could you?" Letting his head fall forward to one side, he waved the servant toward him. "Come closer, boy, and heed some words of wisdom." Then sprawling back, with rolling head and heavy-lidded eyes, Heracles began to lecture him, his forefinger waving in the air:

"Death—my boy—is a debt we all must pay. Who knows if he will be around tomorrow—for where the Fates will wander is anyone's guess. So what does it all mean? What is the answer? I will tell you, boy. Enjoy yourself! That is the answer. Drink! Today is yours—tomorrow can care for itself.

"And always be reverent, boy," he went on solemnly. "Worship the sweetest of all the gods—the Love Goddess!

A-h-h-h, but she is good to men! Now, do I make sense? Yes, I think so, too. Well, then, rise above your troubles, my friend. Have a drink with me. Let it trickle down and relax your soul. We mortals must think and act like mortals. But, if you ask me, a mournful sour-face does not really live. He just exists in misery."

"You may be right," the servant said uncomfortably, "but our misery goes far too deep for revelry or laughter."

"What? Tears for a mere stranger? Now if your master or mistress were dead it would be different."

The servant groaned: "You do not know our loss."

"Indeed, I do," said Heracles, "unless your master lied to me about that orphan girl."

"Orphan girl!" the servant exclaimed. "Oh, he is too considerate of his guests by far."

"Considerate enough not to turn me out with an empty stomach," Heracles growled. "But wait—are you all holding something back from me?"

"Sir, if you will excuse me . . ." The servant tried to leave, but Heracles seized him by the tunic and whirled him around.

"Out with it!" he demanded.

"Oh, sir, you came at a terrible time. If it had been just a stranger's death we would not have minded you so much. But did you not see our shorn heads and black garments?"

"You mean . . ."

"The wife of our master is dead, and our hearts have died with her."

Heracles sprang up and cried:

"Oh, I should have known it. I saw his garments, his eyes, his face—and yet I believed him. The best of hosts and the worst of guests! To think I was making merry and he in such agony! Where is he burying her? Where shall I find her?"

"She would be carried past the marketplace that all might see and mourn," the servant said, "but yonder is a straight path—the road to Larissa—and you will see the marble tomb Admetus built her close by the city gate."

"Am I not stronger than Death?" asked Heracles. And, thanks to Bacchus, he believed he was. "I shall go to her tomb and lie in wait for this black-robed king of cadavers. Perchance I can seize him as he comes to swill the drink offerings. And once I lay hands on him—see him or not—I shall coil my arms about him and squeeze his ribs till there is little death left in him and he will be willing to give her up.

"If need be I shall fight my way clear down to the King and Queen of Hades to make my plea. Never let it be said this noble, most gracious host in Thessaly wasted his kindness on a thankless guest." And, seizing his club, he strode off.

When Admetus returned from Alcestis' burial he could not bear to enter the hateful, empty halls.

"Would to the gods I had never been born!" he exclaimed to the friends who sat around him in the courtyard. They tried to console him, for grieving could not bring her back.

"I wish to the gods I had never married her," he said. "Only those without wives or children are happy. For Death can strike them only once."

"Yet every man must suffer in some way," they said.

"Why did you stop me from hurling myself into her tomb?" he moaned. "I could be lying with her still and we could be making the journey together."

"You must hold your grief in measure," one friend told him. "I had an aged kinsman who lost his one and only son, yet he did not give way."

"Oh, how can I enter this house?" Admetus asked again. "I remember when I first came here with Pelian torches and bridal songs, holding my dear wife's hand in mine. And joyful revelers hailed us with shouts for . . ." His voice broke. ". . . for long life and happiness."

Perhaps he had been too happy, they told him, unschooled by ills to meet a blow that many others had endured.

"Her lot is really happier than mine, my friends," he said, "though some of you might doubt it. No grief can touch her any more, while I, who should have died, am doomed to the bitterest of lives. Where can I turn? With whom can I speak? How can I bear to see her empty bed, her empty chair, the floors unswept by careless servants, and my children weeping at my knee? Every gathering will torture me, seeing other men with happy wives. And behind my back they will whisper, 'Look at that coward still alive because he gave his own wife in ransom to escape from Hades. What kind of a man is he who hates his parents because he feared to die?' How can I endure such talk on top of all my grief?"

"Your affliction must be borne," said one. "For I have long searched all the poets and philosophers, and none has ever found anything more powerful than That Which Is and Must Be, call it 'Fate' or 'Doom' or 'Necessity.' Nothing in all the mystic writ of Thracian Orpheus or the healing drugs of Asclepius.

"Necessity has no altars, no shrines, no statues. No one worships her, for she heeds no prayers or sacrifice. She is ruthless and her bonds are stronger than the strongest iron of the Chalybes.

"Necessity has you in a hold the strongest wrestler could not break. For all men must die—even those the gods beget when they lie with mortal women. Alcestis was dear to all of us and always will be, though now she must lie in a tomb. So it must be, but hers will be no common tomb. It will become a shrine, to which the passer-by will turn aside and pray, for great should be her power to bless."

Thus were they sharing grief and consolation when Heracles came through the gate, still in his tawny lion skin and swinging his mighty club. But over his other shoulder he bore a burden, and they saw it was a woman. She seemed ill or faint, for when he sat her down on a bench she hardly moved and did not speak a word. Her face was veiled against the dust, but casting their eyes over her body they could see she was young and well endowed.

Mopping his brow with the back of his hairy forearm, Heracles began to chide the king.

"A friend should speak his mind straight out, Admetus," he said, "and not let anger rankle in his heart. Surely I was worthy of sharing your grief, but you lied to me. You let me wreathe my head in revelry and drown my wits with wine when your house was plunged in deepest mourning. Thus I besmirched my own good name and yours. It was wrong, my friend, wrong—though I have no wish to wound you further now."

"Oh, Heracles," Admetus said, "I counted you very much my friend in hiding my wife's unhappy fate. It was enough for me to mourn. And I would have added only pain to pain if I had turned you away to another's house."

"Well, let it pass," said Heracles, "for I have come back to ask you a favor. I must go to Thrace to fetch those murderous horses, even if I have to kill their cruel master. Take care of this woman for me while I am gone. If anything should happen to me—not that I expect it—she will be yours to serve you as you will."

"Oh, please," Admetus begged, "not me! Ask it of some other friend, for you must have many here in Pherae who are not bowed down in woe. The sight of her young body in my home would make me weep the more, and I have tears enough already."

"You must not refuse me," said Heracles, "for she was

hard to come by. I won her in a wrestling match—the hardest, I think, a man ever fought, and for a noble prize. Not horses or cattle but this fair lady—a treasure I would not trust with every man."

Admetus was distressed. And most distressed to find forbidden whisperings already in his mind.

"Where could I put her?" he asked Heracles. "For her body is young and tempting, I can plainly see, and my young men are passionate. She would not be safe in the servants' quarters. In your interest alone I should have to take her in with me. But can I put her in my dead wife's bed? Then I should be doubly blamed—not only by the folk who called me false to the one who saved my life but even by my own dead wife herself."

"You must look after her," said Heracles, "for she was hard to win and I am sure she must be pleasing to your eye."

"Ah, yes, she has Alcestis' height and grace . . . but, no, by the gods! Take her away. She is much too much like my wife."

"Would that I only could bring Alcestis back," said Heracles. "But you must curb your grief. What good can it do to mourn forever?"

"I know, but love compels me."

"Your grief is young, but Time will heal it."

"Only if Time be Death."

"A young wife would be a quicker cure."

"Enough of that!" Admetus said in horror. "What are you saying? I would not think of such a thing."

"Now what good will a bed of joyless purity ever do the dead?"

"I would rather die than betray her."

"Good, good," said Heracles, "but surely utter foolishness. Take this woman in your house."

"No, no, by your father Zeus! I wish you had never won her."

"But remember your duty to your guest. Friends must share their winnings, if not their losses."

"True," said Admetus, "but please, as a favor, take her away."

"If you force me," said Heracles, "but must you force me?"

"Yes I must—unless you are going to be angry."

"I would be angry, indeed."

"Then have your way," said Admetus. He told his servants to lead her in, but Heracles would not have it.

"No," he said, "you told me yourself we cannot trust her to servants. You must lead her in yourself. Here, take her by the hand."

"I will not touch her," Admetus said.

"You must," said Heracles, "for friendship's sake."

He drew the woman to her feet and placed her hand in the hand of the king. Admetus trembled at the touch but would not look at her.

"Some day you will bless me for this," said Heracles. "I am indeed no thankless guest." He drew the veil from the woman's face.

"Look at her! Look at her!" Heracles demanded. Reluctantly Admetus turned his head and gave a cry:

"Alcestis! Or is this some trick? Is this my own dear wife I buried? No, you are mocking me. She must be a ghost."

"You hold her hand," said Heracles. "Does a ghost have hands that are warm? Speak to her, for now you have all that you wished."

"Oh, dear heart, dear face, dear body," cried Admetus. "Do I really have you with me once again?"

"You have, indeed," said Heracles, "wrestled, if I may say so, right out of the greedy hands of Death himself. May the gods not be too jealous of your joy. She cannot speak to you yet, not until three days have passed, for the rites of consecration to the gods below must be undone. But take her in, for I must go about my task."

"No, stay," said Admetus. "Share our happiness. Let it be proclaimed to all the citizens. Let there be songs and dancing and wine—and altars heaped high with sacrifices to the blessed gods. Come, son of Zeus and Alcmena, you must stay and share our feasting."

"No," said Heracles, shouldering his club, "I must be off for now. But when I pass this way again I know I shall find a bounteous welcome."

Euripides could have made a prettier story if he had let Alcestis make a bargain with the Fates without her husband's knowledge. But that was not Euripides' way. He approached each legend with the question, "What kind of a person would . . . ?" The resulting picture of Admetus—a man who would let his wife die for him—was one more of Euripides' subtle jabs at the Greek male ego.

Happy endings, according to Aristotle, are for weak minds.

Had this been a tragedy, Admetus would probably have found his rescued life too bitter to endure. But this play is only a tragic postcript. True tragedies were presented each day in series of threes, or trilogies, and were usually followed by a lighter dramatic form called a satyr play. *Alcestis* was performed in this last position as a sort of light dessert after a tragic three-course meal. It is probably the earliest play we have from Euripides.

OEDIPUS THE KING

CHARACTERS

Oedipus (EED-i-pus or ED-i-pus): King of Thebes.

Jocasta (Jo-CAST-a): The queen, wife of Oedipus and widow of Laius, the former king who was slain on the road to Delphi.

Creon (KREE-on): Brother of Queen Jocasta (not to be confused with King Creon of Corinth, in *Medea*).

Tiresias (Ti-REE-see-as): An aged and blind soothsayer, or prophet.

The priest of Zeus: Leader of a group of suppliants.

A messenger from Corinth.

An old shepherd, a former servant of King Laius.

Theban elders.

Antigone (An-TIG-o-nee) and Ismene (Is-MEE-nee): Little daughters of Oedipus and Jocasta.

Oedipus the King is often rated the greatest drama of the Greeks. Certainly it is tragedy in sheer classic form—as clear-cut, proportioned, and integrated as the Parthenon, as logical as a proposition of Euclid. It could never be cut and rearranged like *Hamlet*. Its characters, like Greek statues, are more ideal types than the close-up portraits of Euripides.

The play is a detective story—it's crime, murder, and worse. But the theme runs far deeper. Sophocles loved to exalt man's divine heroism in a cruel universe. In this play man's heroism is his unswerving pursuit of truth in the face of terrible consequences. This fearless quest has been man's tragedy—and glory—from the first. Eons ago, he, alone of all creatures, discovered he must die. Today's Oedipus may be the guilt-ridden atomic scientist who has probed the secrets of nature only to find the worst horror of all. But probe he must.

Although this was a detective story, the story was not a mystery to those who saw it first about 429 B.C. Like the gods, they knew the shape of things from the beginning. But they must have sat entranced as the story unfolded in all its grim irony. They could sense the false goal of every action, the hidden doom in every word. In the background lie superstitions—not all dead—about ancestral sin, soothsaying and oracles, but the action is real and believable.

Although the "Oedipus conflict," arising from repressed sexual feelings toward parents, is one of Freud's best-known theories, it has little bearing on the play. True, great art can suggest many "meanings" to many minds, but Sophocles, for all his insights, was no more a conscious creator of Freudian symbols than he was a Christian moralist creating parables of divine justice.

OEDIPUS THE KING

(SOPHOCLES)

For years the gods had seemed to smile on the city of Thebes. Its flocks were fat and its harvests rich in grain and wine. No enemy threatened its seven gates, and the laughter of children filled the streets. "Rejoice!" each citizen hailed his neighbor. The greeting had never seemed more right.

"Our ship of state sails well," the people said, "with Oedipus, our deliverer at the helm." They almost worshiped their chosen king. Clear-eyed he was, and handsome and wise, and the gold of Apollo shone in his flowing locks and beard. He had only the slightest limp to free him from such perfection as might have stirred the envy of the gods.

How well the people remembered that distant day when Oedipus came to their gates as a wandering stranger. Their king was dead, and their land was plagued by the strangling Sphinx. That loathsome creature, with a woman's face and breasts and the body of a winged lioness, had been pouncing on hapless Thebans at every crossroad to ask her deadly riddle: "What walks on four legs at dawn, on two at noon, and on three in the setting sun?" Those who did not know had to pay with their lives, and none had known the answer. Indeed, it had been to save his people from this monster that old King Laius had set out for Delphi to consult the oracle of Apollo. Alas, the old king and most of his men had been murdered along the way.

The city was mourning its king, and the Sphinx still taking her fearful toll that day the wanderer Oedipus of the swollen foot arrived at the gates of Thebes. He heard their woes, then, eyes flashing, he faced the foul Sphinx, heard her riddle, and roared out the answer:

"Man!"

The Sphinx vanished in a dying shriek, and the plague was ended. At last the tangle-witted Thebans saw the light. Of course, they told each other, man must crawl before he walks, and in the evening of his life he hobbles with a cane. But, they agreed, that Oedipus, who had seen it first, must indeed share the wisdom of the gods.

Their king was dead, and who but Oedipus should take his place? The queen long since had lost her only son, and who else should make her fruitful again and seed a dynasty that would surely find favor in the eyes of gods and men? There was joy when Oedipus took to himself the widowed Jocasta and mounted the throne. Joy when Jocasta, still comely although the silver of Artemis shone in her hair, brought forth a son, then a second child, a third, and a fourth . . .

But now the gods smiled no more. A new evil was abroad —a fiery plague, an unseen thing, more fearful than the strangling monster. It was spring, but not spring. No buds grew on the boughs. Folk and flocks alike were parched and dying. Women suffered childbirth pangs and yet brought forth no young.

High in his palace Oedipus heard the moaning of his people and suffered with them. This was a new, more awful riddle for which he had no answer. No answer, for he knew not the question.

Up from the city came a suppliant procession—old men, youths, and children of the nobly born—led by the priest of mighty Zeus. All clad in white they were, with white ribbons of wool bound in their hair and twined through the olive branches they laid on the altars before the palace doors. The air grew thick with their prayers and incense.

Then Oedipus came and stood before them, a golden hope, dazzling in his kingly robes.

"My children," he said, "why come you thus to me? Let me hear the tale from your own lips, and Oedipus renowned of men, will give all aid in his power. Hard of heart your king would be not to heed such suppliants."

"And there are many more," the old priest said. "All our people are praying in the marketplace or at the shrines of Pallas Athene, for the flaming plague is robbing the city of Thebes to fill the house of Hades with groans and tears.

"Once, O mightiest Oedipus, you saved us from the riddling Sphinx. Do not desert us now. Listen once more to the voice of that god they say counseled you then or the whisper of your mind. Let no man hereafter say that you lifted us once only to cast us down again. End not your days as ruler of a city of the dead."

"Oh, my poor children," Oedipus said. "I know your longings and woe, and yet none of you suffers as I do. Each of you has your own pain to bear, but I bear the sorrows of all. But days ago I sent Creon, my own wife's brother, to inquire of Apollo's oracle what word, what deed, of mine could save this city. As truly as I am a man, whatever the god shows, that will I do."

Even as he spoke there was a stir. Creon and his men were back from Delphi. Prayers turned to cries of hope as the people saw that his white hair was crowned with laurel berries, a sign that the tidings were fair.

"What news, dear kinsman?" asked Oedipus. "What news do you bring from the god?"

"Good news," said Creon. "Misfortune, when all ends well, is all for the good."

"But the word, what was the word?" Oedipus cried. "Your rambling gives me neither heart nor fear."

Creon seemed loath to tell more.

"Should we not go inside?" he asked.

"No, let everyone hear," said Oedipus, "their suffering means more to me than my life."

"I can tell you only so much as the god made plain," Creon said. "Phoebus, our lord, declared there is something rotten within our land; we harbor a festering sore which must be driven out."

"But how may we purge ourselves?" Oedipus asked. "What is this evil thing?"

"It is blood guilt that wrecks our city. We must banish a man or take a life for a life."

"And who is this guilty man?" Oedipus hurled the question at Creon, but Creon began to talk of Laius, the old king, and his murder on the road to Delphi.

"All this I have heard before," Oedipus broke in, "although it happened before I came and I never saw the man. But what is this to me?"

"The god says plainly that we must take vengeance on his murderers, whoever they may be."

"But where could we find them now that the trail is cold?" asked Oedipus.

Creon trembled.

"Here—in this land—the god declared. He revealed no more."

Who in this land could have profited from the king's death? thought Oedipus, looking sharply at Creon. Did his brother-in-law know more?

"Was there no witness?" he asked.

"Only one," said Creon. "He fled in terror when all the rest were slain, and he could remember only one thing."

"What was that? Even a single clue might be a key."

"Only that it was a large band of robbers who fell upon them."

"Unless there was some bribery, some corruption here," asked Oedipus, "why was the murder never avenged?"

"We made inquiry," Creon replied, "yet little could be done, so great were our other woes at the time from the riddling Sphinx."

"Then I will take up the trail afresh," said Oedipus, "and once again bring darkest things to light." He turned to the people.

"Phoebus has spoken well," he said, "and I shall join your cause. Not to avenge some distant kinsman but for my own soul's sake, shall I purge this taint of blood. In righting your wrong I can only serve myself, for the very hands that slew Laius might well wreak worse on me."

As he led Creon inside the palace, the people prayed in hope and fear. They prayed to Athene for wisdom; to Artemis and her brother Phoebus to sheathe their silent arrows of sudden death; to Ares to cease from a war more terrible than any ever waged by men in arms; to Father Zeus to slay Death himself with his fiery thunderbolt; and again to Phoebus and Artemis to bring back the golden light of day and the silver beacon of night; to Bacchus for the return of fruitfulness to barren fields and barren wombs.

But Oedipus had little time for prayer. He said to Creon, "That man, who lost his wits and fled—he must be found."

"I fear he could do us little good," said Creon, "but, if I might speak . . ."

"Speak on," said Oedipus. "Only your cautious silence could be a crime."

"The god made only so much clear. But there is a blind man who might tell us more."

"And are we all not blind?"

"This man, Tiresias, has no eyes but only empty sockets in his aged skull. Yet wise he is, they say, and sees all things known only to the gods. Of all men he is most like Phoebus. And feeling sure that you would approve, I sent for him as I returned. Perhaps he can interpret the message of the god."

"Then let him come and try his craft," said Oedipus. "And meantime I must ply mine, for nothing ought to be left undone."

Then Oedipus once again appeared before his people.

"Your prayers will soon be answered," he said, "if you heed my words and help me to heal your woes. I cannot be a stranger to your suffering, yet being a stranger to its cause, I could not track it down alone. So I proclaim:

"If any man knows the slayers of Laius, the son of Labdacus, let him speak out. Let the guilty man not cringe in fear but purge himself by confession. His penalty will be no worse than to leave this land in peace.

"But if anyone keeps silent to shield himself or a friend, then hear my command: No man shall speak to that murderer, whoever he may be, or give him food or shelter, or join him in any prayer or sacrifice, for he is hated by the gods and has defiled our city. May I, too, suffer the same curse if ever I take him into my home.

"Even if the god had not so decreed," he continued, "it was wrong for you not to avenge your king. But now his cause is also mine. I hold his throne and the wife who bore him a child—a child who might have been brother to my own. So I shall pursue the cause of Laius as though he had been my father. And may a curse far worse than the plague that wastes us now fall on the man who hides the guilty truth."

None of the elders spoke at first. Then one came forward

and said, "I swear, my King, that I was not the slayer, and I cannot tell you who he was." Others, too, began to swear their innocence.

Then up through the crowd, half led, half pushed, there came an aged man whose beard was long and white.

"No, let me go," the old man cried. "Let the king bear his own burden, and let me bear mine."

And Oedipus saw that the old man was blind. It was Tiresias.

"O seer of Apollo," Oedipus said, "to you all things above and on earth are known. And although you cannot see, you must feel our misery. To save ourselves we must drive out the murderers of Laius. If you can tell us who they are, do not deny us the secrets of your art."

Tiresias moaned.

"No, ask me nothing," he said, "for wisdom is an awful thing to one who can only suffer from it."

"Your words are strange," said Oedipus. "They are not friendly to this city. The noblest use of wisdom is to aid your fellow men."

But Tiresias said nothing, as he clasped his feeble hands more tightly on his staff.

"For the love of the gods, old man," cried Oedipus, "do not deprive us of your knowledge."

"I do not wish to hurt myself—or you," the old man said. "The things I know, you will never learn from me."

"Traitor!" roared Oedipus. "Can nothing cure your evil temper?"

"Look to yourself," the old man said, "to find that fault. The future must come. My silence cannot change it, nor can your words, rage on as you will."

"Then it was you!" cried Oedipus. "It was you who helped to plot that murder. If you had eyes, I would swear that you did it with your own hands."

Stung by the charge, the old man looked straight at the king as though his empty eyes could see.

"Your curse be on your own head," he said. "From this day on, never speak to me nor to any man in Thebes. You are the defiler of this land."

"You slanderer!" Oedipus cried. "Who put such vile words in your mouth? Not the god, indeed!"

"It was you who forced them out—you who killed the very man whose slayers you are seeking."

"You shall pay for this, old man," cried Oedipus.

His threat only drove the old man into saying more:

"And you have been living in secret shame with your nearest kin."

"You wretch!" cried Oedipus. "You have no eyes—no ears —no mind. You live in darkest night and cannot harm me nor any man who sees the sun."

"No, not I," said the seer, "but Apollo."

A new thought flashed on Oedipus.

"Are these your tricks or Creon's?" he demanded.

"It is yourself, not Creon, who is your enemy," Tiresias told him.

It must be Creon, Oedipus thought. I, who sought nothing for myself, was given all the wealth and power that Creon coveted. Creon, my pious friend! And all the time he was scheming against me with this tattered holy man, this tricky fraud.

"A seer, indeed!" he said, turning back to the old man. His mouth twisted in contempt. "And when did you ever prove your power? When the Strangler plagued this city with a riddle that cried for a seer's skill, did you then practice your art to save the people? No, it was I, Oedipus, an ignorant stranger with no priestly tricks but only my own wits, who found the answer. And now by trickery you hope to find favor when Creon seizes the throne."

"I do not serve Creon nor you nor any mortal man," the old man said. "Yes, I am blind, but it is you who cannot see. You cannot see from where you came, or with whom you live, or the awful web from which you cannot escape. A mother's and a father's curse will haunt you from hell in a world of darkest night."

"Why was I persuaded to listen to such a fool?" asked Oedipus angrily.

"Your parents had more respect for me."

My parents? thought Oedipus. Surely this seer has never been in Corinth where my parents live—nor were they ever here.

"Then, tell me," he mocked. "Who of men *is* my father?"

"This day," Tiresias said, "will reveal your birth and seal your doom."

"Riddles!" scoffed Oedipus. "Always you speak in riddles."

"And you are the clever man who solves them." Tiresias turned to the youth at his side. "Lead me home," he said.

"Yes, take him away," said Oedipus. "Then he can do me no further harm."

"Nor can you harm me," said Tiresias. "But I can see a late-come stranger doomed to find that he was born in Thebes. I can see a blind man who now has eyes, a beggar who now has gold, groping his cheerless way through an alien land. For he shall be found brother and father of his children, son and husband of the woman who bore him, defiler of his father's bed, shedder of his father's blood. Think well on this, and if it proves not so, then tell the world that I am no prophet but a fool."

The old man was led away, but the Thebans remained, stunned by their king's unbridled rage and the awful sayings of the seer.

"If ever any man committed such monstrous deeds," said one, "he would flee from the sight of men, crashing through mountain thickets like a frenzied bull, vainly trying to escape his doom."

"I do not know about seers," said another. "I have no vision of the future. But I know of nothing evil that ever touched our king."

"The gods know everything," a third agreed, "but how can I tell whether any seer among men knows more than I? I must have proof. Oedipus was tested once, before the Sphinx, and proved both good and wise. I cannot change that verdict in my heart."

The angry Oedipus, who had gone in search of Creon, found him indignantly protesting the charges before a group of elders. Some tried to calm him, saying the king had spoken in anger and did not mean it. Others said nothing. It was better to stay out of palace quarrels.

"How dare you be so brazen?" Oedipus cried at Creon. "Did you think I was such a fool or coward I would not see and thwart your scheme?"

The older man's quivering pallor seemed to Oedipus to show his guilt as he sought to trap him with swift questions about his dealings with the seer.

"Where was Tiresias when Laius was slain?" he asked.

"Here in Thebes," said Creon, "a wise and honored man."

"And did he whisper a word about me then?"

"Not within my hearing," Creon admitted.

"And were you trying to solve the murder?"

"Yes, but we found nothing."

"Then why," demanded Oedipus, "did your clever friend not tell his story then?"

"I do not know," said Creon. "And when I do not know, I have the sense to make no rash surmises."

The gibe was lost on Oedipus.

"But this you do know," he charged. "If you had not conspired with him he would not now be blaming me for Laius' death."

"But why should I conspire?" asked Creon. "Do I not already possess all that I could desire?"

"That makes your crime the worse," said Oedipus.

"No, stop and reason it as I do," Creon said. "First of all, what man in his right mind would choose the terrors that haunt a king when he could sleep at peace while living like a king? I am not so ambitious for an empty title to all the power and luxury I already have gained from you. There would be no profit in it. A king is not his own master but must do many things he hates. I can freely pass the time of day with any man I choose. And if any man needs anything from you, I am the one on whom he calls. Would I be minded to change this happy state of things? Or would I suffer anyone else to do it?

"But if you do not believe me, then go to Apollo yourself. Ask him if I lied about the oracle. If you can prove I have ever plotted with Tiresias, then, by my own decree as well as yours, take and slay me. But do not judge wildly in a moment's heat. It takes years to prove a good man just; one day unmasks a villain."

"He has spoken with reason," one of the elders said to the king. "Swift judgments cannot be trusted."

"Unless I am swift," said Oedipus, "this traitor will pin me before I can move."

"You seek my exile . . . ?" Creon began.

"Not exile," Oedipus shouted, "but your death, that all may see where treason leads!"

"O cease, my lords," said one of the elders, "for the queen is here." Jocasta already had heard enough. Firmly she stepped between them.

"You foolish men," she said, "are you not ashamed? Have

we not troubles enough without a quarrel like this between you. Come in with me," she told her husband. "And Creon, go to your home. This is no place to show such bitter feelings."

"May the god strike me dead if I ever have harmed him," Creon swore.

"Then Oedipus, for the love of the gods, believe his oath," said Jocasta, "for my sake and for all of us."

"Then let him go," said Oedipus sullenly, "but I yield to you, not to him."

"Just as slow to yield as you are quick to lose your head," Creon muttered. "Such a nature deserves to be a burden to itself." He caught Jocasta's warning glance. "I shall go," he said, "justified in all men's eyes but his."

Tenderly Jocasta led Oedipus into her chamber. With soothing words she drew him down beside her on a couch and gently stroked his golden hair.

"Come, tell me all that is troubling you," she said, drawing his head to her breast. But when he had told her, Jocasta laughed.

"What nonsense!" she said. "My brother Creon is far too fearful and pious to do any wrong. And as for seers, why, no man possesses the knowledge of the gods. I have had experience with their kind before, and I can easily show you that all seercraft is a fraud." And then she told this story:

"Many years ago an oracle came to Laius—not from Apollo surely but from his witless priests. It told him that he would be slain by a child of his and mine.

"And then our child was born." She sighed. "When it was only three days old, despite my tears, Laius pinned its ankles together and had it tossed out to die in the mountains. Thus Laius thwarted the false oracle, and of that we now have proof. For when Laius died, there where the three roads meet, it was at the hands of foreign robbers. So pay no heed to the rantings of a seer."

But Oedipus had leaped up from the couch.

"By the gods, woman, what was that you said?"

"Oedipus, what is wrong?" she asked.

"Did you say 'where the three roads meet'?"

"Why, yes, where the roads from Thebes and Daulia and Delphi come together. But Oedipus, my love, what is torturing you?"

"Wait! Tell me, how did Laius look."

"Ah, he was tall," Jocasta murmured, "in form and figure much like you, but silvered in his hair."

"By the gods," cried Oedipus, "I fear I have put a curse on myself."

"What do you mean? You frighten me."

"Tell me one more thing," Oedipus demanded. "Did he travel with many soldiers, like a king?"

"No, his was a humble journey," Jocasta said. "He rode in a carriage, and there were only five in all."

"O I am fearful," Oedipus moaned. "Where is the man who fled and told what happened?"

"He is not here," Jocasta said. "He loved his master dearly; he could not abide to see you reigning in his stead. As soon as he saw you, he came and begged that I let him leave the palace and tend our flocks in the hills."

"Then I must see him," said Oedipus, "for I must know the truth."

"But what has stirred your heart, my love? Surely I have the right to know?" Then Oedipus told her of his forebodings and of troubles he long had kept to himself.

"You know," he said, "that I am the son of Polybus, King of Corinth, and of Dorian Merope. But till now I have kept secret the reason I fled from home.

"My youth was happy there till one day at a banquet some drunken fool began to babble that I was not my father's son. I could have strangled him for such a vile insult to my mother. Next day I told my parents, and they were angry that anyone would dare to say such a thing. But the rumor spread, and the doubt rankled in my heart. So secretly I went to Delphi to ask the god for an answer. Instead, the oracle of Phoebus told me a fearful thing. It said that I was doomed to slay my father and in my mother's bed beget children of incest that men would look upon in horror. I dared not go back to Corinth then, to my parents' home, for fear these awful things would happen. And so I wandered far away.

"And now I must tell you the truth. When I reached the place where you say the king was slain I met five men, and one, as you have described, was seated in a carriage. A servant, at the old man's bidding, tried to push me off the road. I struck the fellow back. The old man watched his chance, and, just as I was passing him, he raised his heavy goad and struck my head a blinding blow. For that he dearly paid. With one stroke of my staff I hurled him from his carriage, lifeless, to the ground. In the fight I killed them, every man —or so I thought.

"If that fiery-tempered stranger could by any chance have been Laius, then I am by far the most wretched of men. Upon my head I have already laid a curse for the deed, and I have defiled you with a murderer's hands. I am unclean. I must be banished. Yet where will I go? Not to Corinth surely. For then that awful prophecy might come to pass—that I should slay Polybus my sire and wed my mother Merope. And may I die before I ever see that day."

Jocasta, too, began to feel alarm but clung to hope.

"You must not fret yourself with idle fears," she said, "for you can learn the truth from the man who saw the deed."

"If it was a band of robbers," Oedipus admitted, "then I

am not the one. But if his story points to one lone wanderer, then I am guilty beyond all doubt."

"No, there were many," Jocasta said. "He told the same tale many times to all the people." She paused. "Even if he changed his story now, the facts would still be far astray from the prophecy. For the god who speaks in riddles clearly said that Laius' own child would be his slayer. But that poor babe perished in his swaddling clothes."

Whatever had been done, Jocasta thought, was done. Better not to stir it now. But Oedipus must be reassured. She would send for the herdsman.

Oracles seldom meant what they said, she thought, but the gods themselves were good. The people's faith should not be shaken. Calling her handmaidens, she gathered some wreaths and jars of incense and went out to the altars.

"My lords," she said, "I have come to join your prayers. Oedipus is overwrought. A wise man judges the future only from the past. But for the moment, he, poor man, has yielded to the terrors of idle talk." And then she prayed:

"O Lycean Apollo, who art near and dear to us, my words have lost their power to heal and so I come to thee. Show us the way to cleanse us from our sins. Like storm-tossed sailors who see their captain, too, is blind with fear, we are all afraid."

Barely had she ceased her rites when a stranger came among them. He was an old man, in the garb of a foreigner, his face and clothing were caked with dust and sweat. He asked for Oedipus.

"The king is within," he was told, "but here is the mother of his children."

"Then may she ever be happy and blessed." The messenger bowed low as Jocasta approached him.

"And may like happiness be yours," she said, "but what have you come here to seek or tell?"

"The people of Corinth call for Oedipus as their king."
"But what of Polybus, his father?"
"He is no more."
"You mean," she cried, "that Oedipus' father is dead?"
"Alas, it is true or may I die myself."

Jocasta turned to a maidservant. "Run, girl, run and fetch your master!"

Now, in truth, she knew that the oracles were false, for Oedipus' hands were surely clean from any death so far away. Then Oedipus came out and heard the news.

"And did my father die of treachery?" he asked.

"No. It takes but little to tip the scales of age," the messenger said. "He died of illness and of many years."

"For that I mourn," said Oedipus. "But look, my wife, how foolish it is to listen to Apollo's seer and the messages he gets from the birds. It may be that my father longed for me and died from grief that I was so far away. Only in that sense could I be called his slayer. But for all clear truth the oracles are dead, dead as my father is."

"And did I not tell you so?" Jocasta asked.

"You did, but I was tricked by fear."

"And now your fears are ended."

"Almost," said Oedipus, "and yet so long as Merope lives one prophecy cannot wholly die. I must still fear my mother's bed."

"Oh, do not fear to live life as it is," Jocasta counseled. "The oracles are riddles, mixing facts with fantasy. In dreams, many a man has entered his mother's bed and dallied with her. I am sure that the oracle meant no more than that. But the man who can easily put such dreams aside will not be tortured throughout his waking hours."

All this was puzzling to the messenger, although he faintly caught its drift.

"What is it you fear, O King?" he asked. "Perhaps I can set your mind to rest." They told him.

"Why, Polybus and Merope were not your parents by blood," he said, "no more than I. It was I who placed you in their arms as a babe. And, being childless, they loved and reared you as their own."

And then he told them how many years before he had taken his master's flocks far up into the mountains of Cithaeron to graze for the summer, and there he had found a baby, half dead, its ankles pinned together. It was because of this that he had given the child the name of Oedipus, which meant "swollen foot."

"You found me?" cried Oedipus.

"No, in truth another herdsman gave you to me. He wept and said he could not bring himself to let you die, and yet he dared not take you back to the city of your birth. This was the city—he said that he was from the house of Laius."

Jocasta gasped. That other herdsman was the very one she had summoned. But Oedipus must never know.

"In the god's name, Oedipus," she screamed, "do not try to find out any more."

But Oedipus' mind was locked and barred against a truth so awful that he could not face it. Like a madman, he grasped at false suspicion. He turned in contempt to Jocasta.

"You thought I was the son of kings," he said. "And now you fear to face the truth. You fear that the blood of common slaves may run in my veins. But how do you know my father was not some god—Pan, Apollo, Hermes, or Bacchus —who sported with some nymph or Theban maiden in the hills? What difference, woman, whether my blood is base or noble? You still can revel in the pride that you are nobly born."

"O wretched man," Jocasta wailed, "may you never find

out who you are . . . Oh, god!" she cried. "That's all that I can say to you—and never will I speak again."

She hurled herself through the doors into the palace.

But Oedipus was calm, calm with the madness that had come upon him.

"She thinks too much of noble birth," he said, "and now she thinks that I shame her. But I am Oedipus, the child of Time and Fortune, the brother of the Seasons that mark my rise or fall. Whatever I am, I could not change. So why should I fear to learn my birth?"

When the herdsman Jocasta had summoned was brought before them he trembled in fear, for he had long kept his awful secret that Oedipus was his old master's slayer. A coward, he had lied from shame at fleeing from a single man, saying that Laius had been set upon by many robbers. But on these facts he was not questioned, for the moment he appeared the messenger cried, "Why that's the very man."

The frightened herdsman did not recognize the messenger at once. Age had changed the messenger's appearance and had dimmed the herdsman's eyes. But when the messenger recounted those summers long ago when both had watched their mingled flocks on Cithaeron, his memory returned.

When the herdsman was questioned about the babe, he grew alarmed. In pity, he had disobeyed the king's command, but on his return he had sworn that the child was dead.

"Why ask me about these things now?" he begged.

"Because, old friend," the messenger said, "Oedipus, your king, is that same babe, now fully grown."

As the whole fearful truth seeped through his mind, the herdsman was stunned to silence. Then only Oedipus' threats against his life forced out the story, bit by bit.

"Whose was this child?" Oedipus demanded.

"O my master, you are lost if you ask me this."
"And you are lost if I have to ask you once again," cried Oedipus.
"It was . . . of . . . Laius' household."
"Of some slave or one of royal blood?" Oedipus demanded.
Both men were trembling on the brink of one dread word. At last the herdsman forced himself to say, "They all reported that it was Laius' own son, but only your wife within would truly know."
At last the dammed-up truth swirled like a torrent into Oedipus' brain.
"O all has been brought to pass," he moaned, "and never again shall I look on the light of day. For I am cursed in birth, cursed in wedlock, cursed in death."
The people recoiled in horror. How wretched is the fleeting hour of man, they thought. High above them had Oedipus risen. Now he had crashed down to a thing so vile they could not look upon it. Not all the rivers of the world, they thought, could ever cleanse this royal house . . .

Inside, the servants in dreadful awe had seen Jocasta running through the halls, tearing her hair with her hands. Straight to the marriage chamber she fled, then slammed and bolted the heavy doors. They could hear her screams and moans as she threw herself on the marriage bed. They heard her cry out the name of Laius. Then all was silent.

Now Oedipus burst into the hall, madly pacing to and fro, calling for a sword, demanding where he should find his wife who was no wife, the mother whose womb had born himself and all his children too.

Then with a shriek he threw his whole bulk against the double doors, smashing them down as bolts and sockets all gave way at once.

Within he saw the woman, her body swinging from the rafters by a slender cord.

With a cry of pain, Oedipus freed Jocasta's body from the strangling knot and laid it on the floor. From her robes he tore two golden brooches and stabbed them again and again into his eyes, crying, "Never shall I look again upon my sins. Be dark forever."

Over his cheeks and golden beard the blood was flowing, yet his pain was only for his soul. He roared for someone to unbar the gates and show him for the thing he was before all the people of Thebes.

"Apollo brought all these woes to pass," he cried, "but I myself struck out my eyes, and would that I could destroy my hearing too. For never again will anything in this world be lovely to hear or look upon. And when I die, in Hades, I shall still be blind. It is well, for never could I endure to see my father again or my wretched mother."

On and on he went, shouting out for all to hear the full story of his guilt till Creon came—Creon who alone was left to rule.

"I cannot find it in my heart to reproach him now," said Creon to the people. "Yet I fear lest the gods will not approve that all should see such naked horror." Then he told the servants: "Lead him within, for piety demands that we his kinsmen should hide our shame within the family walls."

"O Creon, I have played you false," said Oedipus. "But now, for your sake and mine, grant me this wish. Obey Apollo's command and my decree, and cast me from this city."

But Creon would not consent. Oedipus' decrees no longer stood. As for the gods, so much had passed that Creon felt he must learn their will anew.

Then Oedipus begged that Creon give Jocasta the burial rites of one's dearest kinsman.

"But let me go out on Cithaeron," he cried. "It is the place appointed by my parents for my tomb, and yet, I cannot even seek rest in death till the gods ordain. My sons," he said, "can make their way as men, but have pity on my poor daughters. How terrible is the fate I have brought upon them. Who will ever speak to them? Shunned, at every festival, they will come home in tears. And, when they are ripe for marriage, what man will have them? Taunted and despised, they will wither in barren maidenhood."

"Enough," said Creon laying a hand on his shoulder. "You have had your fill of grief."

"Oh, let me but touch my daughters' hands again," Oedipus pleaded. In pity, Creon had Antigone and Ismene brought out, and, holding them so they might not see their father's face, he placed their hands in his.

"O my poor girls," the father said. "Much counsel I would give you, though as yet you could not understand . . . But pity them like a father," he said to Creon, "and do not suffer them to wander friendless and unwed. Good man, touch my hand, in solemn promise that you will care for them.

"Now, cast me from this city and the eyes of men," he cried.

"I cannot," Creon said. "First I must consult the gods again. Now you must go within . . . Come, let the children go."

"No, do not take my children from me," Oedipus cried. But Creon reminded him:

"Many times you have tried to be master of your fate. Now you must curb your will at last."

Slowly the people went back to their homes. They thought of Oedipus, Oedipus who had solved one riddle to become the mightiest of men—and then the most pitiable when he had solved another. And in his heart each held the thought:

"Count no man happy till the day he dies."

From this play, more than any other, Aristotle formulated his famous definition of a tragic hero: a man of high estate, but no saint, whose downfall comes not from depravity or vice but from some human weakness.

In short, he must be high enough to fall, good enough to win our sympathy, hurt enough to frighten us, and treated unjustly enough to stir our pity.

A certain blind rashness helped bring Oedipus' troubles on himself, but the dice of destiny were loaded against him. It is foolish to try to find enough black sins to say the gods were just—if they were responsible for his fate. His incest was innocent. He killed—but in self-defense. He suspected a soothsayer—but the oracle at Delphi itself could be corrupted.

Did Sophocles believe that in some mysterious way the Universe was just even if his play seems to show the opposite? Critics may chide me for leaving out a chorus that seems to say so. Actually it only begs the question. For who knows when the chorus is the mouthpiece of the poet and when it is merely reacting in character?

OEDIPUS AT COLONUS

CHARACTERS

Oedipus (EED-i-pus or ED-i-pus): Former king of Thebes, now a blind, wandering exile.

Antigone (An-TIG-o-nee): Daughter of Oedipus and the companion of his exile.

Ismene (Is-MEE-nee): Oedipus' other daughter.

Creon (KREE-on): Brother of Oedipus' dead mother-wife Jocasta; ruler of Thebes from the time of Oedipus' blinding until Oedipus' sons came of age.

Theseus (THEE-see-us or THEE-syoos): King of Athens, son of Aegeus.

Polynices (Poll-ee-NI-seez): Eldest son of Oedipus, about to wage war on his younger brother Eteocles (Ee-TEE-o-kleez), who banished him to gain the throne of Thebes.

A man of Colonus (Ko-LO-nus), a village on a hilltop overlooking Athens.

Elders of Colonus.

Sophocles was almost ninety when he wrote this play, which those of a mystic frame of mind consider his finest. Perhaps the Athenians themselves had debated the question of Oedipus' guilt for many years. The superstitious view would be that he must be "polluted"—an untouchable—or the gods would not have afflicted him so. The enlightened view would be that he was a great soul, ennobled by the unjust blows of fate.

Athens and Thebes were bitter enemies when this play was written. Naturally, the superstitious view is given to the Thebans, the enlightened one to the Athenians. The Thebans are further represented as tricky and selfish in wanting Oedipus though they refuse to honor him. The Athenians honor Oedipus as a man.

Two things may puzzle the modern reader—the importance of a hero's tomb and the nature of the Furies.

The Greeks had a feeling that the remains of a hero had power to bless the city where he was buried. Only a few years before, the bones of Theseus himself had been brought back to Athens. Some people still have similar feelings about the relics of saints, and even a sophisticated person today often feels a sense of awe at the place where some great man is buried.

The *Erinyes*, or Furies, were the personification of a tormented conscience, but very real to the ancient mind. Older than the Olympian gods themselves, these foul creatures were supposed to lie sleeping in hell until someone pronounced a curse on an evildoer. Then they would pursue the guilty man relentlessly with their wrath. No prayers could buy them off.

Early Greeks felt such terror for these demons that they even feared to speak their name. So they called them euphemistically the *Eumenides*, or Kindly Goddesses. Athens had two shrines for these Kindly Goddesses—one on the Areopagus (Mars' Hill) where their court of religious and criminal justice stood, and the other at Colonus, the suburb which is the setting of this story.

That the Kindly Goddesses promise peace and rest—and revenge—to Oedipus may symbolize his coming to peace with his own conscience.

OEDIPUS AT COLONUS

(SOPHOCLES)

Youth lusts for life. Age longs for rest.
And none but a fool would seek
Too long a span of winter years
When joys are few and griefs are many,
Until the Deliverer comes
Without marriage song or lyre or dance.

Not to be born at all is best.
The next prize comes to him
Who runs the shortest race.
For when the folly of youth is past,
Come envy, quarrels, strife, and slaughter;
Then age without honor, strength, or love.

So Oedipus in the course of years
Stood firm and bleak
As a darkened, windswept northern cape
Lashed by the waves from every side,
A sea of troubles breaking on his shores—
Rejected by men, but dearer to the gods. . . .

All the Furies of hell had seemed to lash out at Oedipus that day he discovered the awful truth—that he was stained with his father's murder and the sins of his mother's bed. With the blood streaming down from his blinded eyes, he had cried aloud to be stoned to death. He had begged the brother of his mother-wife to cast him out of the city.

But Creon, instead, had kept him within the palace walls, hiding his shame—though he could not blot its memory—from the people. There Oedipus, comforted by his daughters Ismene and Antigone, in time became more reconciled to fate.

I have suffered more than I have sinned, he reasoned, for how can all the guilt be mine if my destiny was fixed before I was conceived or born? I must have been doomed to suffer for the sins of my fathers—to expiate their crimes by mine.

Thus he came to peace with the hideous Furies that torment the unpurged conscience day and night, the unrelenting Erinyes that men in fear are wont to call "the Kindly Ones." Surely Oedipus had paid the gods in full. Yet he was still to suffer much at the hands of men—even from his own two sons on whom the dark curse of the house of Labdacus descended.

Polynices and Eteocles had grown from youth to manhood in fear and hatred of their father-brother. Never did they minister to his needs or seek his counsel. But, proud and ambitious, they schemed to grasp the rule from Creon. Through Oedipus, they felt, the throne was theirs by right. Yet Oedipus, as symbol of their tainted birth, was also a stumbling block.

So they spread false rumors among the people, stirring fears that their father's presence might bring another blight on Thebes. The folk began to clamor for his exile. And Creon, never sure himself of what was right, cruelly banished Oedipus to beg his bread—or die.

Steadfast Antigone went out to be her father's eyes and strength. Ismene stayed to plead his cause and watch his enemies. Too late did timid Creon and those headstrong youths learn from the oracles what their hearts should have known:

Oedipus, in life or death, would be a blessing to those who pitied him, a curse to those who cast him out.

Through many lands Oedipus and Antigone wandered, weary, barefoot, hungry—through many driving rains and the pitiless burning of many suns. Sometimes they were kindly treated; more often they were driven on in horror, for their tale was widely known.

"But do not fear," said Oedipus, "for I have a vision from the gods. Some day before I die I shall reach a city where Justice rules, a haven for the tired and poor. There the Kindly Goddesses will receive my body in rest; for they will be Furies to me no more but will save their wrath for the sons of Thebes. And when the time comes, the thunder of Zeus will be my sign."

And so one day the two drew near to Athens. They stood upon a hill in Colonus—Antigone still young and beautiful despite the dust and rags, Oedipus gnarled and scarred, his gray hair and beard matted with the filth of travel, no pleasant sight to look upon. Below them spread the promised city. Oedipus could see its towers and temples in his heart as Antigone saw them with her eyes.

"Let me stop here," the old man said, so Antigone led him into a shaded grove of vines and olives. There she found a ledge of rock where Oedipus could rest and listen to the nightingales above.

But a passer-by was dismayed to see them there in a holy place where no man dared set foot.

"Oh, come away," he cried. "That grove is sacred to the Kindly Ones—the fearful offspring of Earth and Darkness." He avoided the name of the furious Erinyes, but Oedipus understood.

"It was fated that I come to them," he said, "and here I shall remain."

The Athenian was distressed.

"I wish you no harm," he said, "for beneath your rags and scars I think I see a man of noble birth. Yet I do not dare go in to save you." As he hurried off to consult his neighbors, Oedipus prayed:

"O goddesses of vengeance, too frightening for men to look upon, grant me sanctuary and have regard for Phoebus' word. Here, he said, you would give me rest and bless me as you do this city, while bringing ruin on those who drove me out. Now I wait for other signs from the trembling earth or from Zeus' thunderbolts. O grant that Athens, of all cities most renowned, shall pity this poor shadow of the Oedipus I was."

Soon anxious voices were heard along the road. Who was this blind profaner of their shrine? Who dared provoke the dread, yet blessed, goddesses? Did he not fear their curse? He must be from a far-off land indeed.

The village elders came as close as they dared to the grove, then called to Oedipus not to utter any ill-omened words but to come out to them at once.

"Respect our ways—we shall not harm you," one shouted.

"We must trust them, Father," said Antigone, "and not offend them." Slowly she guided his steps down to the roadside.

"Now, wanderer," said one, "tell us first of your birth, your native land, and what misfortune brings you here."

"Good friends, I am a man without a country," Oedipus pleaded. "Do not ask me more."

But ask they did until at last they forced out the name of Oedipus. Then a cry went up.

"Get out of here," they shouted, "beyond our borders—quickly—both of you!"

"Your promise," Oedipus pleaded, "your justice!"

"Justice smites the wrongdoer," one cried. "Be off before you put your curse on our land too."

Then Antigone addressed them:

"Good friends, my father's deeds have made you deaf to his pleas. But pity his poor daughter who looks at you with a daughter's eyes. I beseech you by whatever you hold dear —your children, your marriage bed, your duty, or your gods. Be gracious; do not drive us out. All that my father did he did unknowingly and against his will. Search as you will, you will never find any man who can flee from such deeds as a god compels."

They listened, then, as Oedipus said:

"Good men, can this be Athens, famed beyond all other cities for piety and justice, a shelter for the world's oppressed? Surely you cannot fear an old and helpless man. It must be my name you fear. Yet ask yourselves if I should be condemned.

"Could any court hold me guilty for striking back at the man who tried to slay me—even had I known he was my father? As for my mother, alas, I knew not where it was I went. The only ones who knew were the gods themselves who afflicted me. But you will show them no reverence now by trying to thwart their will. Do not blot the name of Athens with a wicked deed, but receive and protect me as a suppliant who brings not ill, but good."

His words had weight but called for wiser minds. They let him rest and sent for Theseus their king.

As they waited there, Antigone watched the road. From time to time a lonely traveler passed, or a farmer with a laden beast bound for the marketplace. Oedipus noted the passing sounds, the scent of sweat, and the wisps of stirred-up dust. Then Antigone caught sight of one young woman, richly dressed but travel-stained, riding a Sicilian colt, her face half shaded by a Theban hood. Beside her walked a servant.

"Father, it is Ismene!" Antigone exclaimed.

"Father! Sister!" Ismene cried, rushing to their side. "How hard I have tried to find you! The gods be thanked that many saw which way you came." All three were quickly linked in one embrace.

"Oh, how I have yearned for you," Ismene said.

"And that is why you came so far, my child?"

"Yes—but I also had news. So I took the only slave I could trust and escaped to find you."

First she told about her brothers—and at their mention Oedipus groaned. Greed for power had made them bitter enemies, she said. Eteocles, the younger, had subtly worked on Creon's feelings and stirred up the passions of the people until they had banished the older brother Polynices and made Eteocles their king. Polynices had fled to Argos and married the daughter of King Adrastus. From there he was leading back the armies of seven princes, sworn to conquer Thebes or die.

In the face of this danger, Ismene said, Thebes had sent Creon out in search of Oedipus, for the oracles had prophesied that after his death, his spirit would aid the land that received him and bring destruction upon its invaders.

"Then when I am nothing I shall be worth the most," sighed Oedipus.

"O Father, you are dear to the gods even now."

"Would that I had been dearer to them in my youth," said Oedipus bitterly. "A cheap gift they give me now . . . But, tell me, what does Creon plan to do?"

"To take you back to Thebes," Ismene said, "that you may in time be buried not far from the city's walls. Not in the sacred dust of Thebes itself—for they still fear the taint that the gods put upon you—but close enough so that many offerings can be brought to your tomb to appease your angry spirit."

"Never shall Creon lay hands on me," said Oedipus angrily. "But what of my two sons?"

Ismene admitted that they, too, had heard of the oracles.

"Then if they seek me," Oedipus said, "it is not for any love they bear me but only their evil lust for power. Then may the gods never quench their fated strife, but let its course fulfill my wish. May the usurper lose his throne, the exile never see his home. I was their father, yet neither one breathed a word to save me, and but for you, dear daughters, I should have perished. Never shall I aid any cause of Thebes no matter whom they send.

"If Creon comes," he said turning to the elders, "I beg you to join your Kindly Goddesses to protect me."

"Then first," said one, "you had best appease those deities for treading on their sacred ground."

They prescribed the rites, but Oedipus lacked the strength and sight to perform them.

"Let me go, Father," Ismene said, "for I can fulfill them as your closest kin."

"The guardian of the shrine will aid you," one elder said.

"And surely those dread deities will listen to one so pure in heart," said Oedipus as Ismene left them to do her task.

Meanwhile, Theseus, the King of Athens, was hastening up from the city. He had known the pain of exile in his youth, and he, too, had unwittingly caused his father's death. For when he sailed home in victory from Crete, he had forgotten his promise to hoist a white sail if all were well. From a high cliff, his father Aegeus had scanned the ship in vain. Then, thinking all was lost and Theseus dead, he had hurled his aged body into the sea.

No stranger then to human ills was Theseus as he greeted Oedipus:

"I have heard of your suffering from many men, O son of

Laius," he said, "but nothing has moved me so much as to see you now with this helpless maiden. Tell me what you ask of this city and of me?" Oedipus greeted him in turn, then said:

"I come to offer you this worn-out body—not a pretty gift but one of value if you will but give it those burial rites that every soul requires to rest in peace."

"This and nothing more?"

"With that I shall gain everything," said Oedipus.

"It is a little thing you ask," said Theseus.

"Yet fraught with danger," Oedipus replied, "for I must warn you that some would try to force me back to Thebes."

"Why, then," asked Theseus, "should you prefer this ill-becoming exile?"

Then Oedipus explained it all—from his cruel exile by his sons down to the prophecy that his tomb would some day aid a city against its enemies.

"But our city is at peace with Thebes," said Theseus.

"Dear son of Aegeus," Oedipus replied, "time changes everything except the deathless gods. The might of men and nations must decay, and honor die. Between men or cities love can turn to hate or hate to love. Today a friendly sun shines down on you and Thebes. But every day must yield to night throughout the endless years. One little word can shatter peace and call a host of men to arms.

"And in my grave, if Phoebus and his father Zeus speak true, some day my cold and buried corpse shall drink a hot invader's blood. Enough. If you will only give me your word, no one shall ever say that Oedipus came to this land as a gift-less guest, unless the gods themselves have lied to me."

The elders murmured assent as Theseus replied:

"Who could reject this suppliant who comes so well disposed toward this state and me? Our hearts and treaty laws uphold his claim on us. He shall be a citizen of this land. Guard him from any harm."

"Zeus bless you," said Oedipus. "I have your word and that is all I need."

"My oath could be no stronger," said Theseus. "So do not fear the empty boasts of your enemies. Be brave, for Phoebus brought you here. And, wherever I am, my name will always protect you."

With that he left them, for he had sacrifices to perform at the altar of Posidon. Then the village elders sang to Oedipus their praises of Colonus:

> This fairest piece of earth
> In all the steed-famed land—
>   Bright Colonus
> Where nightingales trill clear
> In wine-dark ivy bowers,
>   Untrod by men,
> Unmarred by sun or wind,
> Where Bacchus and his nymphs
>   Are wont to play—
>
> Where in each morning's dew
> The white narcissus shines
>   And golden crocus;
> Where sleepless springs well up
> That fields below may bless
>   Cephesus' stream;
> Where the choir of Muses sings
> And golden Aphrodite
>   Loves to dwell—
>
> Where the gray-leafed olive grows
> To nurture Athens' sons
>   Who fear no foe;

> Gray-eyed Athene guards it—
> Unplanted and untilled—
> Zeus guards it, too.
>
> And by Posidon's grace
> The city's name spreads far,
>   For Kronos' son
> First taught its folk to rule
> With bit and oar his steeds
>   And stormy seas.

Meanwhile, Ismene had walked around the grove until she reached the shrine. From its attendant she received three golden bowls of intricate carving and filled them with purest honey and water from a living spring. Each bowl she wreathed with fresh-shorn wool from a yearling sheep. Then facing the rising sun she poured the draughts one by one into the thirsty earth. Over the spot she laid nine olive branches, then nine across, and still another nine. And kneeling down she prayed in silence to the deities beneath.

Just as she finished, a shadow loomed over her. She rose and turned. There stood Creon with a band of men in arms.

Stopping her cries, some held her there while Creon and the rest went around the grove. Antigone first saw them coming and cried a warning.

Oedipus pleaded: "Dear friends, protect us."

"Have no fear," one said, "for though we are weak and old, Athens is young and strong."

"And do not fear me," said Creon in silken tones, "for I too am feeble although the might of Thebes is great. I have come only to plead with this poor man to come home with me. All of Thebes yearns for him and I, his kinsman, most of all.

"Tears overwhelm me," he said to Oedipus, "when I see you like this—a sightless, begging wanderer, with only this poor girl to tend you. Alas, I never thought that she would be brought so low—ripe but unwed—ready to be despoiled by any passing stranger. This is a bitter reproach to you, to me, to all our race. So come home to your father's land. Bid farewell to these kindly people, but reverence the claim of Thebes who nurtured you."

This was too much for Oedipus. His ancient temper flared.

"You shameless weaver of words," he cried, "throwing a cloak of piety over your evil schemes. Enough of your tricks. When I cried for exile, you imprisoned me. When I craved to stay, you drove me out. No kinsman then. And now I have found a welcome haven, you want me back to bury me—out beyond your walls. Not for my sake, but yours. Your tongue is keener than a sword, but it can win no victory here."

"Poor fellow," said Creon, "has age still brought you no wisdom?"

"Enough to know," said Oedipus, "that no honest man has honeyed words for every cause."

"I call these men to witness how you revile your dearest kinsman," Creon said.

"They are sworn not to let you take me."

"Then you shall smart for this. Already one of your daughters is in my hands." Creon turned to his men. "Now take the other, unless she will go willingly."

The Athenian elders protested as Creon's men laid hold of the weeping Antigone: "This is not just."

"I keep to the letter of your law," said Creon. "I shall not touch this man. But, as guardian of these girls, I take only what is mine."

"O men of Athens, save us," cried Oedipus. But Creon warned them:

"Stop! If you lay a hand on me, it will mean war with Thebes."

My prophecy so soon, thought Oedipus. Then, at a sign

from Creon, the men carried Antigone off despite the cries of the girl and her father and the angry protests of the crowd.

So far Creon had remained within the doubtful boundaries of right, but now he forgot all caution in his insolence.

"See!" he jeered at Oedipus. "You have lost both your crutches. Enjoy your victory over your friends and country if you can. Once more you will find you only destroy yourself by yielding to your fatal rage."

But Creon's trick was failing, for Oedipus did not consent to go, as Creon had hoped. Now some of the elders blocked his way and demanded that he give up the girls. Then Creon went further to excess and began to threaten that Thebes would have Oedipus, too.

"O goddesses," cried Oedipus, "grant me just one curse. May this evil man who tears away a blind man's only eyes suffer an old age as miserable as mine."

"See how he attacks me," Creon shouted. "Old as I am, I shall take that man myself."

"Not while Athens stands!" the elders shouted. As Creon rushed toward Oedipus, they seized him.

Creon was struggling in impotent rage—for many, though feeble, were the hands that held him—when Theseus returned, summoned from the temple of Posidon. Quickly he ordered horsemen out to man the passes and bar the escape of the maidens' captors; then he turned to Creon with scorn.

"Has old age robbed you of your wits?" he asked. "Surely if I were a stranger in your land of Thebes, I should know enough not to act like this, however just my cause. By seizing these suppliants you have flouted our gods, our laws, the might of our land, and me."

Creon quickly changed to a humbler mood. "I meant no disrespect to your state," he said. "But I never thought its people could be so smitten with love for my sinful kin. Know you not that this man slew his father, aye, and took to himself an unholy bride—his very mother? Your sacred court of the Areopagus, I am sure, condones no such wickedness in your city. Even so, I did not try to seize him until he began to curse me. Only a dead man would not have been stung to rage. Still you may do what you wish with me, for though my cause is just, I have not the might to enforce it."

"O shameless insolence," Oedipus retorted, "do these taunts smear my old age or yours? Murder—incest—misery—I knew them all. But those deeds were planned before my birth. I was born to suffer, and when I met my father it is true I killed him. But I knew not who he was.

"And my mother—for shame to speak of her! She was your sister. You force me to admit she bore my children. I did not know it then, nor did she. But you know full well what you are doing, and do it willfully, when you choose to speak of unspeakable things and heap shame on your sister's memory and on me.

"Just answer me this. If right now someone should come upon you and try to kill you, you fountain of righteousness, would you stop to ask if by any chance the killer happened to be your father? No, as you love your life, I think you would act swiftly and not stand debating the right and wrong of it. That was my god-given plight. If my father's spirit came back to life, he would not refute me.

"Your tongue balks at nothing that serves your ends. You think it clever to flatter Theseus and Athens. But one thing you forget. No land surpasses this in proper rites and reverence to her gods. And now to these goddesses I pray for help that you may learn what breed of men guards this city's honor."

The elders clearly sided with Oedipus in this debate, but Theseus called a halt to words. The sisters were still to be rescued. He suspected they were hidden close by and demanded that Creon lead him to the place.

"You will learn," he said, "how soon ill-gotten gains are lost, and that no man is stronger than the state."

"I am not master here," said Creon; but added, "when I am home I shall know how to act."

"Save your threats for our journey," Theseus told him. "But now be off and lead the way."

As they left, the village elders fell to wondering where the maidens would be found. They thought of many likely spots. Warriors once themselves, they conjured up wild scenes of battle with the maidens' captors brought to bay—sword against sword, horse against horse, chariot against chariot. Victory in the end, of course, must come to Theseus and to Athens—to Athene, Posidon, Zeus, Apollo, and Artemis.

The old men's dreams of romantic battles quickly ended when Theseus reappeared with the sisters at his side. They had not been carried far away. Ismene and Antigone rushed to their father's side and embraced him with joy.

"And now, if I die, I cannot be wholly wretched," Oedipus said, "for I hold my darlings in my arms." He turned to Theseus. "It was you alone who saved them. I pray the gods will favor you and your people. In you alone of all men have I found reverence, fairness, and lips that never lie. Give me your right hand, O King, that I may touch it, your cheek to kiss . . ."

Then he caught himself.

"Oh, what am I saying? How can I ask that you even touch one who has dwelt with so much sin? Only those who share my burden dare approach me. No, I could not let you touch me if you wished. But hear my thanks from where you are."

"Your joy in your daughters is thanks enough," said Theseus. "But now I must ask something of you. A suppliant stranger threw himself at my feet beside Posidon's altar and begged to have a word with you. He said he was your kinsman—though not from Thebes."

"Not from Thebes, you say?" asked Oedipus.

"Think, then, have you any kin in Argos?"

"O no!" cried Oedipus. "My son, my hated son, whose words would pain my ears like nothing else."

But Theseus begged that he at least listen to the plea of one whose supplications were made in the name of the god. Antigone, too, pleaded with him to hear her brother. It would be a slight to Theseus' good faith to do otherwise. If Polynices' plans were evil, she said, his speech would betray him. Let Oedipus remember the past and all the ills his wrath had caused, and then be gentle even to the son who had sorely wronged him.

After much persuasion, Oedipus agreed, though against his will.

Polynices, though full of pity for himself, could not hold back a cry of anguish at the sight of his father and sisters.

"I am the vilest of men in everything I have done to you," he said to Oedipus, "yet I plead for mercy."

But Oedipus only sat in stony silence. In vain the son begged his father for a single word.

"Tell him your story," Antigone said, "and perhaps his feelings will give birth to speech."

Polynices then spoke bitterly of Eteocles, his younger brother who had roused the rabble to hurl him into exile when he had tried to mount his father's throne of old. He told of his flight, and his marriage in Argos. He told of the league of seven princes, who had sworn to cast the usurper out of Thebes.

"By your children, by your life, my father," he said, "I

implore you to relent in your wrath against me, and help me chastise my brother, for the oracles say victory will be with those you join.

"Like you," he continued, "I am a beggar and an exile who has found a welcome in a distant land. We share one common doom. *He* mocks us both. But if you join me, we shall cast him out. You and I shall both be restored in our rightful home. Without you I cannot return alive."

At last his words stung Oedipus to speak—but not to forgive. Bitterly he recounted Polynices' crimes against him.

"You," he cried, "you—more willfully than I—are the murderer of your father. You sought my death when you cast me out. You are both murderers and no sons of mine."

Instead of a blessing, he called down a curse on Polynices.

"Never shall you capture Thebes," he said. "You and your brother both shall die, each stained with the other's blood. I have cursed you before and I curse you again. I call on all the dread spirits of this place and on the Destroying God to bring the hatred you nursed for me and each other to its just conclusion. Go, tell all Thebes—tell your allies—how Oedipus honors his sons equally for the way they honored him."

Then Polynices knew he was doomed. His father's wrath would never be assuaged. Oedipus' curses would prevail and the oracles be fulfilled. Yet Polynices was a soldier, sworn to lead men that he must not desert. No, he could not disclose these things, not even to his allies. A leader must always keep the look of assurance, no matter how hopeless the odds against him. Not even in speech could he share his doom with anyone. All he could ask was that when his time came his sisters would not dishonor him but give him proper burial.

Antigone begged him to speed back to Argos and bid his allies disband.

"I cannot," he said, "for I am sworn, and honor forbids that I live in cowardly exile so long as my brother rules."

But when he saw his sisters' anguished tears he feigned a lighter mood.

"Weep not," he said. "My life will be in Fortune's hands. And for you two I pray no misfortune may come, for in all men's eyes your lives have been innocent and pure."

Then he departed, and the folk marveled at all the evil the blind man's coming had revealed. Had these been a father's words or was Oedipus an instrument of Fate, working out the will of the gods who can overthrow the great and exalt the humble?

Then the clear sky was rent with lightning and thunder, striking terror in all except Oedipus. He bade his daughters have Theseus summoned quickly from Posidon's temple.

"This is the sign," he said. "The winged thunder soon will lead me hence."

Again the sky flashed and roared. The panic grew.

"O Zeus, save us!" the people cried.

"My daughters," said Oedipus, "your father's end is drawing near. He can no longer turn away. But hasten to bring the king of this land."

For a third time the sky blazed with a fearful rumbling roar.

"Zeus, be merciful," the people cried, "for we have looked on a man accursed."

"Is Theseus near?" asked Oedipus. "Will he find me still alive?"

"Hasten, O hasten, our King!" they cried.

"What means this summons?" Theseus asked as he came to them. "What awful ill does this storm from Zeus portend?"

"Be of good heart, most welcome King," said Oedipus, "the gods have shown their love for you by their summons. My life is now in the balance. We must make our pledges before I die.

"Soon, O son of Aegeus, I shall disclose an ageless boon

for this city. Guided only by the gods I shall show you the way to the place where I must die. But that place must never be revealed to anyone save to your heir when your own end is near, then by him to his down through the years. And this will be a defense—better than ten thousand shields.

"Not even to my own children shall it be revealed. But it will forever remain as a bulwark against the Dragon's brood of Thebes. For the gods are slow but sure when men spurn godliness and turn to madness. And now I hear the summons. Let us go."

Oedipus turned his scarred face to the heavens and led the way into the grove with slow but certain steps, neither seeking out the path with his staff nor suffering any hand to aid him.

"Come with me, O King," he said, "you, too, my children, but touch me not. I shall guide your steps now as you have guided mine. The hands of Hermes and the Goddess of the Dead will lead me to my sacred tomb.

"Now at last my body feels the light—that light I lost so many years ago. Blessed be you and all in this land; and when your days are blest, think once again of me."

The people did not follow but stayed and prayed to all the feared and unseen deities of death to give this man of many sorrows passage without pain to the realms below.

Oedipus led his daughters and the King up close to the hill of Demeter. Then he sat down on a rock and unfastened his ragged garments. At his bidding, his daughters fetched water and washed and dressed him.

The thunder pealed again. Antigone and Ismene shuddered and fell weeping at their father's knees.

"My children," he said. "Hard has been your burden of tending me; for that I can repay you only with my love. But now you shall have me no more."

From Theseus he gained a ready pledge to care for them. Then, clinging to each other, the father and his daughters wept. But out of the heavens rolled voices:

Oedipus, Oedipus, you tarry too long!

Then he groped for their hands once more and said: "Now, my dear ones, you must be noble and brave and leave this place. Only Theseus must remain to witness the mysteries that come."

Desolate and weeping, the maidens slowly walked away; when at last they turned and looked back Oedipus was no longer there. King Theseus stood in that place—alone, still shielding his eyes with his hands from some overpowering sight. Then he saluted the earth and the heavens and slowly came away. Only he knew what had happened in that last moment—whether a messenger of the gods had taken Oedipus or the kindly earth had split open to receive him.

"He has gone as one might wish," Antigone sobbed. "For he perished not in war or at sea, but Death called him home in some swift, mysterious way. Oh, what will be our fate without him?"

"Let me join him," Ismene cried. "I cannot go on living."

"Peace, Sister, the joy we had in caring for him is not lost," said Antigone, "and even in that dark underworld he shall never lack our love. It was his wish to die here, in an alien land. Yet I should have been with him to the end."

The folk tried to comfort them.

"Oh, cease from lamentation," they said. "Every mortal is an easy prey to misfortune, but your father found a blessed end."

Then a wild desire seized Antigone.

"Let us hasten and go back. Let us see the place our father died."

"It is forbidden," Ismene said in horror.

"Take me there," Antigone cried. "Then slay me, too."

"No, no! Do not leave me," Ismene begged.

As the others tried to calm her, Theseus returned.

"The Dark Powers have received him kindly," he said. "Weep no more, lest you provoke their divine anger."

"Son of Aegeus," said Antigone, "we beg you to let us look with our own eyes upon our father's tomb."

"No, it cannot be," said Theseus. "Your father charged me that no one should ever draw near or hail that place where he sleeps. That was his wish and my promise. So long as I keep my word I shall keep this land unharmed. And the gods who guard all oaths heard me give my pledge."

"If this be his will," said Antigone, "we must be content. Then send us quickly back to Thebes that we may perhaps prevent our brothers' bloodshed."

"That I shall do," said Theseus, "and all else that may help you and bring pleasure to that one who has just left us."

And so the two sisters returned to Thebes to pit their love against a father's curse and, perhaps, the wondrous and fearful will of the gods.

This was the last of some 125 plays that Sophocles wrote—plays which never won less than second prize in the competitions. The Athenians revered him in life; in death, they made him a hero and performed yearly sacrifices at his tomb. What, then, was his final message?

Sophocles would hardly have been shocked by Critias' suggestion that the gods were invented by some politician to whip the masses in line. But beyond these false gods of custom, so bitterly attacked by Euripides, he sensed some Power of nature. He could not fathom it, nor did he try to rationalize it in terms of human justice. He might well have said,

"To thine own self be true and it must follow thou canst not then be false to any god."

It is tempting to see Oedipus' end as some sort of divine redemption. But Oedipus never repents anything except the woes the gods have inflicted on him. Almost his last act is to curse his kin for their treachery. In his own mind he is always justified. The Athenian Theseus recognizes his moral goodness, and symbolically the gods are forced to recognize it too.

But how did the pious Creon of *Oedipus the King* become so treacherous? Though written a quarter of a century apart, these plays seem closely linked. Psychological insight should show an inner consistency in Creon. His piety is never a moral virtue. Creon lacks the integrity of a hero. He is the inadequate man who always tries to play it safe.

Creon's piety in the first play is superstition; he is trying to play it safe with the gods. He keeps Oedipus in the palace, not through kindness but to hide his shame from the people. When his superstitions are worked on by Oedipus' scheming sons, Creon cruelly casts Oedipus out. Then when superstition, as symbolized by the oracle, tells him he needs Oedipus back, he will stop at no low trick to get him. Only those who confuse outward piety with moral rectitude can see Creon as a Sophoclean hero. And how this inadequate man without moral fiber acts when he gains the power of a king, we shall see in the following story.

ANTIGONE

CHARACTERS

Antigone (An-TIG-o-nee): Daughter of Oedipus (now dead) and sister of the slain Polynices (Poll-ee-NI-seez) and Eteocles (Ee-TEE-o-kleez).
Ismene (Is-MEE-nee): Sister of Antigone.
Creon (KREE-on): Uncle of the two sisters and the slain brothers, who suddenly finds himself King of Thebes.
Eurydice (Yoo-RID-iss-ee): Wife of Creon.
Haemon (HEE-mon): Son of Creon and Eurydice, betrothed to Antigone.
Tiresias (Ti-REE-see-as): A blind prophet.
A soldier, set to guard the body of Polynices.
Theban elders.
Servants of Creon.

Before his mystical death in Colonus, Oedipus had cursed his cruel sons, praying that each should destroy the other. Polynices' repentance had come too late, yet Sophocles almost made him a tragic hero. By deliberately portraying this exiled brother as the older of the two, and tricked by his younger brother Eteocles, Sophocles made his the juster cause. And the old playwright, who twice had served Athens as a general in war, drew a memorable picture of Polynices as a military leader, sworn to a cause of honor and compelled to uphold his men's morale, marching knowingly to his doom.

That doom has now fallen. Each of the brothers has slain the other as the attack of "The Seven Against Thebes" is repulsed.

Our story begins next day at dawn. This act of fate has made Creon the King; our inadequate man has become a tyrant. The question at issue: Shall Polynices the "traitor" be decently buried? The timid tyrant says "no," but the conscience of any ancient people would be shocked to its depths by such sacrilege. Antigone defies the tyrant.

Many claim that this is really the greatest play of the "Oedipus Trilogy." Perhaps it is. But its theme is not, as so often held, a conflict between the laws of God and man—unless we are to assume that the voice of the people—if free from terror—is the voice of God. Antigone, like all of Sophocles' heroes, is guided by an inner light. The real question raised by this play is: When does personal conscience demand disobedience whatever the risk? This is the theme of *The Andersonville Trial* and many other plays. Moreover, it is a theme of life—exemplified in the Nuremberg trials and, more recently, in the Eichmann trial.

Sophocles, when he wrote the play, believed that democracy was the collective expression of personal conscience, more to be trusted than the assumed "divine right" of any dictator.

ANTIGONE

(SOPHOCLES)

The night was almost over. Soon the sun's bright eye would rise above the streams of Dirce. And those who had no dead to mourn would hail it as the fairest light that ever shone on Thebes. For the city was saved; its enemies from Argos had fled leaving their seven leaders dead by its seven gates.

Among the dead lay Polynices, the proud son of Oedipus— the prince, the exile, the avenger. Like a shrill eagle he had come upon them, a mad beast thirsting for their blood. His followers had stormed against their ramparts in waves of clanging gold. But even as they were shrieking victory, Zeus struck them with his fire, and Ares, the war god, spread panic through the white-shielded ranks. Now they were gone. They would not return.

Thus were Theban prayers fulfilled. But so, too, was the curse of Oedipus against his sons. For beside the fallen Polynices was found the bloodstained body of his brother, King Eteocles—each slain by the other's hand in a final frenzy of hate. Two sisters' prayers had been in vain.

Now for a third time the city's rule fell to the faltering hand of Creon. But it could not be for long. Creon was old and grieving for his son, the slain Megareus. Only his younger son Haemon remained to succeed him—Haemon, who was betrothed to Antigone.

For many hours that night Creon tried to console his aged wife Eurydice. But when at last her tears gave way to sleep, he rose and paced the palace halls.

I must be firm, thought Creon, for I alone have the duty and the power to declare what is right for the city. And before dawn he had decided on his first decree: The corpse of the traitor Polynices must be left to rot in the sun and be torn to pieces by the carrion birds. Its spirit must have no rest.

Let no one give that body burial on pain of death.

Haemon was dismayed. He feared for Antigone and for his father, too. Could Antigone endure her anguish for her brother's soul? Was not Creon pursuing a vengeful justice in realms he did not rule? For surely the dead belong to the gods, not to men. And could the gods themselves abide such outrage to a kinsman in death, whatever the crime?

Yet Haemon held his peace. He knew his father lacked the greatness that easily yields to reason. A hasty plea might only harden his resolve. Haemon knew that he must be subtle.

Antigone had no such patience.

"It is for us, for me, that Creon plans to publish this edict," she whispered angrily to her sister when she had drawn Ismene deep into a corner of the palace walls. "Whoever disobeys shall be stoned to death before all the people."

"Oh, my poor brothers," Ismene wept. "Both torn from us in a single day!"

"But now," said Antigone, "now you can prove whether you are nobly born or false to your own brave heritage."

"Poor sister," said Ismene, "what can I do or change?"

"Help me honor the dead."

Ismene trembled. "You mean—to bury him—when all the city has been told . . ."

"Yes, for he is my brother—and yours, though you might not wish it so. At least I will never be false to him."

"But Creon . . ."

"Creon has no right to keep me from what is mine."

"Oh, my sister," Ismene sobbed, "have you forgotten how Oedipus our father was blinded by his own hand for the sins he discovered, then died in hate and scorn; how his mother-wife hung by the twisted noose; how our brothers shed each other's blood in common doom? Then, think how we—the only ones left—will perish even more miserably if we defy the law and the power of the king. No! We must remember we were born women and no match for men. The strong must rule; we must obey in this—or even worse. O my dead brother, forgive me if I yield to force, but meddling would be madness."

"Then I shall not ask your help," Antigone told her. "Indeed, I should not want it now, even if you were willing. Go your way. Let me bury him—and die for it. I shall rest by my dear brother, purified by my crime, for my debt is more to the dead than to the living. But you may dishonor, if you will, the laws of the gods."

"I do not dishonor them," Ismene pleaded, "for I am helpless. Yet how I fear for you."

"Have no worries for me," said Antigone. "Just take care of yourself."

Ismene was too concerned to feel the sting.

"Be careful not to let anyone know what you are doing," she begged. "I, too, will keep it secret."

"Oh, go and denounce me," Antigone taunted her. "You will reap only hatred for your silence unless you tell everyone."

"You have a hot heart for a cold deed," said Ismene, "but your daring is doomed. It is wrong to try what is hopeless."

"Do not talk that way," said Antigone, "or I shall hate you, and so will the dead—forever. Just leave me to fate and my folly. No matter what I suffer, it cannot be worse than a death of shame."

Ismene realized talk was useless. "Then go if you must," she said. "But even though you are out of your mind, remember this: I love you."

Antigone left in silence. She could have thrown her arms around her sister and forgiven her weakness, but she did not trust herself to yield this much. She must go on alone and tell no one—not even Haemon. Going back to her chamber, she filled a small, bronze ewer with pure water, wrapped herself in the dark, drab cloak of a mourner, and slipped out through the palace gate.

The streets were almost empty. The mingled scent of sacrificial meats and incense still lingered in the air, but the last tired revelers were now at home asleep. She saw only an occasional palace messenger darting by or a sleepy elder toiling up to the citadel in answer to Creon's summons. None of them recognized her, wrapped as she was in the rags of mourning. Nor did the nodding soldiers at the city gate take notice as she passed. A peasant woman, probably, on her way to gather wood.

Antigone shivered in the dawn chill as she went toward the place where they had told her her brothers had fought. Large patches of mist still lay upon the plain. Perhaps no one would see her perform her rites. No one except the gods.

Back in the courtyard, Creon faced the gathered elders who waited in silence for him to speak. He could not tell what they were thinking.

"My brave people," he began, "we have been sorely tossed on stormy seas, but the gods once more have brought us safely through on even keel. I have summoned you knowing how steadfast and true was your reverence for the royal power of Laius, for Oedipus until he was destroyed, and for Oedipus' sons until they fell.

"And now, since I am closest of kin to the dead, the throne and all its powers are mine."

Their silence seemed to give assent, but would they murmur at his decree? He must justify the dread words before he uttered them.

"Whatever his authority," he said, "you cannot know the temper, soul, and wisdom of a man until he has shown his skill to judge and rule. I have no place for anyone who puts friend or kin above his fatherland. As all-seeing Zeus is my witness, I can never be silent if I see ruin threatening the welfare of our people. I would never make any traitor to the state my friend. Our country is our common shelter, and only when our country is safe do we dare have friends.

"By these rules shall I lead our city to greatness. And this is my proclamation to its citizens:

"Eteocles, who nobly perished in the defense of our city, shall be laid in a tomb and duly accorded all the rites that follow the noblest souls in death;

"But as for Polynices, his brother, who returned from exile bent on burning to ashes the city and holy shrines of his fathers, who sought to slake his thirst with Theban blood and lead our people into slavery, I order that no one shall give give him either tomb or tears, but leave his ghastly corpse unburied for the birds and dogs to eat."

For a moment there was no response.

"If these are your thoughts, O Creon, son of Menoeceus," the oldest among them said at last, "you have the power to enforce them on the dead as you do on us who are living."

"Then see my words are carried out," said Creon.

"Nay, put this burden on younger men," the old man said.

"Younger men are already guarding the corpse," replied Creon. "But see that you aid no one who would defy me."

"No man is so foolish as to love death," one muttered.

"And death will be the reward," said Creon, "but some men are destroyed by love of gain."

As his eyes searched them sharply, seeking out those who might dissent, he saw a soldier moving hesitantly toward him through the crowd. The poor fellow was looking this way and that as though seeking to escape some force that held him against his will.

"My king," the man began, "I can't say that it is from running that I am out of breath. My feet had no wings. I had many thoughtful pauses on the way, and sometimes I almost turned back. My soul had great consultations with itself. 'You fool,' it shouted to me, 'why rush to put your head straight into the noose?' But then it whispered, 'Poor fellow, why not get on with it? If Creon hears about this from somebody else, how will you save your hide anyway?' Turning these things over in my mind, I made a long journey of a short one. Coming here to you finally won out. All I can hope is that I won't suffer anything that wasn't fated from the beginning."

"What troubles you?" asked Creon impatiently.

"Well, first I want to tell you about myself. I didn't do it. I didn't see who did. So it wouldn't be right to punish me."

"A sharp eye for your own good," said Creon, "but what terrible thing are you hiding?"

"Well, bad news makes a fellow stop and think...."

"Oh, tell it, will you," Creon broke in, "and then get out of here."

"Well, this is it. Somebody sprinkled earth over the body, performed the pious rites, and got away."

"What is that you say?" Creon shouted. "What man would dare?"

"I don't know," said the guard. "There was no trace of who it was, no wheel tracks, no marks of a spade or mattock. The ground was dry, hard, and unbroken. The corpse wasn't buried, just thinly covered with dust. It looked as if someone had done it to avoid a curse.

"We all swore at each other. We accused each other. We almost came to blows. Everybody guilty; everybody innocent. We were ready to hold red-hot irons in our hands, to walk through fire, to swear by all the gods we knew nothing about it. Finally we decided someone had to tell you. So we drew lots, and I was doomed to win the prize. That is why I am here—unwilling and unwelcome, I'm sure. For no one likes the bearer of bad news."

"Perhaps it was the work of the gods," suggested one elder.

"Hold your tongue," cried Creon, "before you fill me with rage and prove yourself a witless old man. What god would care for this corpse? Have you ever known the gods to honor the wicked?" His eyes narrowed as he searched their faces, then he continued slowly:

"But there are some in this city who long have muttered against me and shaken their heads in secret. They could not endure me nor keep their necks properly bowed under my yoke. It is by their bribes and wiles, I am sure, that this deed was done. There is nothing among men so evil as money. It destroys cities, drives men from their homes, and perverts upright minds to deeds of shame. But the hirelings who wrought this deed have sealed their doom.

"By my reverence for Zeus," he said, turning to the guard, "unless you find this strewer of dust and show him to my very eyes, death alone will not be enough for you. Hung up alive, the lot of you, you will be forced to reveal this outrage and learn what comes of ill-gotten gains."

"May I speak?" asked the guard. "Or should I just go?"

"Your words vex my ears," said Creon.

"Yes, but it is the deed that vexes your soul," said the guard, "and that was never mine."

"Then show me the doer," said Creon, "or you will find your cheap bargain has cost you your life."

"Then may he be caught," said the guard. As he left he muttered to himself, "But whether he's found or not, you certainly won't see me again." And with that he breathed a prayer of thanks to his gods that fate had not decreed his death for that day at least.

Who had dared to defy the law, the elders wondered. Yet what was law? Was it the voice of one fearful and fallible king? Or was it the wisdom of the gods that spoke in all men's hearts? In the people's hearts the king had been wrong in his harsh decree. Now someone had dared to say so.

> Of all the wonders of this world,
>   Most wonderful is man,
> Who bravely plows the towering seas
>   As surely as he tills
> The gods' own mother, tireless Earth.
>
> He snares blithe birds in cunning nets
>   And creatures from the deep,
> While horses with their rippling strength
>   And fearsome mountain bulls
> Are tamed to serve beneath his yoke.
>
> Speech he has learned and lightning thought
>   And all the statecraft arts.
> Not frost nor rain nor any ill—
> Save one—can foil his endless wit—
>   He cannot conquer Death.
>
> His cunning skill, beyond all dreams,
>   Brings good or evil ends.
> But while he heeds the city's laws

> And the justice he has sworn
> On heaven's altar to uphold,
> He shares the common good.
> If not, he dwells in blackest sin.

Antigone had fled when she heard the soldiers coming in the morning mist. From the shelter of a thicket she heard their bellows of rage at what she had done, their curses, and their wrangling. And then the lone messenger passed by, no doubt to tell it all to Creon.

But the deed was done. Her brother's soul could join the dead in peace. She could probably slip away now and never be discovered. Her pious teachings told her the rites could never be erased. Yet something held her there, to watch over that body in love as others did in hate.

As the mist cleared, she could hardly choke back a cry at what she saw. Holding their nostrils against the stench of death, the soldiers were brushing away every trace of the sacred dust. At last the white flesh again gleamed naked in the morning sun. Then they withdrew a little to the windward and sat waiting.

At first Antigone could do nothing. Then, as if in answer to her prayers, the wind freshened; fierce gusts whipped up eddies of dust. The soldiers covered their faces against the stinging blasts, and Antigone dashed out. To the dust that whirled around the body she added three handfuls of her own. She was pouring water from the bronze ewer to consecrate the act when suddenly she was seized from behind and heard a gruff voice shouting past her ear:

"I have her! I have caught the doer of the deed."

It was the messenger returned from the palace. The other guards closed in. This time there was no casting of lots.

"The prize is mine!" her captor shouted. And quickly he

led her back to Creon, forgetting his vow never to return. And this time he poured out his story with no delay.

The elders were dismayed to see Antigone. What would Creon do now?

"Do you admit or deny this deed?" Creon demanded.

"I admit I did it," she replied, her head bowed.

Creon turned to the guard. "Be off with you." Then to Antigone he said: "Tell me—and make no long speeches—did you know my edict?"

"Of course," she said. "How could I help it? Everyone knew."

"And you dared to transgress that law?"

"Yes," she said, raising her head proudly, "for it was you, not Zeus, who proclaimed it. And no edict of yours can override the unwritten laws of the gods. For they are not of today or yesterday, but live forever. And no man's anger will force me to break them. Die I must, some day, whatever your edicts. And if it is before my time, I count it gain. For what gain is there but death in a life surrounded by evil? The pain will be slight. The only pain I could not endure would be to let my own mother's son remain unburied. If that seems foolish, perhaps it is but a foolish judge who condemns my folly."

"Her father's strength and her father's passion," one elder said. "Like iron tempered in fire, she cannot bend."

"Aye, but she can be broken," said Creon. "I have seen fierce colts submit to rein and bit. Pride has no place in a slave. This girl was insolent to break the law—twice insolent to boast of it. Verily I am no man—she is the man—if she can usurp my power unpunished. No, she shall not escape her fate—neither she nor her sister, for I accuse them both. Bring that other one before me!"

No, not Ismene! Antigone thought. Creon's anger must be directed against herself alone.

"What more do you wish than to slay me?" she asked. "Then why delay? I could not enjoy hearing any more from you, nor you from me. I have won my greatest glory. And every man here would approve if fear did not hold his tongue. Only royalty enjoys the luxury of speaking its mind."

"No true Theban shares your view," said Creon. "Are you not ashamed to be at odds?"

"There is no shame in honoring my brother."

"But you dishonored your only true brother who died for Thebes," said Creon. "It was blasphemy in his sight to honor the wicked equally with the good."

"Who knows how these things seem in the world beyond?" Antigone sighed. "I can only love, not hate."

"Then go where you can love your dead if you must have love," said Creon. "But while I live, no woman shall rule me."

He turned on Ismene as she was brought before him.

"You viper in my home," he shouted, "secretly feeding on my blood. Will you confess your share in this treason or swear you knew nothing about it?"

"I share the blame," she said.

"No!" cried Antigone. "This is unjust. You opposed it. You had no part in it."

"In these troubles," Ismene said, "your cause is mine too."

She looked in vain for acceptance in her sister's eyes.

"A friend in words," Antigone chided her, "but not in deeds."

"Do not reject me, Sister," Ismene pleaded. "How could I live without you?"

"Ask Creon," said Antigone. "Your pleas were all for him. You chose to live. I chose to die. Men will approve your choice; the gods will honor mine."

"But now I choose your cause and fate," said Ismene.

"See them!" Creon told the elders. "The one as insane now as the other was from the beginning."

"But will you slay the bride of your own son?" Ismene asked.

"He will find other fields to plow."

"But never again such a love as was theirs."

"I cannot abide sons with evil wives," said Creon.

O dearest Haemon! Antigone thought. How your father wrongs you.

"But will you really rob your son of his bride?" one of the elders asked.

"Not I, but Death," said Creon, and he ordered the girls taken away under guard.

How fortunate are those who have never tasted evil days, the elders thought. But a house blasted by the gods is cursed forever. Divine wrath rages like the wind that churns up black sands from the very depths of the sea. And generation after generation must suffer. There is no escape.

What human trespass can curb thy power, O Zeus, who dwellest in the splendor of Olympus?

Never, from the beginning to the end of time, can greatness enter mortal lives without a curse. It lures men into false desires. And sooner or later evil seems good to those whose minds the gods drive to destruction. Their respite is brief.

And now these two girls—these last frail roots of the house of Oedipus—must perish. And for what? A handful of blood-stained dust, a foolish tongue, and a vengeful mind.

Haemon would have spoken to his father alone. But there was no time if Antigone was to be spared. May the gods grant me wisdom and guide my tongue, he prayed, as he came out to face Creon before the elders.

"Have you come to rage against your father?" Creon demanded. "Or do you still respect whatever I do?"

"Father, I am yours," said Haemon humbly. "Your counsels rule my life. No marriage could mean as much to me as your good guidance."

"You are right, my son," said Creon more quietly, "to hearken to your father in all things. Every man prays for obedient children who will honor his friends and take vengeance on his enemies. But he who begets profitless children sows only trouble for himself and reaps the scorn of his foes. So do not let pleasure rob you of reason. The joy of an evil woman in your bed would soon grow cold."

Haemon flinched, but said nothing.

"No wound strikes deeper than a false friend." Creon's voice rose. "Despise this woman as an enemy. Let her find herself a husband in hell. Of all the city, she alone disobeyed my order. I will not make myself a liar before the people. I will slay her!"

He turned to the elders. Antigone was of his own royal blood, he admitted. But if he allowed mischief in his own home, how could he check it anywhere?

"No!" he shouted. "The King must be obeyed in all matters —small or large, just or unjust. Disobedience is the worst of evils. It ruins homes. It destroys cities. We must support the law and never yield to a woman. If we must fall, let it be at the hands of men."

"Unless age has addled our wits," said one, "there seems wisdom in what you say."

But Haemon began to speak softly but earnestly.

"Father," he said, "it is the gods who planted reason in men, something priceless beyond anything else we possess. And though I am not able or learned enough to say you did not speak rightly, there might still be merit in another's thoughts. For your sake I have been watching everything that men say or do or murmur at. No ordinary citizen will risk your frown to tell you anything displeasing. But in the shadows I hear other voices. The city weeps for this girl who could not dishonor her brother. 'No woman,' they say, 'ever deserved less to suffer so shamefully for deeds so noble.'

"Such are the whispers that seep through the city. And, believe me, I treasure nothing so much as your welfare. For what greater adornment could any son have than the good name of a prospering father? So ponder the wise words of others. Even a wise man is not ashamed to learn and to bend at times like the pliant tree that saves itself from the winter torrent while the stiff and stubborn one perishes root and branch. The sailor, too, who keeps too taut a sail only upsets and ends his voyage keelside up.

"It is the soul of vanity to think oneself alone is wise and has no equal in speech or mind. So forego your anger and allow your heart to melt. I am young, but if my thoughts have any weight let me say that it would be fine if any man were all-wise by nature; but as it is, no one dares close his ears to the good advice of others."

The elders then pleaded with each to listen to the other, for there was wisdom on both sides. But Creon's anger grew.

"Are men of my age to be schooled by children?" he exclaimed.

"Think not of my years," Haemon begged, "but only of what is right."

"Is it right to honor traitors?"

"All Thebes approves of what she did."

"And shall the city tell *me* what I should do?" Creon shouted.

Unable to control himself, Haemon cried: "Now *you* are speaking like a child. No city belongs to one man alone. Your kind of rule befits only a desert."

"Infamous whelp," Creon exclaimed, "arguing with your own father!"

"I argue for justice."

"My power is justice here."

"Not when it tramples the laws of the gods," said Haemon.

"You are nothing but a woman's slave," sneered Creon. "Every word you utter is for that girl."

"And for you," said Haemon, "and for me—and for the gods."

"She shall never be your bride alive," said Creon.

"Then," said Haemon ominously, "she will not die alone."

"Threats!" Creon scoffed. "You and your stupid talk of wisdom!"

"If you were not my father . . ."

"Say no more of that," Creon said. "I am not proud of it."

"You only want to talk," said Haemon, "and never listen."

"Yes, by heaven!" cried Creon. "And you shall see . . . Bring out the wench! Let her die right here beside her bridegroom, before his very eyes."

Haemon took one step toward his father. The guards blocked his way. It was hopeless.

"No, I cannot endure it," Haemon cried, "nor will you ever see my face again—you maniac!"

And he fled, his twisted face ablaze with thwarted rage.

"Good riddance!" said Creon, though he was shaking. "Let his passion carry him beyond all mortal bounds but he shall not save those girls from doom."

"You still mean to slay them both?" the elders asked. Creon hesitated. He could not misread their horror nor wholly free himself from fear.

"No, not the innocent one," he said at last. "You speak well."

"And the other?"

Again Creon hesitated. He had vowed that she should be stoned to death. But now he recoiled from such open violence against his kin.

"I shall take her to a lonely cave," he said, "and imprison her there with only such food as piety demands. Thus the city will avoid all stain."

A little food, he meant, but not enough. A mere token —like the handful of dust Antigone had cast—to avoid a curse. Then he could believe that time and nature, not he, would take her life.

"There," he told them, "she can pray to Death, the only god she worships, for release. Too late she will learn what fruitless toil it is to honor only the dead."

What a fearful power is love, the old men thought. It brings great fortunes crashing down, yet nestles softly in a sleeping maiden's cheek. Far and wide the Love Goddess ranges, driving men to madness, warping just minds to ruin, and turning kin against kin.

Antigone had already been told of her fate and as she was led out from the palace, its full reality swept over her.

"See me, citizens," she cried, "going on my last sad journey, gazing for the last time upon the sun. No marriage chant will ever be sung for me, but only the dirge of death."

"Yet you go with praise and honor," one tried to assure her feebly, "not stricken down by sickness or a sword, but of your own free will—almost like a goddess."

"Must you mock me to my face?" she cried. "In the name of our ancestral gods, wait till I have gone! Gone unwept to a prison tomb to dwell with neither the living nor the dead —and by what laws you well know."

"You scaled the heights of bravery, my daughter," said one, "then fell at the throne of Justice—doomed to pay, I fear, for your father's sins."

Antigone cursed the bitter truth. What horrors had beset her family. No marriage had been blessed; Laius begetting his own slayer, her father sleeping in his mother's bed. And now, but for her brother's union with a daughter of the enemy, she might even now have been on her way to the bridal chamber instead of a tomb.

"Your reverent act deserves some reverence," one told her softly, "but those in power can brook no rivals. Your willful temper has worked your ruin."

But Antigone could only repeat to herself, "Unwept—unfriended—and unwed."

"Away with her!" Creon ordered. "If weeping and mourning could hold off the coming of death, no one would ever cease. Take her to that cave, as I told you, to live or die as she pleases. Our hands will be clean. But never again shall she see the light of day."

"Look at me, you princes of Thebes," Antigone rebuked them. "Know what I suffer, and at whose hands, judged a sinner because I could not sin against the gods. Do you think your acts are pleasing in their sight? Soon I shall know if any deed of mine was evil. For when I meet my doom all will be revealed to me. And if it is my judges who have sinned, then may they suffer in fuller measure all the agony they have brought to me."

And with this curse on her lips, she was led away.

Down in the city one man knew the answer. It was the ancient Tiresias—sightless, yet ever seeing what no other man could see, outliving many generations, afflicted but instructed by the gods. Each day he would take his seat by the haunts of the birds and read messages from the sounds of their voices and the whirring of their wings in flight.

And this day he had heard a strange, dire sound among them. A fierce frenzy had raised their voices to discordant screams of pain and anger. He could hear them tearing each other to pieces with their beaks and talons.

"They have been feasting on human flesh," Tiresias cried in horror. Quickly he told his boy to help him prepare a sacrifice to the gods on his altar. Fat-wrapped thighs of sheep were laid above the kindling, but the Fire God brought no flame. Only a foul moisture oozed out and dripped on the embers which smoked and sputtered and filled the air with the scent of bile.

"Our city is polluted with sin," Tiresias moaned. "The gods reject our prayers and sacrifices."

He called the boy to lead him to the palace.

"What news, old man?" Creon asked as he approached.

"Will you heed the warning of a seer?"

"Have I not always?"

"And so you have guided the city well. But now you stand on the brink of disaster." And Tiresias told of the dire omens.

"Your own decrees have brought this sickness upon the city," he said. "Now our hearths and altars are defiled by birds and dogs and the unburied flesh of the slain son of Oedipus. Think of this, my son. Every man is prone to error. But once a wrong is discovered, a man of wisdom and virtue is quick to mend it. I speak only for your welfare. What valor is there in stabbing one already slain? Give the dead their due, and heed a good counselor who speaks only for your gain."

But the seer's soft words only steeled Creon's anger and roused his suspicions.

"Everyone aims his arrows at me," he said, "and now I must be the target of your seercraft, too. You have made a bargain to deliver me to my enemies. Go trade in the white gold of Sardis or the yellow gold of India, if you wish, but do not make me your merchandise. Even if the eagles of Zeus carry the dead flesh up to his very throne, you shall not bury that body. No mortal act can defile the gods. But how shamefully the wisest fall, old Tiresias, when they clothe evil designs in fair speeches for the sake of gain."

"Know you not," Tiresias chided him, "that good counsel is far more precious than riches? Have I ever prophesied falsely?"

"The whole tribe of seers loves money," said Creon.

"And every generation of tyrants loves oppression."

"Do you realize you are speaking of your king?"

"That I know, for it was by my guidance that you saved Thebes."

"You are a wise seer," Creon admitted, "but nonetheless a lover of evil."

"Then you force me to reveal the awful truth I would rather hide in my soul. You will not live many days before those you love will give you corpses—two for two—because you have thrust a living soul into the grave and denied a grave to a corpse still kept in the land of the living. The avenging Furies of the gods above and the gods below are lying in wait to ensnare you in these very evils.

"And before many circles of the sun's chariot you will learn for yourself whether I spoke from truth or from love of gold. For your halls will echo with the mourning of men and women, and hatred will spread from city to city. Those are my arrows, O King, which your anger goaded me to shoot, but you will not escape them. . . . Boy, lead me home and let him vent his spleen on younger men."

He left them standing in an awed silence until one elder spoke at last.

"The man has gone, O King, and I tremble at his words. For, though my hair has turned from black to silver, in all my days I know his prophecies have never failed."

"I know it, too," said Creon, "and my soul is troubled."

All at once he seemed to shrink in stature before their eyes. The robes of kingly power now seemed but a hollow shell, a masquerade—a mockery of the foolish, frightened man who had put them on.

"Son of Menoeceus," said one, "you must take wise counsel."

"What, then, should I do?" Creon asked. "Tell me, and I will obey."

"Set the maiden free and make a tomb for the dead."

"This is your counsel? Then I should accept it."

"But quickly, for swift is the stroke of the gods that cuts down folly."

"It is hard to give up my resolve," Creon confessed, "but I can no longer battle fate."

And calling his servants to bring the implements, he went forth in humility at last to appease the will of the gods. There might yet be time, the old men fondly thought, and when he had gone their thin voices rose in a hymn of praise and joy to Bacchus.

The body of Polynices was a grisly sight. For with the guards standing apart as ordered, the carrion creatures had done their work unchecked. Nevertheless, Creon and his servants washed what was left as best they could. With prayers to Hecate and Pluto they gathered boughs from the nearby thicket and heaped them in a funeral pyre. Then, when the flames had consumed the body, they heaped high over the ashes of Polynices a mound of his native soil.

Thus Creon humbled himself before the gods, but the

harder task he had put off. Now he must abase himself before a mortal—a mere woman who had defied him.

As they drew near the cave in which Antigone had been imprisoned they could see that someone had wrenched apart the great stones that had blocked its mouth. From within they could hear bitter cries of anguish. Creon listened, then groaned:

"Oh, wretch that I am. If my fears be true, this is the saddest road I have ever taken."

For the voice was the voice of Haemon.

The servants rushed ahead. In the depths of the cave, as their eyes grew accustomed to the dark, they saw her—like her mother Jocasta—her body hanging from a jutting rock by the fine-spun linen sash that had girdled her dress of mourning. Haemon had clasped his arms around her waist, mourning his bride in death and cursing his father's deeds.

"Oh, my poor boy," Creon cried. "What misfortune has destroyed your reason? Come out, my child. With these hands I implore you."

The youth sought out his father with frenzied eyes, then advanced and spat full in the old man's face. Without a word he drew his sword from its sheath and drove at him. Creon shrank back and the blow missed. Then, with a groan, Haemon turned the point into his own side and leaning on it with all his weight drove in the blade halfway to the hilt.

As strength and sense were failing, he groped for the body of Antigone and pulled it down. He fell upon it, gasping. And there, as they lay on a couch of flint in close embrace, his life's blood gushed over her pale breast in a marriage of death.

As the slow procession made its way back to the palace, Creon bearing the saddest burden that ever a father bore, a messenger sped on ahead.

"Oh, what a change of fortune I have seen," he told the elders at the palace. "Creon, whom once I counted blest—for thrice he saved our city—now, for all his power and riches, is only a living corpse."

"What is this grief you bear?" they asked.

"Antigone and Haemon are slain."

"Surely not by Creon?" they asked in horror.

"No, by their own hands—but in dire rage at the king's cruelty."

"O seer, how truly your words have come to pass!"

A hush fell on them as Creon's wife Eurydice came out of the palace. She, poor woman, was on her way to pray at the shrine of Pallas Athene, but as she heard them check their speech and saw the dark tidings in their eyes, she reeled back and almost fell into the arms of her handmaidens. When she recovered, she asked the meaning of their grim silence.

"The news is sorrowful, my Queen."

"Then tell it to me quickly, for I am no stranger to sorrow."

She listened to the blunt tale without a sign, then turned and fled within.

"What means this?" one asked anxiously. "Not a word she said of good or bad."

"I, too, thought it strange," said another. "But she is a queen, and any public show of grief would be unseemly. Within, no doubt, she is now pouring forth the anguish of her soul where only her handmaidens can see her."

"So may it be—but listen!"

Their ears were drawn to sounds of lamentation outside the palace gate. It was the voice of Creon.

"O Haemon, my son, my son! You have died through no folly of youth, but by an old man's stubborn madness."

Through the gate they came, Creon and his servants bearing the two shrouded bodies. Gently they laid them down.

"Behold us," cried Creon bitterly, "the slayer and the slain! Woe for me, for I have sinned. Woe for the blindness of my rule!"

"Too late," one said, "you seem to have seen the right."

"Ah me," said Creon, "some god must have dealt me a crushing blow to send me reeling down the path of cruelty till every joy was trampled underfoot. Harsh and bitter has been my lesson."

But even then it was not ended. A servant rushed from the palace and threw himself at Creon's feet.

"Sire, the queen your wife, too, is dead!"

"O merciless Hades," Creon cried, "can you never be appeased?"

He staggered through the palace doors and there on the marble hearth beside the family altar lay Eurydice, her frail, veined hand still clasping the knife that pierced her heart.

The servant and some elders had followed Creon inside.

"We did not know; we could not stop her," the servant said. "She cried first for Megareus, then for the son who lies without. And with her last breath, before she struck the blow, she called down a curse upon you as the murderer."

"O wretch that I am," moaned Creon, "let me die! Is there no one here who will strike me down with a two-edged sword? I am the slayer of my son and my wife. I confess the truth. Let me never see the coming of another day."

"Pray not for that," one of the elders admonished him. "For it is not for mortals to decree their fate or escape the woes of destiny."

"Then lead me away, a rash and foolish man," said Creon. "O my son, unwillingly I killed you—and now you, my wife. I know not where to look nor where to lean for aid. For everything I touch is doomed to go amiss. My head is crushed by fate."

The lesson was ended. Without wisdom there can be no happiness. Men turn their backs on the gods in vain. For the gods will smite the proud with mighty blows until they have learned wisdom with their years.

As *Antigone* had no sources in ancient legend, it is thought to be Sophocles' own democratic parable, based on some anti-Theban propaganda. Not to bury a slain foe was considered the worst form of atrocity. We find the complete atrocity reflected in a later play of Euripides where all of Thebes' slain attackers, not Polynices alone, are denied burial, and Theseus of Athens goes to war to right the wrong.

Thus, the whole Athenian audience—and the intimidated "Thebans" on stage—knew Creon's decree was immoral. The issue, however, is not religious but political, though dramatically heightened by its confinement to a single family. This is spelled out by Haemon. His plea is not for love or religion, but for justice and democracy. The gods gave no man wisdom enough to rule alone, he says.

Equally significant is the fact that Antigone buries her brother *twice*. This does not come from faulty structure to allow the comic scene with the soldier. Sophocles is too much a master craftsman for that. Every move he makes has a clear-cut purpose. With the first burial he removes the religious issue from the play completely. Everyone knew that no human acts could erase that rite. It remained as valid as baptism. Therefore the repetition is a "civil ceremony." It is the assertion of conscience against injustice—an overt act of nonconformity. One burial might have confused the issue with religion. But the second burial makes it stand out clearly.

Reading through theologically tinted glasses, many have misinterpreted the entire "trilogy." In the first play, they wrongly see Oedipus punished for sin, and find in Creon a model of piety. Then, in the second play they are forced to assume that Creon was made a very different, vicious character for purely dramatic purposes. In the third play, they elevate Creon to a tragic hero—a man who is almost right but unfortunately a victim of his own excess.

But Creon is the very antithesis of the Sophoclean hero who clings to his one ideal regardless of any outside force. Oedipus pursues truth to the bitter end; Antigone, justice; Ajax, heroic honor. Such characters are "inner directed" come life or death. Creon is not of this mold, but is weak and "other directed." He has no inner sense of right. Superstition, fear, and conformity, rather than any moral code, impel his acts whether they happen to be kind or cruel, seemingly honest or deceitful.

Above all, let us remember that this "last" play was actually the first, written many years before either of the other two plays of the trilogy. It was for this play, not the others, that the character of Creon was created, and he was created as a symbol of unrestricted monarchy.

HIPPOLYTUS

CHARACTERS

Aphrodite (A-fro-DI-tee), also called Cypris or "the Cyprian": Goddess of love, daughter of Zeus. (In the original play she addresses the audience directly in the prologue, but only her force and her wrath are felt in the story.)

Artemis (ART-e-mis): Daughter of Zeus and Leto, twin sister of Apollo, goddess of the moon, wild life, and hunting, often called the Huntress or Virgin Goddess.

Theseus (THEE-see-us or THEE-syoos): King of Athens, father of Hippolytus, and husband of Phaedra.

Hippolytus (Hip-POL-it-us): Illegitimate son of Theseus and the Amazon queen Antiope; a handsome youth, but a hater of women.

Phaedra (FEE-dra): Beautiful young wife of Theseus and mother of two children, daughter of King Minos of Crete.

An old servant of Hippolytus.

An old nurse of Phaedra.

Women of Troezen (TREE-zeen).

And Joseph was a goodly person and well favored. And it came to pass that his master Potiphar's wife cast eyes upon Joseph and said, "Lie with me." But he refused and said, "Thou art his wife; how then can I do this great wickedness and sin against God?" . . . And she caught him by his garment, and he left his garment in her hand and fled. . . . And when his lord came home she said, "The Hebrew servant came into me to lie with me, and I cried out, and he left his garment with me and fled." And Joseph's master's wrath was kindled. And he took Joseph and put him in prison.

Condensed from *Genesis 39:6-20.*

A similar folk tale was used by Euripides in an earlier *Hippolytus*. He then reworked his story into the present play with its more subtle psychology. For once, he pleased the critics and won first prize with this play. But in developing the moral conflict in Phaedra, he made her the really central figure of the play.

Aphrodite (the Phoenician Astarte or Ashtoreth) was widely worshiped in many forms, from the chaste *Venus Genetrix* to a *Venus*

Meretrix, with harlot priestesses in temple-brothels. In this story, the goddesses are more symbolic than real. Aphrodite stands for erotic desire, Artemis for its opposite evil (in Greek eyes) of a harsh and loveless purity. The story of *Hippolytus* lies in how these drives and inhibitions can afflict human lives.

HIPPOLYTUS

(EURIPIDES)

All the people of Troezen held the love goddess Aphrodite in high esteem—except Hippolytus, son of Theseus. Born himself of a violent love, Hippolytus shunned the goddess' rites. And although his handsome bronzed body and auburn locks were enough to set all maidens afire, he was cold to their charms and abhorred any thought of a marriage bed.

Instead, he made chaste vows to the goddess Artemis. For in his proud frigidity, he felt himself most akin to that virgin sister of Apollo. He sought the sound of her voice by the forest streams. And whenever he rode with his hounds in pursuit of the woodland beasts, he imagined the Huntress Goddess was riding by his side.

Hippolytus was the son of Antiope, queen of the Amazons, whom Theseus ravished when he conquered her tribe of warrior-women. His mother died soon after his birth. So he never knew the tenderness of a woman's hand nor the warmth of a woman's love. Yet it was for a woman's sake that he was sundered from his father when Theseus took a fair young bride to warm his middle years. The boy was sent to Troezen then, for his great-grandsire (the wise and saintly Pittheus) to rear.

The woman Theseus chose was Phaedra, daughter of Minos of Crete. Hippolytus saw her once as a youth, that day he went to Athens to join in the rites of the Great Mysteries. From her seat of honor, Phaedra gazed with limpid, violet eyes on his lithe, young body, then blushed and turned away her golden head. What thoughts she held for him he did not know, nor did he care. She was just a woman—the symbol of his father's weakness and the mother of his father's children. And those children she bore in holy wedlock were bitter reminders that he—though dear to his father, too—had been born in bastardy.

Now that Theseus and Phaedra had come to Troezen this woman's presence irked him all the more. So Hippolytus took to spending his days far away from the palace, seeking the hills and woods of his Virgin Goddess.

With whoops and halloos, one day, Hippolytus and his young companions rode clattering home from the hunt and reined up their snorting steeds in the courtyard of Pittheus' palace. The chase had been good, and they shouted their praise of Artemis.

"She is the loveliest daughter of Zeus!" they cried.

Ignoring the nearby altar of Aphrodite, Hippolytus leaped from his panting stallion to present his offerings to Artemis alone. He had gathered a garland of flowers in meadows untouched by plow or scythe.

"O mistress pure and undefiled," he prayed, "accept these gifts from the fields of innocence far from the wicked ways of men." And he placed his wreath on the gilded hair of her painted statue. Some day he would surely see her face to face. For he had vowed to leave this world as chaste as when he had entered it.

But the old attendant who held his glistening stallion shook his silvered head in dismay. How intemperate, he thought, how reckless, even in virtue, a youth could be who had never felt the powerful forces and passions of life!

"My prince," he said—for he called no one "master" except the gods—"would you heed a well-meaning word?"

"Of course," said Hippolytus. "Else I should be a fool."

"Have you never observed how men dislike a proud and unfriendly soul?"

"And why not," Hippolytus asked, "for who loves a churl?"

"Then surely the gods demand courtesy, too."

"No doubt," Hippolytus agreed, "for we pattern our lives on theirs."

"Then why do you spurn the holy Goddess of Love?" the old man asked.

"I merely keep at a pure and proper distance when I greet her."

"But most men welcome Aphrodite's gifts and worship her."

"Each to his own," Hippolytus replied. "If men may choose their special friends, why not their special gods as well? As for me, I find no pleasure in a goddess of the night."

"Then I wish you luck," the old man sighed, "and wit enough to go with it."

But Hippolytus paid him little heed. "Go in, my friends, and spread the board," he shouted. "A hard day's hunting calls for a hearty meal. And someone rub my horses down. I will yoke them later for a run." To the statue of Aphrodite he tossed a curt and casual "Rejoice!" in passing, then followed them in.

But the old man lingered behind to pray to Aphrodite: "Forgive him, holy Lady of Cyprus; do not deem that he speaks for me, his slave. For I am wiser with years, while he is only a youth, declaiming his folly in thoughtless fervor. But gods are slower to anger than headstrong men. So be gentle, Cypris, I pray, and pretend that you did not hear him."

The bridle jerked in his hand as his young master's horse caught the scent of a distant mare and began to neigh. He led the animal, prancing sidewise, to the stable.

Not far from the palace a spring gushed forth from a rock where the women of Troezen were wont to fill their jars with water—and their ears with gossip of the city. Here, too, they would wash their clothes and set them out on the shelving rock to dry in the warm bright sun. This day the talk was all of Phaedra, the queen, and her strange affliction.

"I hear she is wasted by a fever," one woman said as she swirled a purple garment in the stream. "She stays in her room and hides her fair blond locks beneath the coverlets."

"For three days now," another said, "not a crumb of bread has touched her lips. She shuns all food as though it were tainted. They say she longs for the harbor of death."

What was afflicting the beautiful Phaedra? they wondered. Had she been bewitched by Pan or Hecate? Could the Huntress Goddess be punishing her for some neglected vow?

"Perhaps some wench has stolen the noble Theseus from her bed," one whispered. They savored that thought for a moment till another said, "No, she feels more sadness than anger from what I hear. Some sailor from Crete may have come to the harbor with sorrowful tidings about her kin."

An older woman smiled. Had they all forgotten how lost and fretful a woman feels when her time is near? Let Phaedra but pray to Artemis and her pangs would be eased.

But this last surmise was as far from the truth as the rest.

Even Phaedra's own nurse knew not what troubled the pallid queen as she led her out on a portico to feel the warmth of the sun. Handmaidens brought out a bed and laid the coverlets. As the old nurse fluffed the cushions, she grumbled:

"You would give me no peace till I brought you here. Yet soon, I know, you will fret to get back to your room. Everything disappoints you now, and nothing pleases. Your eyes have a sad and distant look as though set on some fancy far away."

Phaedra's only reply was a deep-drawn sigh as the nurse helped her lay her weary limbs among the cushions.

To be ill was bad enough, the old nurse thought, but having to care for the ill was a double evil. A plague on feeble folk and their dismal diseases! Life was nothing but toil and grief —yet people clung to it desperately. For what lay beyond was forever veiled by clouds and fables.

Soon, as the nurse had surmised, Phaedra grew restless again.

"Lift up my body," she said. "My head should be higher . . . Hold my hand, I am feeling faint . . . This cloth on my head is too heavy. Take it off. Let my yellow hair flow around my shoulders."

"There, there," the old nurse said. "Do not tire yourself, my child. You must bear your sickness nobly. We all have to suffer at times."

Phaedra began to murmur feverishly: "Let me lie in some grassy meadow under the poplar trees and drink from a cool, clear stream."

What madness was this?

"Surely the water is cool enough right here by the palace," the old nurse said. But Phaedra raved on.

"Take me out to the woods and the mountains, where the hounds chase the spotted deer. Let me poise the javelin beside my ear and send it whirring to its quarry. O Artemis, let me go down by your shores to break in the wild Venetian colts . . ."

"Springs—mountains—shores!" the nurse exclaimed in bewilderment. In heaven's name, what ailed the queen? These were haunts for lusty youths like Hippolytus, but surely no place for a frail, young mother and ill at that. "It would take a seer to know what you want," she muttered, "or to tell what god is afflicting you."

"I am sorry," Phaedra said. "Some frenzy seized me. Cover my head. I am ashamed."

"I will cover you," the old nurse said, "but if you go on so, the earth will soon be covering me. How wise is the ancient saying, 'All things in moderation—even love.' For I love you far too much, my child. And so I must bear your sorrows as well as my own. At least let me know what is wrong, why you sigh and fast and long for death. It will not do for Theseus to come home and find you like this."

At the sound of her husband's name, Phaedra hid her face in her slender hands.

"Come, dearest child," the old nurse begged. "Never mind my chiding. Away with frowns and wayward words. We must both use reason. If some woman's ill is what you suffer, there are many women here to help you. If not, you should tell me just what is wrong that I may inform a physician. But do say something—anything. Even scold me if I am not speaking aright."

But as Phaedra said nothing, the baffled nurse put a sharper edge to her voice.

"Oh, why be as heedless as the raging sea?" she demanded. "Look! If you die you will only betray your children. Theseus' throne will never be theirs. They will have to bow instead to the bastard son of the chariot-riding Amazon—the pure-minded lord Hippolytus."

"No, no!" cried Phaedra.

"Ah," said the nurse with a gleam of hope, "I have stung you to words at last."

"By the gods I beg you," Phaedra cried, "never speak that name again!"

"Have you no care for your children, then?"

"I love them, but I am caught in another storm."

"Surely you have no blood on your hands?" the nurse asked anxiously.

"No, the stain is not on my body but in my soul."

"Has some enemy cast a spell?"

"No, but alas, a loved one destroys me all unknowingly."

"Theseus?"

"O gods, no! If only I were as faithful as he!"

"Then what is wrong?"

"Oh, leave me alone!" cried Phaedra. "It is only myself that I hurt."

"But you will destroy me, too," the old nurse pleaded. "For if I lost you I could not live."

"Oh, the curse of love!" sobbed Phaedra. "It brought my mother to ruin, then my sister, and now me."

Her mother? What did she mean? The nurse grew pale. The frenzied Pasiphaë had been enamored of a bull and given birth to the monstrous Minotaur. It was to cheat this monster's jaws of the captive children of Athens that Theseus first had come to Crete. There, with the help of Minos' daughter Ariadne, he had tracked and slain the beast in its labyrinth.

Her sister? Ariadne had lain with Theseus in love, but he soon grew weary of her. He left her to the gods in Naxos. Weeping she had sat upon a rock, gazing after his ship till its ill-omened sail had vanished beyond the horizon.

Phaedra was wrong, the old nurse thought, ever to wed the man who betrayed her sister. But that was past.

"What crushes you now, my child?"

"I cannot speak of it," Phaedra sobbed. "But tell me, what is the meaning of love?"

"The sweetest of thrills, my child, or the bitterest sorrow."

"The sorrow is all I know," sighed Phaedra. "Oh, why did the noble Theseus ever lie with the Amazon?"

If this was jealousy, the old nurse thought, it was flowering late. Then suspicion burst on her like a crashing blow.

"Hippolytus!" she cried. "Is *he* the one you love?"

"Ah, you spared my saying it," said Phaedra, turning her head away in tears of shame.

"Now you *have* destroyed me," the old nurse groaned. "I would sooner lie in Hades than see your purity so defiled —however unwillingly. Aphrodite is no god, but some evil mightier than a god, if she can bring such ruin down upon this house."

"Do you think I have not tossed through many long night hours," asked Phaedra, "wondering how such miseries can wreck men's lives? It is not through ignorance that we sin. For we know what is right however much we may yield to malice, idleness, or shame. I know too well how wrong I am. No drug can cure me of that knowledge.

"When first I felt the wound of this shameful desire, I built a shrine to Aphrodite and sought to allay her curse by prayers and sacrifice. Alas, I could not. Each prayer only conjured up another vision of him standing there—young, strong, and proud. I vowed to hide my love in silence, for I dared not trust my tongue. I tried to guard my chastity with reason. But reason flees in the face of love; now death alone can kill the flame."

"No, no! There must be some other way," the old nurse cried.

"There is no other way," said Phaedra. "As I value my virtuous name, I want no one ever to witness my fall. A man might outlive such a scandal, but never a woman. A curse on the wife who first took lovers to her bed. High-born she was, beyond a doubt, for low-born folk only ape the sins of their betters. How I hate all women whose speech is chaste but whose deeds are vile. How can they face their husbands and not be afraid the very walls that hide their lusts will cry out?

"I must die before I disgrace my husband or my children. Let them live forever free in glorious Athens and not be enslaved by the taint of a mother's shame. Time holds a mirror to all our lives; may I never look therein and behold evils I could not endure."

Now the nurse was gripped with fear, for her greatest concern was Phaedra's life.

"O mistress, forgive me!" she said. "Your sudden tidings quite robbed me of my wits. I was wrong to chide you. One's second thoughts can be more discreet. After all your plight is not so unusual; many have felt the sweet goading of Aphrodite. Indeed, if she did not sow her seeds of passionate desire, what one of us would be here on earth today? But to die for love is profitless. When love grows too strong to fight, to yield is the only cure."

Phaedra's violet eyes opened wide with horror. But the nurse went on in soothing tones. "Oh, do not think that love is a shameful thing, my dear. From the ancient poets we know that even Zeus once burned for Semele. And the shining Goddess of Dawn carried Cephalus off to heaven to be her lover. There, I fancy, they still abide—quite happy with their fate, not shunning the paths of the gods for shame. Under these same gods and their laws you were begotten by your father. Who are you to reject them?"

"But I have a husband," Phaedra said, "which makes my passion far more shameful."

"I grant that you should not flaunt it before the people," the old nurse said. "It is only common sense to conceal some things. But how many men do you think, and the wisest ones at that, merely close their eyes when their wives take lovers? And how many pious fathers connive to aid their sons' amours? Oh, do not strive for perfection, child! If a carpenter had to have every joint and every beam perfectly straight and true, he never could build a house to shelter us. So it is in shaping our lives. A mortal must take what comes and be well content if the good outweighs the bad.

"Moderation alone is the way of a happy life. Perfection is the goal of pride and just a sinful desire to be better than the gods themselves. Be brave, then, and love, for the gods have willed it so. Seek charms and spells to aid your cause. We shall surely hit on something—a woman's wit can always find a way."

"Oh, these are glittering, guileful words," cried Phaedra in rebuke, "such words as break up homes and corrupt well-ordered cities. I need simple words of truth to save my soul, and you fill my ears with forbidden honey."

"This is no time for preaching," said the nurse. "You need no words at all, but a man—and someone to speed the truth to his ears. Believe me, if you had not fallen already in your heart I would not be luring you on to pleasure and lust. But who can blame us now when it means your life?"

"Stop saying such wicked things!" said Phaedra.

"Wicked, perhaps, yet wise," said the nurse. "It is better to love and live than to carry the empty name of chastity to the grave."

"Stop, by the gods!" cried Phaedra. "You know I am weak, and your words will be all the more wicked if they persuade me."

"Your mind should have ruled your heart from the first," the old nurse said. "It is too late now." She paused. "But no, I have just remembered I do have some philters to charm away the pangs of love. They will heal you harmlessly if you will be brave. But first I must have some token from you"—she drew a ring from Phaedra's finger—"and something from him, to join together to make this spell."

Phaedra shuddered, but did not resist.

"This charm?" she asked. "Is it some ointment or potion?"

The nurse was caught unawares.

"I do not know," she said, then hastily added, "but what you want is relief, not the recipe."

"I fear you are too clever," Phaedra said.

"You tremble at everything, my child."

"I fear you will tell my secret to Theseus' son."

The nurse was vague.

"Oh, you must trust me," she said. "I promise to be discreet." But as she hurried into the palace with Phaedra's ring, she breathed a prayer: "O Aphrodite, be my helper now."

> How sweet is love when it comes in season—
>   The first awareness,
>   The quiver of hope,
>   The pain of desire,
>   The flame of passion,
> And the soft, mystic glow when the flame subsides.
>
> But Semele died in the blazing embrace
>   Of her lover—Zeus—
> And Heracles' lust for Iolé,
>   In scorn of his vows,
> Brought vengeance, agony and death.
>
> For deadlier than the thunderbolts
>   Of mighty Zeus
> Are the arrows of forbidden love
> That fly from Eros' bow to smite
>   Tormented souls.

The skies grew darker as clouds began to veil the sun, and a chill crept over the portico. The nurse had not returned. So Phaedra called to her maids to help her back to her room. Part way down the corridor, where the curtained doorway led to the hall of men, they were checked by the sound of voices beyond the curtain. Phaedra froze as she heard Hippolytus cursing the hapless nurse.

"Away from me, you pandering hag," he cried, "betrayer of your master's bed!"

Fear and dismay pierced Phaedra's breast. The foolish old woman, although with the best intent, had betrayed her secret. The cure she had sought was proving more deadly than hemlock. For Hippolytus raged; there was not even pity in his voice.

"O Mother Earth and all-seeing Sun!" she heard him exclaim. "When have I ever heard so wicked a plea?"

Phaedra silently waved for her maids to go on and leave her there. Then, sick and faint, she clung to the cold, gray stone of the doorway and listened.

"Hush, my son!" she heard the old woman pleading. "Someone might overhear."

"How can I hide such sin in silence?" demanded Hippolytus.

"Please, I implore you!"

"Keep your filthy hands from my cloak!" Hippolytus cried. "They soil me."

"By your knees I beg you, do not ruin me!"

"Ruin you?" he sneered. "How could I ruin you if your plea were pure?"

"It was meant for no ears but yours. And you swore by holy Artemis to keep my secret before I shared it. Can you now break your sacred oath?"

"I swore with my tongue," Hippolytus said bitterly, "but not with my heart."

"Surely, my son," the old nurse pleaded, "you will not destroy your friends."

"Friends?" said Hippolytus with scorn. "The wicked are never my friends—least of all my father's harlot wife."

Phaedra choked back a gasp. She could not endure any more. Reeling, she fled down the corridor to her room.

Beyond the curtain the nurse continued her forlorn plea.

"At least," she said, "you can find it in your heart to forgive. For to err is only human."

"Human!" Hippolytus exclaimed. "Are women human? No! They are brazen counterfeits." He rolled his eyes to the skies. "O Zeus," he cried, "why in heaven's name did you ever allow your sun to shine upon them? If you wanted to breed a race of men, why did it have to be by women? Why could we not buy our children for silver and gold in your temples and dwell at peace in a land not plagued by females?

"Women! Even the sires who beget them pay dowries to rid their homes of the evil. And love-sick fools who wed them must clothe and adorn them till all their wealth is squandered. Sometimes for the sake of a family tie a man forces himself to smile on a vicious wife. But if by chance he should find one any good, then her kin would surely turn out to be worthless parasites.

"The best one can hope to wed is some simple, useless fool without enough mind for mischief. But the gods deliver me from a clever woman with more than a woman's wit! She is a willing tool for Aphrodite's wiles and ought to be guarded by fierce dumb brutes with teeth—not wicked servants to aid in her lecheries."

He turned again on the trembling nurse.

"Oh, you were lucky to trick me into an oath. Nothing else could stop me from telling my father. But I shall leave these halls in silence till he returns. Then I will be back to watch how you and your mistress dare face him—though you are brazen enough. I have learned that already. May both of you perish! I hate all women, for they are vile. For saying as much before, I have been reproved—but never yet have I found a good one. So women must learn to mend their ways or my curses will never cease."

Still in a rage of righteousness, he turned and strode away. The nurse clutched the curtain in despair. How could she face her mistress now?

Back in her room, Phaedra sat gazing into her mirror. Its smooth bronze surface concealed her pallor but revealed the anguish in her face and the glistening rivulets of tears. She deserved all this, she felt, and she knew her guilt. Now others would know it too. Theseus would hate her beauty—hate even the children she bore him. Nothing could save her.

"Oh, I am most wretched of women," she moaned.

Then, past the tortured image of her face, she caught sight of the nurse in the doorway. She sprang to her feet.

"Vile woman," she cried, "what have you done? May Zeus destroy you with his fire! I suspected your purpose and begged you to hide my woes. But no, you could not. You told him and made him angry. Now he will go to his sire and accuse me of sins that are yours. He will surely unburden his soul to old Pittheus. The whole world will hear the awful truth. Then not even death will save my honor or protect my children. The fiends seize you and every evildoer who strives to help friends against their will!"

"O my mistress, you well may curse me for doing wrong," the old nurse said, "for the hurt you feel outweighs your reason. But remember, I nursed and loved you. For your sake alone I was seeking a cure, though I gained what was far from my wishes. Yet with any luck you would have blessed my wisdom. For all who win are accounted wise."

"Your deeds have wounded me enough," said Phaedra. "Spare me the salt of your sophistry."

"Well, let us admit, then, that I was foolish," said the nurse. "I am sure I can still find a way of escape."

"No. Leave me alone!" cried Phaedra, driving her out of the room and bolting the door. "Keep your evil schemes to save yourself. No more will I trust my fate to any hand but my own."

Frantic thoughts coursed through her mind. She had wanted to die. And now she must. She could never face Theseus again nor the shame she would bring on her Cretan kin. Yet somehow in death she must save her honor, if only for her children's sake. They must be free of taint and never forced to bear the yoke of the Amazon's bastard son.

She would destroy herself as a final appeasement to Aphrodite, who had smitten her with a hopeless love. But she would destroy another, too. In his pride and scorn he would learn a bitter lesson. She seized a stylus and waxen tablets. Passion, hatred, and despair engraved her cryptic message:

Theseus, my lord, farewell. The Amazon's son has ruined me. I can no longer live nor look upon your face. So pity me and protect our children.

She sealed the tablets with wax and the print of her golden ring, then tied them to a bracelet on her wrist. Already the nurse was knocking at the door and calling her name, but she did not answer. Soon others came and began to beat on the stout oak planks. There was little time now—she must hurry. She mounted a bench and fastened a silken cord to the rafters, then drew a noose about her fair, white neck. . . . For a moment she fluttered like a wounded bird. Then she was still. The pounding increased. At last the door was smashed from its bolts and sockets and fell to the floor with a crash. They found her hanging there.

Theseus, returning from a holy pilgrimage, was irked to find no one standing by the gates to greet him. Then he heard the wailing of women. *Pittheus!* he thought, as he leaped from his chariot. Old though his grandsire was, his death would be deeply mourned. He seized hold of a servant near the door.

"The old man?" he asked. "Is it he?"

"O King, it is not for the old but the young that your tears will flow," the servant replied.

"My children?"

"They live—but, alas, they grieve for a mother dead."

"My wife! Dead? What are you saying? How can it be?"

"She knotted a strangling noose on her neck."

"But why?" His voice was choking with sudden grief.

"Master, I weep for you, but I know no more. Just now they have laid her body out in the hall to await your coming."

Theseus clapped his hand to his brow and his fingers touched the pilgrim's crown of leaves.

"Oh, why do I wear this holy wreath," he cried, "when I am cursed by the gods?" He tore the wreath from his head and flung it away as he ran inside. The servants fell back before him. There she lay, pale as an ivory statue on the rich, purple coverlets, her body sheathed in a shroud of white. The lids of her violet eyes had been closed and her hair flowed over the silken pillow like waves of gold in the sunset.

Theseus moaned and fell to his knees beside her bier.

"Oh, why have I lost you?" he cried. "What mad blow was this you struck? Your death is my death, too. How heavy the heel of fate that crushes me—how vast and shoreless my sea of woe! How can I name this cruel doom, my wife? Like a little bird you flew from my hand and are lost in the gloomy clouds of death. But why? What is this curse that has doomed us both? What dim and far-off sins of my fathers have vengeful gods now heaped on my hapless head?"

Around him flowed the hollow words of sympathy, but his ears were closed.

"O my loved one," he wept, "what joy you brought to my home, and what sorrow—beyond all telling, all enduring! My house is empty, our children motherless. You are gone—gone—my dear one—the purest of wives ever seen by the radiant sun or the eyes of the night."

Then he stood and faced them, his eyes ablaze.

"Will no one tell me what happened," he asked, "or does my royal roof just shelter a flock of useless knaves?"

They could not say, but their eyes were fixed on the letter whose seal they had dared not break. Then Theseus saw it too.

"What is this message tied to my dear one's wrist? What does it seek to tell me? Poor woman—some dying wish, perhaps. Fear not, my lost one, no other woman shall ever enter Theseus' house or bed."

Gently he freed the letter from her bracelet and broke its seal. He began to read. Then his eyes almost leaped from their sockets. He let out a cry of rage.

"What is it?" they asked.

"This letter—O horror of horrors! It cries aloud. It shrieks of a sin unspeakable, unendurable. Where can I hide my head from its weight of woe? Oh, what an evil curse these words are chanting! A deed so vile that I cannot keep it locked in my lips. . . . O my people, Hippolytus, the son I cherished, has dared to rape my dearest wife, sinning in the very eyes of Zeus."

They gasped in horror and disbelief. But Theseus flung his hands to the heavens and prayed to Posidon, the lord of the trembling earth and the raging seas:

"O Father Posidon, once thou didst promise to fulfill three curses for me. Now I claim the first. *Destroy my son Hippolytus!* Let him not escape this day if thou art a god whose word is true."

"O King, for the love of the gods call back that curse!"

The old nurse fell at his feet. "For you will learn you are wrong, believe me."

"Never!" cried Theseus. "I shall drive the sinner from this land. Whether the god heeds my prayers or not, his doom is sealed. For either Posidon will speed him to Hades' gates or he will drag out a bitter life as a lonely exile in friendless lands."

With a cry of despair, the nurse rushed out of the palace she knew not where. But she knew that she, too, could only join her mistress in death.

Hippolytus frowned as he came from the stables and saw his father's chariot. He had meant to be at the palace on Theseus' return, to shame the lustful Phaedra with silent reproach when she greeted her lord. But something was clearly amiss. There were sounds of moaning. He entered the hall and had hardly begun to hail his sire when he spied her corpse.

"Father, what happened?" he asked. "I cannot believe it. A short time ago I beheld her in the sun. They said she was ill—but *this!*"

Theseus glared at his son without speaking.

"Come, Father, tell me," Hippolytus pleaded. "Silence can bring you no ease to your grief. My heart that would share your joys should be still more eager to share your sorrows. It is wrong to conceal your woes from your friends—or from one who is more than a friend."

Then Theseus spoke, but more to the world than to his son.

"How is it that men can devise and master ten thousand arts but none has learned how to teach restraint to a brutish fool?"

"Any man who could teach a fool to be wise would be clever indeed," said Hippolytus. "But, Father, I do not understand. Has grief overwhelmed your wits that your thoughts go so far astray?"

"Oh, why is there no true test for friendship?" Theseus exclaimed. "Every man should be forced to have two tones of voice—one to show when he speaks the truth and one to betray his lies."

"Your words lack cause," Hippolytus said. "Has someone been slandering me?"

"Oh, where is the end of such brazen infamy?" Theseus cried. "If sons go on to outsin their fathers, the gods must create a new earth to contain so much wickedness. Look at him! Fruit of my loins—befouler of my bed! Her death cries out his guilt."

Hippolytus covered his face with his hands, but Theseus roared:

"No! You cannot hide from it now! Show me your face!" His voice seethed with scorn. "So you were the chaste, the holy one who consorted with gods? Faugh! I do not believe that the gods are such fools. Go preach the teachings of Orpheus! Go eat your meatless meals! Read your empty scriptures, they will not save you. For you are caught—you prater of pious words and doer of evil!"

Hippolytus helplessly glanced at the corpse of Phaedra.

"Do you think you are safe because she is dead?" demanded Theseus. "Her death condemns you more than any oath—her death and *this!*" He thrust the accusing letter into Hippolytus' hands.

Hippolytus read the words in dire amazement.

"Oh, how she must have hated me!" he murmured.

"For no more cause than your bastard birth?" scoffed Theseus. "What wife would be so wasteful as to fling away her precious life to feed her hate? Or do you say that women are a different breed—more rash than men? No, it is men in the heat of youth that lose their reason, especially when Aphrodite goads them, though they plead their manhood as an excuse.

"But why need I prove your guilt by argument when this body alone convicts you? Begone, an exile from this land! Never set foot in god-built Athens nor in any realm beneath my spear. Else Theseus' conquered enemies will rise from their graves to brand him a liar for calling himself a scourge of evildoers."

Hippolytus flinched at his father's wrath, appalled by his harsh decree. How he yearned for eloquence now! Ever ill at ease except with his closest friends, he had scorned all glib-tongued swayers of men as fools in the eyes of the wise. But now—condemned by all but dumb truth itself—he, too, stood in need of words. He must plead for his very life.

"In all this earth and under heaven's dome," he said, "you will not find one soul more innocent than mine—though your jeers deny it. Old Pittheus taught me to love the gods and to walk with godly men; to choose as friends only those whose thoughts and deeds were pure and who never would lead me into temptation. Could I mock such friends by doing wrong? No, never—within their sight or out of it.

"I swear by Holy Artemis I have always been chaste. Since the day my poor, dear mother died my body has never felt the touch of woman's flesh. I know nothing of the acts of love except through poems and pictures. Even these disgust me. Do you think this woman so alluring, then, that she could fill me with lust?"

Theseus groaned.

"Or do you think that possessing her I thought to possess your kingdom? I am not such a fool, for I know that kingly power can only corrupt the man who craves it. I would gladly win an athlete's crown in the Grecian games, but ever be second in any kingdom, content with wealth and friends, but free from the terrors of a throne.

"Only one thing remains that I cannot cite in my defense, for I am sworn. But if I had witnesses as incorruptible as myself, or if she who is dead could speak, you could soon track down where the real sin lies and where the evildoers lurk. For I swear by Zeus, the god of oaths, that I never touched your bridal bed nor wished to—even in my dreams. And may I die without a name, and may earth and sea refuse to receive my body if any word I speak is false. Whether she slew herself through fear, I do not know—and more I cannot say. Consider her chaste, for she kept her chastity in her fashion. But I am the truly chaste one although accused."

All but Theseus were moved by his plea. They begged the king to heed his fearful oath and relent. But Theseus said:

"Is this fellow not a clever juggler of words, hoping to conjure away the wrath of the father he shamed?"

"Father, I marvel at you," said Hippolytus. "For were I your father and you my son I should slay you on the spot. I should never let you flee in exile if I thought you had lain with my wife."

"Ha! You confess!" said Theseus. "But you give yourself too light a sentence. Swift death is too easy for such a crime."

"Will you not wait for Time to reveal the truth?" Hippolytus asked. "Must you banish me at once?"

"Yes," Theseus said, "beyond the boundless Atlantic if I could, so much do I hate your face."

"Do oaths and pledges mean nothing? Will you not even question a seer?"

"Her letter is pledge enough. Her death is an oath. These need no seer's art. So let the soothsaying birds fly about as they will. 'Begone,' I say to them—and to you."

"O gods," cried Hippolytus, "why should your faithful

servant perish? Why must I keep the truth locked in my lips? And yet," he reflected bitterly, "could I persuade him even if I broke my sacred oath?"

"Enough of your injured piety," Theseus said. "It kills me. Away with you! Leave your fatherland at once!"

"Where can I go?" moaned Hippolytus. "Who would receive me?"

"Any who welcome traitors with open arms and bid them make free with their wives."

"What brings me closest to tears," Hippolytus said, "is not my fate but your belief in my guilt."

"The time to repent was before you ravished your father's wife."

"Oh, if only these walls had a voice!" cried Hippolytus.

Theseus jeered: "How clever to keep on crying for witnesses void of speech. But even her dumb corpse swears to your crimes."

"If only I could stand aside and see myself," Hippolytus sighed, "I should weep at the wrongs I saw."

"You have always had eyes for yourself alone," said Theseus, "adoring your own perfection and scorning your parents."

"My parents!" Hippolytus groaned. "O my poor mother and my wretched birth! May no one I love have to suffer a bastard's woes."

"Get him out of here!" Theseus cried to his servants. "Did you not hear my sentence long ago?"

"If anyone touches me he will rue it," Hippolytus said. "Only you, my father, can thrust me out if that is your wish."

"It is—and go!" said Theseus. "I have no pity for your exile."

"Then all is lost. I will obey," Hippolytus said. "For though I know the truth, I know not how to tell it."

He bowed his head and left the hall. For a moment he paused before Artemis' altar.

"O daughter of Leto, dearest of gods," he said, "and chaste companion of all my ways, never shall I see glorious Athens again nor Troezen, the home of my happy youth." Then he went on to bid his friends farewell.

Swiftly the news swept the city, and people wondered. Was their faith in the gods but a soothing drug if mortal affairs could go so awry? Was nothing sure in this life but change? The sands of the shore and the mountain glades would mourn for the banished youth. No more would they hear his baying hounds or the thud of his horses' hoofs. No more would the halls of his father smile when he wakened the sleeping Muse with his lyre. No more would Artemis wear his crown of flowers, nor the virgins of Troezen vie— as they long had in vain—for his love. A golden star had fallen from Hellas' skies, and many would murmur against the gods.

Down by the wave-beaten shore the weeping servants were combing his horses' manes when Hippolytus came with a sorrowing throng.

"No more tears," he said. "My father must be obeyed. So harness my horses. This city no longer is mine." And when he had mounted his chariot he stretched forth his hands and cried, "O mighty Zeus, strike me dead if I have sinned. But whether I live or not, let my father learn how grievously he has sinned against me."

Then he lightly touched the four horses with the goad and set his course toward Argos and Epidaurus. But his friends were still loath to let him go. They ran along by his chariot wheels exchanging words of parting sorrow.

Theseus might have forgotten his angry curse. But a god cannot forget. As the grieving throng reached the lonely plain beside the Saronic Sea, a deep rumbling roar was heard from the bowels of the earth. Hippolytus' horses pricked up their ears at the ominous muttering of Posidon. Then in from the sea rolled a mighty wave—a wave so high that its crest hid the cliffs of Sciron. And crashing down on the beach in a thunder of foam it belched forth a beast whose bull-like bellowings shook the echoing hills.

Straight for Hippolytus' chariot the sea monster came. The horses reared up shrieking and whirled about, then plunged in panic back through the scattering throng. With practiced hand Hippolytus tried to curb their headlong flight, pulling the reins this way and that like a valiant helmsman caught in a raging sea. But his horses were heedless now of the hands and the voice they had known so well. Freezing their jaws on the brazen bits they plunged on in reckless terror. Soon the chariot was dashed against a rock, its wheels and axle-pins and planks all shattered. And out of the wreck Hippolytus was dragged along, hopelessly tangled in the reins.

In dismay his friends heard his piteous cries: "Oh, help me! Help me! For I have done no wrong!" But his body was hurled against jagged rocks that battered his head, splintered his bones, and tore at his flesh. At last, someone braver than the rest leaped in behind the plunging horses, slashed through the leather reins and cut him free. But now his young body lay cruelly mangled and racked with pain. They took their cloaks and hunting spears and made a litter, then gently laid him on it and slowly bore him home to die. A messenger sped on ahead to tell the king.

"Your son Hippolytus is dead," he said, "or at best has little time to see the light."

Theseus was grim, but showed no feeling.

"Who killed him?" he asked. "Some other outraged husband?"

"No. The horses he fed with his own dear hand—and the deadly curse that came from your lips imploring the Sea God's vengeance."

"O Posidon," said Theseus, "thou art indeed a father who hears my prayers."

"I am only your slave," the messenger grew bold enough to say, "but I cannot believe your son did evil, not if the whole race of women should hang themselves to prove it and fill every pine of Ida with accusations."

"I should rejoice at his suffering, I hate him so," said Theseus. "Yet he is my son and I fear the gods. So his fate brings neither joy nor sorrow."

"Then where shall we bear him?" the messenger asked. "Oh, do not treat him harshly."

"Bring him here to face me," Theseus said. "He swore he never stained my bed, but heaven's wrath refutes him now."

"No, Theseus, no! He spoke the truth." An unseen voice was heard from above and a mystic woodland fragrance filled the air. *"The doom of heaven falls not on your son—but on you."*

Theseus trembled. "Who speaks?" he cried.

A silvery, luminescent cloud floated down till it shrouded the goddess' image and lightly hovered above her altar.

"Proud son of Aegeus, know it is I, Artemis, the child of Leto. What joy can you find in your wickedness, O cruel slayer of your son? Where can you flee your wretched lot —where in the darkness of earth or the boundless sky—unfit to dwell among men? Your son was pure. Let him die with honor. And hear the truth though it tears your heart. . . ."

As the goddess told of the bitter course of Phaedra's passion, each word dealt Theseus' soul a bleeding wound, and he groaned in pain.

"Well may you grovel in remorse," the voice went on. "It

was you who forged the final link. Once the Sea God pledged you to grant three prayers. And one of these that you should have used to thwart your enemies you hurled against your son. Think you Posidon wished to slay him? No! But even a god must keep his oath. Yet in his eyes as well as mine your son was pure and your prayer evil."

"Have the blessed gods no mercy?" Theseus moaned.

"Your deed was infamous," Artemis said. "Yet two things may win you pardon, though they cannot quench your grief. The first is ignorance. For though you believed too readily, your wife was most lavish with her proofs. Then both you and she were blinded by Aphrodite's fury—that queen of passions detested by every virgin heart. She used you both to destroy the one who scorned her. No god may thwart another's will, and fear of Zeus alone kept me from saving the mortal I loved beyond all. A god cannot weep, but I share your grief. For there is no joy in heaven when a good man dies."

The courtyard was bathed in the glow of the setting sun when they brought Hippolytus home. His brain was afire, a fearful pain throbbed through his limbs. He screamed at the tenderest touch of his friends. He bemoaned his father's curse, his thankless horses, and even Zeus who had failed to save him.

"What sins of my bloodstained ancestors have the gods requited on me who never harmed any man?" he cried. "Oh, set me down and quickly bring a sword to end this agony. Come Death and give me rest!"

"Poor man," said Artemis, "your noble heart was yoked to a cruel fate."

"Ah!" Hippolytus exclaimed, "I know that voice. I feel her fragrant presence, and my pain grows less. She is here, my goddess Artemis!"

His dying eyes pierced through the mists and he saw her then—the silver maiden with the silver bow.

"I shall always love you, even in death," she said. "How evil is Aphrodite who hated your pride and purity!"

"Then it was she who struck me down?"

"Yes—you and your father's wife and your poor deluded father."

"I am ruined, my son," wept Theseus. "There is no joy in life."

"Father, I mourn for you even more than myself."

"Oh, would to the gods I could take my curses back!"

"Or that men in turn could curse the gods," said Hippolytus.

"Your death shall not go unavenged," said Artemis. "There is one that Aphrodite dearly loves—the youth Adonis. My shafts will smite him down. And you shall have honors in Troezen's land. Long will your death and Phaedra's love be recalled in song. And every maiden, before she weds, will cut off her hair for you—an endless harvest through all the years. Forgive your father. Though blinded by a god, he loved you. And now, farewell, for the end is near. It must not pollute my eyes."

"Farewell, O blessed Virgin Queen," Hippolytus said. "How easily you vanish from my sight. . . . Father, take me in your arms. I see the gates of death."

"Oh, do not leave me," Theseus cried, "with murder on my soul."

"You are forgiven, Father. The taint is gone."

"O to lose a son so noble!" Theseus moaned.

"You have true-born sons," Hippolytus said. "Only pray that they, too, may be pure in heart."

"Do not leave me, my son!" cried Theseus.

"The end has come," Hippolytus gasped. "Farewell . . ."

They carried his body into the hall, and the sounds of mourning arose afresh.

Alone in the twilight, between the altars, an old servant stood alone. This day he had seen two souls struck down in their years of golden youth. One smitten by an impure love, the other by a loveless purity. Old though he was, some things would ever remain beyond his understanding. Only this he knew—when great souls die, whole cities must weep.

Only a puritan could confuse Hippolytus with a single-minded Sophoclean hero exerting his inner moral force against fate. That Hippolytus is other-directed is indicated specifically in many ways and symbolized by his devotion to Artemis. Hippolytus consciously maintains his purity as a sort of bargain with the gods. So in the end he wails loudly and often that he trusted the gods and they cheated him.

With our black-and-white philosophy, it is hard to capture the Greek view that Hippolytus' bragging chastity is an evil excess. But *sophrosyne*, the golden mean, is sounded as a recurring keynote throughout the play. Lust is one excess, but inhuman coldness is the other. Hippolytus had no pity for the one he hurt. To show compassion would have been to follow the golden mean.

Euripides employs many subtle touches to show the hollowness of Hippolytus' goddess. The last scenes have beauty, but Artemis shows all the aloofness of a rich lady on a slumming expedition. She vows to slay Adonis only to avenge her own insult. And there is irony in the gifts she promises. Phaedra must share his claim to fame. And he will be worshiped, not by pure youths but by maidens, such as he despised, on the point of yielding to Aphrodite.

Euripides was called a "woman hater" by Athenians who resented the way he forced their attention to the sex that Pericles had said should never be mentioned "either for good or bad" among men. His Hippolytus leaves us cold but who can forget his tormented Phaedra?

IPHIGENIA IN AULIS

CHARACTERS

Agamemnon (Ag-a-MEM-non): King of Argos and Commander-in-Chief of the Greek expedition against Troy. He and Menelaos are the sons of Atreus.

Menelaos (Men-e-LA-os): King of Sparta, brother of Agamemnon, and husband of Helen, whose seduction by Paris of Troy led to the Trojan War.

Clytemnestra (Kli-tem-NESS-tra): Wife of Agamemnon, sister of Helen, and daughter of Tyndareus.

Iphigenia (If-i-jen-I-a): Eldest daughter of Agamemnon and Clytemnestra.

Orestes (O-REST-eez): Infant son of Agamemnon and Clytemnestra.

Achilles (A-KILL-eez): Leader of the Myrmidons, son of Peleus and the sea nymph Thetis, destined to become the greatest warrior at Troy.

An old servant of Clytemnestra's from her father's palace, who serves Agamemnon in the army.

A soldier.

(An irrelevant chorus of women from the nearby town of Chalcis is eliminated in the telling of the story.)

The beautiful Iphigenia, delightful in her youthful innocence and exuberance, loved and adored her father Agamemnon. And she was his favorite daughter. What a shock it was when she found he was planning not for her marriage but for her death!

This is the most romantic of Euripides' plays and the most beloved by many moderns who find sheer tragedy too austere. The play was not produced until after Euripides' death, and then it was partly reworked by a brilliant second hand. The manuscripts carry traces of several versions side by side. In general, I have omitted those passages which Miss F. M. Stawell, in her superlative English translation, considered spurious. Her artistic judgment was unimpeachable.

Every character, except the Spartan Menelaos perhaps, is drawn with great sympathy and insight. None is cast in any rigid heroic mold, but each is delightfully human and plastic. In the character of Iphigenia, for the first time in all Western literature, probably, we see significant character growth before our very eyes.

IPHIGENIA IN AULIS

(EURIPIDES AND EURIPIDES THE YOUNGER)

A hundred thousand eager Greeks had mustered in the bay of Aulis to sail against the Trojans, but now they chafed and cursed the harbor as a prison. They burned to be off to avenge the seizure of Helen. Instead, their thousand ships lay beached and useless as day after day they waited for winds that never came. Their food ran short, their tempers shorter.

And now it was another night of hateful, stifling calm. Not a breeze was stirring; not even a ripple slapped on the sands. All was quiet except for the low, soft, organ tones of many sleeping men.

One tent alone was bright and golden from a lamp within, and on its wall was cast the huge and restless shadow of a man.

For Agamemnon, the leader of the host, was trying to write a letter. Many times he wrote, erased, then wrote again—sealing the tablets, only to break the seal, and once he hurled them to the ground. But at last he finished. He drew aside the tent flap, softly calling: "Come here, old man!"

A servant came from the shadows.

"I am here, my lord. These eyes need little sleep."

Agamemnon looked up at the sky.

"What star is that?" he asked.

"Sirius, my lord, by the seven Pleiades."

"Ah, so it is; the night is almost gone." He sighed. "I envy you, old man. I envy the life of every man who has neither power nor honor to uphold."

"We slaves have no glory, either," the old man said.

Agamemnon shook his head. "The paths of glory are beset with danger. Our lives are crushed between the anger of the gods and the clashing wills of men."

"Are these fit words for a king? Then tell me what is troubling you."

The old man had served Agamemnon faithfully since the day Clytemnestra, as a bride, had brought him to Argos from her father's halls. So the king was tempted to share a bitter secret that only he and three others knew.

Not that the seeds of the war itself were any secret. For all the kings of Greece were pledged to rescue Helen. Once they had been her ardent suitors, ready to kill each other for her hand. And crafty old Tyndareus her father, fearing bloodshed in his halls, had made them all swear a solemn oath: Helen herself should choose the one she loved, then all would defend her marriage with their lives. So they swore, and Menelaos was her choice.

True to that oath, no other Greek thereafter laid an eye or a hand on her. But a foreign prince, young Paris, son of Priam king of Ilium, had come to Sparta. Glittering in all his gold and rich barbaric finery, he stole her from Menelaos' bed and carried her off to Troy.

Then Menelaos in his rage called all his former rivals to make good their oath. So they came to Aulis with ships and shields, and steeds and chariots to sail against Troy in vengeance.

"Perhaps because Menelaos was my brother, they chose me

as their leader," Agamemnon told the old man. "Would they had named another. For I have failed. Here we are trapped in Aulis. Our ships are drying up. We cannot sail to Troy."

"But that is not your fault, my king," the old man said. "For it is gods, not men, who rule the winds."

"Yes, it is the gods," said Agamemnon, "but there you touch the sorest spot. For the goddess Artemis is angry with me now. She holds the winds and will not let us sail. Many years ago, it seems, I made a vow to sacrifice to her the most precious thing the year brought forth. Then I forgot. But in that year was born my dearest daughter Iphigenia. Surely she was the year's most lovely gift. And now at last the goddess claims her as a sacrifice. This the soothsayer Calchas has revealed to Menelaos, Odysseus, and me.

"So Iphigenia must be slain on Artemis' altar or our fleet can never sail from this shore. When I learned this I wept; I could not slay her. Rather would I disband the fleet. But Menelaos, my brother, by many a crafty plea, persuaded me that I could not shirk my duty.

"And so, some days ago I wrote a letter to my wife. I could not tell her, 'Send our daughter here to be slain.' Instead, I pretended the warrior Achilles had asked me for her hand in marriage. I bade her send the girl to me that the wedding might take place forthwith. And I added such praise for Thetis' son as should persuade a mother's heart to give up her daughter gladly. Calchas, Odysseus, and Menelaos saw me write and send the letter. No others knew.

"But now I have repented. Better far that Troy be lost. And so this night, with many bitter tears, I have written another letter—this!" He showed the letter in his hand. "I have told my wife not to send the girl now; the marriage must wait for another season. Take this and carry it swiftly to Argos. There may still be time."

"But Achilles—will he not be angry to lose his bride?" the old man asked.

"You do not understand. I only pretended. Achilles knows nothing of what I did; he has never spoken nor heard a word of marriage."

"Was it not wrong to use so noble a warrior's name to lure your child to die for the Greeks?"

"I know—I was mad," said Agamemnon. "But hurry now, old man. Forget about your age."

The servant was ready to go. Not just for the king, but to help his mistress, for he had served, even before she was born, in the halls of her father Tyndareus.

"Mind you do not sit by some spring in the shade or fall asleep," Agamemnon warned.

"Do not say such evil things."

"Watch every crossroad keenly to see no chariot passes with my daughter. And if you see her, turn her quickly back to Argos."

"Indeed, I will," said the servant.

"Now go, and guard that letter with your life. The dawn is coming, and better if you were not seen."

The old man needed no further bidding. As Agamemnon returned to his tent, the servant tucked a few things in his tunic for the journey, then started out. But before he had rounded the second tent he was seized from behind and the letter wrenched from his hand.

He turned and recognized the face and golden beard of the man who waylaid him. It was Agamemnon's brother, Menelaos. Fending off the old man's feeble blows, Menelaos broke the seals and read the message with an angry frown.

"Shame on you, Menelaos!" the servant cried. "You have no right to read what I bear."

"Nor you to be bearing such treason."

"Give that letter back to me!"

"No! You serve your master too faithfully."

"I can be proud of that. But give it back, or I will not let you go."

"Take care, old man, or my staff will crack your aged skull."

"I can die for my master, too."

Their words brought Agamemnon out of his tent.

"What means this brawling at my door?" he asked.

"Aha!" said Menelaos. "I saw your light and had my suspicions. It is well I watched, you black-bearded coward! Is this your shameful message?"

"It is mine. Now give it back to me!"

"Not until I have read it to all the Greeks."

"You had no right to break my seal."

"Nor you to break your word."

"Am I not master of this camp?"

"Not when your heart is weak and shifty," said Menelaos. "Oh, you were mad for power once. Your secret heart was bent on being leader of all the Greeks. You fawned on everyone and clasped his hand. You kept an open door, eagerly conversed with all who wished—and even those who wished it not—seeking by every devious way to buy your honor. Then when you won it, you changed. You spurned your former friends and shut them out, scorning the very steps by which you climbed to power."

"These are not a brother's words," said Agamemnon. "Why this panting rage and these bloodshot eyes?"

"Have you forgotten so soon," asked Menelaos, "that when the winds failed and many kings were ready to give up, you came to me? 'Oh, what can I do?' you moaned. 'How can I keep my fame and my command?' And then, when Calchas said you must sacrifice your daughter, you promised and willingly sent for her. No one forced you to write that letter then."

"Is it madness now to repent my wrong?" asked Agamemnon.

"It is a greater wrong to betray us all," said Menelaos. "Like many men who gain the heights of power, you have failed. Oh, I am sick for Greece. She was born to glory, but you would make her the laughing stock of every worthless barbarian. Kinship is no excuse to rule. Only wisdom brings that right."

"Where have I wronged you?" Agamemnon asked. "What do you want? A beautiful wife? You could not hold what you had. Must I be the one to pay for your mistakes? Just to feel that lascivious woman in your arms you have tossed away all reason and decency. Shame on such lust! For a time I yielded, yes, but it would be madness to make such a sacrifice for an evil wife well rid of. Never for such a wanton woman could I justly slay my dearest child."

"Have I no friends left?" asked Menelaos.

"Not if you destroy them—but I am still your brother."

"How can you prove *that?*"

"By wisdom, surely, not by folly."

"Have you no duty to suffer for Greece?"

"If Greece demands this sacrifice, she, too, is mad."

But now a messenger arrived bringing the worst of tidings.

"O leader of Hellas," he said, "I have brought your daughter here from Argos, your good wife Clytemnestra, too, and even the babe Orestes to delight your heart."

"Oh, gods in heaven, no!" groaned Agamemnon. But it was true. The messenger said they had stopped outside the camp by a meadow stream to water the horses and wash the dust of travel from their feet. They would soon be here.

"Your outposts have seen them," the messenger said, "and

already rumors are spreading through the camp. The soldiers are saying, 'It must be a wedding—why else would the mother be bringing her daughter?' They are eager to make the first offerings to Artemis."

Agamemnon clasped his beard and groaned. For it was not just bridal offerings that Artemis demanded but the offering of the bride herself.

"Let us wreathe our heads," the messenger went on. "Strike up the bridal songs! And let us begin our dancing to the flute. A happy day is dawning for your daughter."

"Enough!" said Agamemnon. "Go seek some rest. All may yet be well."

But misfortune had indeed outwitted all his stratagems. With Iphigenia here in Aulis, her doom was almost sealed. The Greeks would let nothing stand between themselves and Troy, if they learned the truth. If only he were not a king. A common man could tell others of his grief and ease it with a flow of tears. But kings were slaves to dignity and to the very mobs they ruled. As a man, he had to weep; as a king, he could not.

And how to face his wife? She never should have come. And yet, why not? Could any mother have sent her daughter on alone and not been there to counsel and wash and deck the bride for marriage. The bride? The bride of Death, he thought. O the ruin that Paris and Helen had brought upon his house!

Though Agamemnon tried to hold his tears in check, Menelaos could read his anguish all too well. And now, too late, he pitied him. Tears answered tears as he seized his hand.

"No, my brother," he said, "by our grandsire Pelops and Atreus our father, it must not be. I take back all I said. I cannot fight you now nor let you slay your child. Why should you mourn that I might rejoice, or lose your Iphigenia while my Hermione still lives? What has your daughter to do with Helen that she should die? There are other brides if I must have one. To regain my wife and destroy my own dear brother would surely be trading good for bad. I was crude and thoughtless. Only now, as I see your face, do I realize all the wrong I have done you.

"You must disband this army here in Aulis. Dry your tears so that I too need not mourn. Whatever Calchas demands, I shall have no part of it. You and I were born of one womb, and foolish strife must never part us."

"Dear brother," said Agamemnon, "your words are straight and true beyond all my hopes. But we are tangled far too deep in fate to turn back now. My child must die."

"But who compels it?"

"Every warrior of Hellas will."

"They do not know. There still is time to send her back to Argos."

"Calchas will tell them of the oracles," said Agamemnon.

"Not if he dies," Menelaos said. "And that could happen."

"Yes," said Agamemnon, "one prophet less would be no loss—but there are others."

"You fear the rabble too much."

"Can you not see Odysseus standing before the Argive host, telling them what Calchas said and how I lied when I gave my promise? We cannot save her now—the army could slay us both. Even if I fled to Argos, the Greeks would follow, tear down the walls, and waste my land. No, I am ground in a mill between the gods and men. There is no escape. So do this, my brother. Go to the others. Make sure that Clytemnestra hears no word of this until my child is dead. Till then, my tears alone will be enough."

The brother-kings embraced in sorrow, and Menelaos left.

Agamemnon returned to his tent. He could not face his wife and daughter in front of his men.

The coming of Iphigenia and the spreading rumors had turned many to thoughts of Love, golden-haired Love, whose arrows could be tipped with bliss or dipped in the poison of ruin. Even this war for which they lusted and would risk their lives had been brought about by the love-spells of Aphrodite. And it all began, as mortal woes so often do, among the gods.

For the gods were happily feasting once, so the story runs, when Discord, the uninvited guest, tossed a golden apple on the banquet table. And on the apple was engraved: "For the fairest of the goddesses." But who should claim it? Hera the wife of Zeus himself? Gray-eyed Athene the wise? Or Aphrodite the goddess of love? No god in heaven would risk an answer. And so the three descended on a mortal.

Paris, they agreed, should be the judge. And they found him on Mount Ida, tending the rich-uddered heifers of his father. Hera's promise of power did not sway him, nor did Athene's offer of wisdom beyond all others'. To Aphrodite, standing in lovely nakedness, he gave the apple. And in return she gave him an aura of charm to win the fairest woman in all the world.

So it was that he came to Greece, to the ivory palace at Sparta, and saw an answering light in Helen's eyes. And that first night of breathless ecstasy had led to this—a thousand ships and a hundred thousand men all vengeance-bound to ravage Troy.

None of the soldiers who guided the carriages through the camp to Agamemnon's tent knew of Calchas' prophecy or the fate of Iphigenia, but they marveled at her fair young beauty. Clytemnestra, too, was a striking figure, with black hair, piercing eyes, and a regal bearing. And little Orestes, sleeping at her breast, brought a tear to the eye of many a man who thought of his own dear son at home.

When her carriage came to a stop, Clytemnestra thanked them all: "Your kindness gives me hope that I am bringing my little bride to a happy marriage." She bade them take from the cart the wedding gifts and carry them in with greatest care. She asked someone to stand by the horses' heads for fear they might start up suddenly and warned her daughter to be graceful and cautious in stepping to the ground. Willing hands took the sleeping child from her arms as she called on others to help her descend from the high carriage seat.

"Wake up, little boy," she said to Orestes, "and smile for your sister's wedding." A soldier led them to Agamemnon's tent and drew back the curtain. "Walk close beside me," she said to Iphigenia. "Let everyone see how happy we are."

But at first sight of her father within, Iphigenia forgot all dignity.

"Forgive me, Mother," she said and ran with a cry of joy to throw her arms about his neck and hold him close, feeling his throbbing heart against her own. But Clytemnestra stood back and said:

"Your majesty, my lord Agamemnon, we are here to do your bidding."

"Oh, Father, I am so happy!" Iphigenia cried, nestling her cheek against his beard. "It has been so long."

"Long indeed," said her father, "for both of us."

"Rejoice!" said Iphigenia. "It was good of you to send for me."

What could he say? He could not lie—much less reveal

the truth. Iphigenia felt him tremble, drew back her head and, seeing his face, exclaimed, "Are you not really glad to see me? Why are your eyes so sad?"

"A leader and king has many cares," he said.

"Then send them all away," she laughed. "This hour belongs to me. So smooth your brow, and let me see the joy in your eyes."

Agamemnon tried to smile and said, "There now, child, see how happy I am."

"But I still see tears."

"It is only because we must part again."

"Oh, Father," she said, "why can we not be together always?"

"I wish we could," he said, "but even a king cannot have his way."

"Oh, perish the war and Menelaos' troubles!" she cried.

"They have ruined us all," he agreed.

She prattled on, sometimes in earnest, sometimes in jest. She asked him how things went in Aulis and how far it was to Troy.

"Will I be sailing with you, Father?"

"No, but you will be always in my thoughts."

"Will I go home with Mother then?" He shook his head.

"Am I to go to another man's home?" she asked, a little frightened. He touched his finger to her lips.

"Little maidens ask too many questions."

"At least you must hurry back from Troy," she said. "Will you be sailing soon?"

"First I must make a sacrifice."

"It is right to honor the gods," she said. "Will I be there? May I lead the dance around the altar?"

Each question stabbed him like a sword. He could not answer more. So he kissed her again and held her hand, gazing at her glowing cheeks, her fresh young bosom, sensing the fragrance of her golden hair. As beautiful as Helen herself, he thought, and cursed the thought for coming. He led her out and bade his servants arrange another tent with whatever comforts she desired, where she might bathe herself and don her saffron festal robes. Then sadly he came back to his wife who sat by little Orestes asleep on the couch beside her.

"O daughter of Leda," Agamemnon sighed, trying to explain his mood, "it will break my heart to lose her."

"I understand—I have my feelings, too," said Clytemnestra. "I shall probably weep at the wedding. But time will heal the pain. So tell me about this man. I know his name, but little else."

Agamemnon traced Achilles' lineage all the way back to Zeus and the nymph Aegina.

"His father was Peleus, son of Aeacus," he said, "and his mother the sea nymph Thetis, daughter of Nereus. Cheiron, who dwells by Mount Pelion, was his teacher; so he did not learn the ways of wicked men."

Clytemnestra seemed pleased. "We could do no better," she said. "But where is his home?"

"In Phthia."

"Shall you be taking her there?"

"I think that should be his task."

"Well may they both be happy!" she said. "How soon will the wedding be?"

"In the next full moon."

"And the first offering to the Moon Goddess—have you slain the victim yet?"

"That rite already lies upon my mind," said Agamemnon.

"When will you hold the marriage feast?"

"After I have made the sacrifice the gods demand."

"And the women's feast?"

"You could hardly hold one here by the galleys," he said. Clytemnestra seemed disappointed. But, after all, a camp was not a palace.

"One thing I must insist on," said Agamemnon.

"Do I not always obey?"

"I alone must give the bride away for both of us."

"But I am her mother," said Clytemnestra. "Where would I be?"

"You must return at once to Argos to care for our other daughters."

"And hold no marriage torch for my child?"

"I can do what is needed."

"I never heard of such a thing," Clytemnestra exclaimed.

"This camp is no fit place for a queen. Besides, our other girls should not be left alone."

"They are safe enough in their maidens' quarters."

"You must do as I say," said Agamemnon.

"No, by the Argive goddess queen!" she declared. "You may go and do all the work of a man, but I shall attend to the mother's duties here."

Agamemnon left the tent in despair. This woman blocked him at every twist and turn. Why did she refuse to leave? Could she not see his task would only be harder? But no—how could she understand what he dared not explain? A stubborn wife was worse than no wife at all. A wife should obey without question. He would go to Calchas and tell him to prepare for the rites.

For, much as it grieved him, Iphigenia must die. The Greeks with their galleys must get to Troy to fight by the silver eddies of Simois. Doubtless, in Troy the mad Cassandra long since had foretold their coming. And the Trojans would be laughing at her prophecies—laughing at the Greeks themselves. No, it must not be!

Achilles, son of Peleus, was troubled as he made his way through the camp toward Agamemnon's tent. Though only four men knew its cause, the delay was chafing all the Greeks. Achilles had led his Myrmidons to Aulis from Pharsalia, and now they were close to revolt. "Either take us home," his men had demanded, "or let the sons of Atreus lead us on to Troy." Achilles was coming to report this to the king.

Outside Agememnon's tent he asked, "Where is the leader of all the Achaeans? Tell him Achilles is here and seeks a word with him."

Within the tent Clytemnestra leaped at the sound of his name. She rushed to the entrance, seized him by the hand, and said, "Achilles, my dear, come in!"

Achilles was startled by her greeting. "Who are you, my beautiful lady?" he asked as she drew him down beside her on the couch.

"Oh, of course you would not know," she said, "for we have never met. But I know all about your fame and your desire."

"A woman like you in the camp? I do not understand."

"I am the daughter of Tyndareus and Leda, the wife of the king. You may call me Clytemnestra." Her dark eyes beamed upon him intimately.

The wife of the king! Achilles tried to excuse himself and go.

"No, stay," she said. "Give me your hand as a pledge of love."

Achilles stammered: "Your husband Agamemnon is a good man and my friend. This is not right."

"Not right when you are going to wed my daughter?" she asked.

Achilles was speechless. Was the woman out of her mind?

"Oh, I know a young man feels ill at ease," she said, "when

he first meets the parents of his bride . . ." Achilles sprang up.

"Lady, I have never wooed any daughter of yours, nor has her sire ever spoken to me of marriage."

"Why, this is odd," she said.

"Odd, indeed," said Achilles. "And yet you seemed to speak with some reason."

"I have been deceived," cried Clytemnestra. "Oh, I am so ashamed to approach you like this!"

"Someone, it seems, has played a shabby trick on us both," said Achilles. "But think no more about it."

"Then good-by," she sobbed. "I cannot bear to look you in the face. I have been made a liar and a fool. This is an outrage!"

Achilles could only agree. But as he turned to leave, he heard another voice:

"Wait, son of Peleus and Leda's daughter!"

They both turned. It was the old servant that Clytemnestra knew so well, for she had brought him to Argos with her dowry.

"Are you both alone?" he asked.

"Yes, except for my baby," Clytemnestra assured him.

"I have always been loyal to you and your children," he began, "and though I came to Aulis with the master I really am yours."

"That is true," she said.

The old man seemed relieved. "Then my duty is greater to you than to him?"

"Yes, but what is all this mystery?"

"O my mistress, the king is planning to slay your child."

"Old man, are you mad?"

"No, but I think the king is mad." Then swiftly he told of Calchas' oracles, the wrath of Artemis, and the sacrifice.

"He lied to bring Iphigenia here?" asked Clytemnestra.

"Yes, he knew you would part with her only for a noble marriage. Yet for a time he repented." He told of the second letter and of Agamemnon's quarrel with Menelaos.

"Oh, my poor daughter!" cried Clytemnestra. "Son of Thetis and Peleus, do you hear this?"

"I grieve for you," Achilles said, "and I am angry with your king."

All pride had fled from Clytemnestra's soul. She threw herself at Achilles' feet and clasped his knees, a desperate mother fighting for her child.

"Help me! Pity me!" she begged. "Save the girl who was called your bride—however wrongly. To be your bride in very truth I brought her here. I washed and scented and adorned her just for you. Oh, do not shame her now, nor shame the noble name you bear! For you can make the name of Achilles a glorious one if you stand beside her. I am a helpless woman among hard and savage men. You can save us or let us die; our lives lie in your hands."

Achilles pitied her. Still more he burned with a righteous wrath, for Cheiron had taught him to hate deceitful ways.

"Lady," he told her bluntly, "I have not seen your daughter nor do I stand in need of any bride, though many another maiden is yearning for my bed. And until now I was never untrue to the sons of Atreus. But a free man should not be bound to evil leaders.

"You and your child have been foully used by the very man who should have loved you most. And my name has been besmirched. I will not lend myself to Agamemnon's trickery. Indeed, I would share some guilt in your daughter's murder if even my name were to lead her to her death. No! By my goddess mother, Agamemnon shall not touch so much as a finger to the hem of her garment. Nor Calchas either. What is a seer? A man of many lies who only by chance ever speaks the truth. If any man lays hands on her he shall feel my sword long before it does its work at Troy. Forget your fears. I am no god, but all the man within me shall rise to protect her."

"O Achilles," Clytemnestra cried, "how could I find the words to praise you. I could stir the envy of the gods and still not say half enough. I am ashamed of what I asked. But you have shown your noble lineage in helping a stranger in distress. How I should love to have you for my son as well as my protector if you desire the girl. Would you have me send her to you? She is beautiful—but shy and innocent—and proud like me. Yet if you want her, she will surely come."

"There is no need," Achilles said. "Her coming would only stir coarse jests among the men. Nor do I need her charms or prayers to save her. My own honor is at stake, so I shall defend her with my life."

"May heaven bless you!"

"But now," said Achilles, "we need some plan. First you must try to change your husband's mind."

"He is too much of a coward," she said with scorn. "He fears his army."

"Still you must try. If he listens to reason, good. You will have no need of me. That would make things better between the army and me—to say nothing of your peace at home."

"A feeble hope, but I will try," she promised, "yet, if I fail . . ."

"Never fear, I shall watch close by," he said. "The daughter of so worthy a man as Tyndareus shall not be shamed."

"I am your slave," she said. "Command me as you will. And if there is a god in heaven (which I sometimes doubt) you will surely be rewarded." She clasped his hand and bade him good-by.

Now, she thought, Iphigenia must be told the treachery of her beloved father. Clytemnestra found her dressed in spotless virgin robes—fit for a bride—or a holy sacrifice.

In wide-eyed disbelief at first, then fear, Iphigenia heard the tale. At last she broke into uncontrollable sobbing. Her father! How well she remembered the many times as a little girl she had climbed upon his knee. He would caress her tenderly and say:

"Will I see you some day, my little girl, living happily in some young husband's home and growing still more beautiful for me?" And she would laugh and run her little fingers through the thick black beard she loved and look in his glistening eyes and say, "What about you, dear Father, when this beard is gray? O, you must be my guest for years and years, for it would take me forever to repay you for all your loving care."

Marriage? It had been her dream that one day she would be married to someone like her father. Not that she wept for Achilles. She did not know him. Enough that he had been her father's choice. Death? She could hardly understand it. But her father! No weeping could ever heal that hurt.

"Dry your eyes, girl," said her mother. "There is hope in Achilles yet. And come to me when you are ready." With that she left her.

When Clytemnestra returned to Agamemnon's tent, the king was there.

"It is good we are alone," he said, "for girls should not hear their bridal plans. Now I want you to send her forth with me alone. All is ready for our sacrificial rites—the lustral water, the barley flour to cast upon the flame, and the victim for the altar."

What innocent words he was using, Clytemnestra thought,

to hide such evil plans! Oh, she would force him to reveal himself for what he was before the daughter who had so misplaced her love.

"Here is your obedient child," she said as Iphigenia came in.

"Why are you weeping, my girl?" asked Agamemnon. "Why do you turn your face away from me?"

"You should know," said Clytemnestra bitterly.

"Is this some conspiracy? Why do you both look at me so?"

"Just answer me this," Clytemnestra demanded. "Did you plan to kill this child of yours and mine?"

"You must not ask such a question!" exclaimed Agamemnon.

"It is the only one I have," she said, "but answer me!"

"I am ruined!" Agamemnon groaned.

"So are we all," said Clytemnestra. "Your silence and your sighs confess your guilt. Do not trouble to put it in words."

"Why should I add more lies to my distress?" he asked.

"Then hear the truth," said Clytemnestra as he cringed before her black and fearsome eyes. "I never loved you. I have hated you since you slew the one I really loved and took me for your wife. Still I was a good wife to you—chaste and thrifty. I gave you the pleasure of my body and made your home a happy one. I bore you three daughters and this little son. For what? That you might slay them for my wanton sister's sake?

"Think hard, my lord, what will happen if you are long away in Troy. What will go on in my heart if day by day I look at her empty room and say, 'Your own father killed you, my poor child'? What more pretext will we need to greet you as you deserve on your return? Beware lest the slayer be slain.

"What favor of the gods can you pray for if you murder

her? That your journey may end in the way it began? And what could my prayers be for you? Are the gods such fools as to bless a slayer? And when you return will our children run to kiss you or flee in hiding from your knife?

"Do you care for nothing except to lead an army? If someone's daughter must be slain, why not cast lots? Or why not Menelaos' own Hermione? The quarrel is his. Why should I, the chaste one, mourn for a daughter slain, while my harlot sister Helen will enjoy her own child once she is safe in Sparta? If I speak wrongly, answer me. If not, repent; give up this fearful crime."

Agamemnon remained frozen where he sat, and Iphigenia wished she had the eloquence of Orpheus whose voice, the poets say, could move the very stones themselves. But she had no eloquence except her maiden tears. And these she poured forth as she clasped his knees and said:

"Oh, my father, do not kill me. Life is so sweet; the grave is so black. Can you forget the many times you held me on your knee? The little gifts we exchanged? I can remember every word we said since the first day I could call you 'Father' and you smiled and said, 'My little daughter.' Yes, every word, but you have forgotten them all. And think of my mother. For your pleasure she brought me forth in pain. Must she now suffer an anguish greater still? Look at me, Father. If I cannot persuade you, give me at least one kiss before I die. One more kiss that I may take with me and you will long remember."

Agamemnon groaned. He clenched his fingers in her dress and deep in her flesh. He closed his eyes. He could not look upon her face. He could not kiss her.

Little Orestes had awakened and was crying.

"See, Father," she said. "Even my little brother pleads for me. He cannot understand this now. Some day he will. Dear

Father, pity your children. Only a madman wants to die. Life is sweet; death is nothingess. The most wretched life is better than the most glorious death."

But when he did not answer, she tore herself from the clenching hands that bruised her flesh and fell weeping on the couch beside the babe.

At length Agamemnon spoke: "Pity has no depths I have not felt. For I am no madman, my wife; I love my children. This is a terrible deed to do, a terrible one to refuse. Look at this mighty fleet, the kings, and all the bronze-clad warriors of Hellas who cannot sail against the towers of Troy unless this sacrifice is made. They will stop at nothing in their passion to fall upon the barbarians and stop their raping of the wives of Greece.

"Suppose I refused the sacrifice. It would not save us. They would slay us all—you and me, even our daughters in Argos. I am no slave of Menelaos, but I must serve Greece. Greece must be free, free forever from her barbarian spoilers. I have no other choice."

In tears he rushed from the tent.

"O my child, your father has betrayed you," said Clytemnestra.

"And I shall never see another day," Iphigenia wept.

Strange were the workings of the gods. Iphigenia might have lived, and the Greeks have had no war if only another king had shown the courage to slay his own child years before. For even before Paris was born the oracles had foretold that he would bring destruction on Troy and its people. And so King Priam tore the suckling babe from its mother's breasts, yet did not have the will to finish the deed himself. Instead he told his herdsman to leave the babe to die out on the snow-capped crests of Ida. But the herdsman, pitying the child, had reared him as his own. Thus in time Paris grew up to herd his father's kine not knowing who he really was.

And there it was, on the slopes of Ida where roses and hyacinths bloomed, that Hermes led the three goddesses for the royal shepherd youth to judge which was the fairest.

Alas, mused Iphigenia now, when Paris gave that golden apple to Aphrodite he was handing me to Artemis to die. I can see him, too, as he must have been that day in the glittering halls of Priam when the old king, forgetting all the warnings of the past, rejoiced and acknowledged him as his proven son. And I can see him now, leading the laughing Helen to his bed in Troy, while here in Aulis my father will lead me to my grave. Oh, why did these bronze-beaked ships with their wings of pine have to come to Aulis and why . . .

She screamed as warriors burst into the tent. They were clad in bronze, with brazen swords and leather shields, and from the crests of their helmets waved frightening plumes. But Clytemnestra recognized their leader clad and armed in shining gold.

"Hush, my child!" she said. "It is Achilles come to save us."

"Oh, Mother, let me hide. I cannot face him; I am so ashamed."

"This is no time to be so coy," said her mother sharply.

"Oh, poor lady," Achilles said, "can you hear those cries?"

For the first time Clytemnestra was aware of distant shouting. "What does it mean?" she asked.

"The Argives are clamoring for your daughter's life."

"But why is no one stopping them?"

"I tried," said Achilles, "and they answered me with a shower of stones."

"They would not dare," said Clytemnestra. "Where were your Myrmidons?"

"They were the first to turn against me," Achilles said, "all except these few with me. The rest called me a love-struck fool when I said they could not slay the bride that was promised me."

"You are right," said Clytemnestra, "and I could show them the letter that brought us here from Argos."

"It would be no use. I was shouted down."

"Oh, we are lost!" moaned Clytemnestra. "That awful mob!"

For the first time Achilles noticed Iphigenia, who was shrinking behind her mother.

"Be brave," he said to her. "We shall still defend you. So long as I live you shall not be taken."

Iphigenia looked up at him—this goddess' son in his golden armor. Strong, handsome, honest, brave! This was the man her father had said she would marry. She would have done as her father said and gone to his bed. Yet she did not think she loved him. Nor could this man love her as her father did. Yet he was ready to die for her—or at least for her honor and his own. A good man, a hero! Well might Hellas be proud of him. And if he died for her sake, Greece would lose her mightiest champion at Troy. She did not love him, but she reached out and clasped his hand. It was a strong hand, and from it she seemed to feel new strength surging through her body. She, too, could be brave.

"How many are there?" asked Clytemnestra.

"Thousands on thousands," said Achilles, "led by Odysseus."

"That son of treachery!" snapped Clytemnestra. "King of murderers! What will they do?"

"Try to seize your daughter by her golden hair and drag her to the altar. But I shall stand against them all."

"Oh, what can I do?" Clytemnestra moaned.

"Cling fast to your child . . ."
"As if that could save her!"
". . . and pray."
But Iphigenia, calm and weeping no more, began to speak.
"Mother dear," she said, "do not be angry with my father. It is hard to wage a hopeless fight. We should thank this stranger kindly for his will to save us, but he would only die in vain. We must save him from the reproach of Greece."

"Daughter, what are you thinking?" Clytemnestra asked.

"It is destined that I must die. And I want to die—gloriously. I see it clearly. I have put away all thoughts of fear."

"No, no!" cried Clytemnestra.

"Mother, listen to me. All Greece depends upon me now. I alone have the power to launch her ships and conquer Troy —to free the daughters of Hellas forever from barbarian lust. I can save my country by my death and become a name forever blessed. Here are thousands of warriors ready to die. Why should I cling to my little life in greedy fear? You did not bear me for your own pleasure or my father's, nor for the pleasure of any man—but for all of Greece.

"And Achilles should not fight his nation for a woman's sake. His life is worth ten thousand women. If Artemis demands my life, we must not fight the gods. This body is mine to give to whom I will. I give it to Greece. Take it—and smite down Troy! For all the ages, that will be my memorial, my marriage, my children, and my fame. Greeks must never bow down to barbarians, for they are slaves, and we are free."

Achilles was deeply moved. This was no longer a girl, he thought, but a woman. And such a woman!

"Agamemnon's daughter," he said, "it would be heaven's blessing to have you for my wife. Greece is my only rival now. I envy her such love. And as I look on the beauty of your very soul, more and more do I yearn for you in my marriage bed. Come, let me serve you, take you to my home. As Thetis, my goddess-mother, is my witness, I shall take it hard unless I can fight the whole host of Greeks to win you. Think! Death is a fearful thing."

For a moment Iphigenia could think of nothing except this man, this godlike man who wanted her. A strange ecstasy thrilled through her limbs, a desire to throw herself into his arms and cry, "Yes, take me! Take me, dear Achilles, forever!" And he would battle bravely for her—for her alone —*and die!* The sudden thought dispelled the dream. It could not be. Already she was pledged.

"You must not kill or die for me, dear friend," she said. "The body of Helen has kindled strife and slaughter enough already. But let me save Greece, if I have the power."

Achilles bowed his head and tried to calm the turmoil in his soul.

"O dear and noble heart," he said. "I have no words to use against the course you deem is right. Your purpose is a glorious one; why should I not admit the truth? Yet if it should change, I and my men in arms will be close to the altar. Even when you see the knife nearing your throat, you may still call upon me to redeem my pledge not to let you die. I shall not stop you if your resolve holds firm to the very end. But no sudden impulse now shall let them slay you then against your will."

But Iphigenia knew she would not change. Clytemnestra was weeping silently.

"Mother, you must not weep," she told her.

"Have I not cause to break my heart?"

"You must not try to weaken me," said Iphigenia. "You must never mourn or cut your hair."

"But, child, if I lose you . . ."

"Lose me? No, I shall be saved, and you will share my fame."

"I will try to be brave, but what can I tell your sisters?"

"Not to mourn, but to rejoice for Greece."

"And this child Orestes?"

"Poor little Brother, we are all as helpless as you," she said with a wistful smile, "but, Mother, rear him to a noble manhood."

"Is there no more that I can do for you?"

"Just this—my father, your husband—do not hate him."

"He shall pay dearly for what he did to you," said Clytemnestra.

"It is against his will that he offers me," Iphigenia said.

"No, it was by such treachery as shamed his fathers."

The shouts grew louder.

"Now I must go," said Iphigenia, "proudly and willingly. It would be ill-omened if men should drag me there by the hair."

"I will go with you," said Clytemnestra.

"No, Mother, you must not."

"I shall cling to your dress."

"No. Heed me, Mother, stay here. It will be better for both of us. Let Achilles lead me to the field of Artemis."

"Oh, do not leave me!" Clytemnestra cried.

"There must be no more tears," said Iphigenia. Two of Achilles' men took Clytemnestra's arms and guided her firmly but gently to the couch beside the little Orestes.

Iphigenia, pure and radiant in her bridal robes of saffron silk, took her place outside the tent beside Achilles in his panoply of gold. His bronze-clad guard fell in behind. Then with a steady step, her head held high, they set out toward the altar—to Chalcas the priest, the knife, and Artemis who would receive her sacrifice for the victory and salvation of Greece.

The shouting ceased. The troops fell back in awe and wonder as she passed, passed between those hundred thousand men and the thousand ships drawn up along the shore. She would set them free.

Her father was waiting at the altar.

This story was unknown to Homer, but human sacrifice, especially for success in war, was practiced in many ancient cultures. The victims should be of the same sex as the god; they should be young, unblemished, virginal, and the nobler they were the more pleasing. But the idea was shocking to later generations. The story (in *Genesis 22:1–14*) of Abraham's sacrifice of his beloved son Isaac, which was prevented at the last moment by the angel of the Lord and the miraculous appearance of a sacrificial ram in the thicket, is presumably an allegorical reflection of the abandonment of such rites.

According to Homer, Agamemnon was a great king, ruling all the others as lesser chiefs. His home was in Mycenae, where archeologists have found traces of great wealth and artifacts such as Homer describes. But Euripides anachronistically makes him a political leader who had to campaign for his position of leadership. Euripides and Aeschylus wrongly name his capital as Argos—a nearby city that had far eclipsed Mycenae in historical times. To avoid confusion I have kept to Argos in all my stories although Sophocles has Mycenae.

AJAX

CHARACTERS

Ajax (A-jax): The mightiest warrior of the Greeks at Troy after the death of Achilles; the son of Telamon, King of Salamis, an island close to Athens.

Tecmessa (Tek-MESS-a): Ajax' concubine, and the mother of his little son Eurysaces (Yoo-ri-SAY-seez).

Teucer (TYOO-ser): Half-brother of Ajax.

Odysseus (O-DISS-yoos): The wisest, or wiliest, of the Greek kings at Troy, the hero of Homer's *Odyssey*.

Athene (Ath-EE-nee): Goddess of wisdom, who traditionally was a guardian deity to Odysseus.

Agamemnon (Ag-a-MEM-non): Son of Atreus; the great king and leader of all the Greeks at Troy.

Menelaos (Men-e-LA-os): Brother of Agamemnon; King of Sparta, and husband of the stolen Helen.

Calchas (KOLL-kas): The priest and prophet of the Greeks.

Soldiers, members of Ajax' own crew on the voyage to Troy.

The Trojan War lasted ten years after the sacrifice of Iphigenia, and Achilles was its greatest hero. Homer's *Iliad* tells vividly of the battles that raged near the end of the war while Achilles, in a quarrel with Agamemnon, sulked in his tent and would not help the hard-pressed Greeks. But at last he returned to avenge his dearest friend. Then he slew Hector, the great champion of the Trojans.

While Achilles was out of the fray, the mightiest of all the Greeks had been Ajax.

Soon after the events of the *Iliad*, Achilles himself was slain by treachery. And after his burial there was to be a contest to award his golden weapons and armor to the greatest warrior left. Obviously this was Ajax, who feared neither gods nor men. But Ajax was hated for his arrogance. Agamemnon called him an ox, as Shakespeare two thousand years later called him "beef-witted." If there were any way to block Ajax' honor, the Greeks were going to find it.

Ajax is a true, if somewhat more primitive, Sophoclean hero. Like Oedipus or Antigone, he has a moral code that no outside force can break. Ajax, with his primitive code of heroic honor, stands apart from other men. His life is cheap, but honor is his dearest possession. To understand Ajax we must realize that honor does not end with brave deeds. It must also include recognition.

AJAX

(SOPHOCLES)

The Greeks stood aghast at the unbelievable butchery. In the night some maniac had carved a shambles through their captured Trojan herds. Bodies of cattle, their legs as stiff as spikes, lay all about. Their necks and chines and flanks had been hewed and hacked in some blind orgy. And among the mangled beasts the purple light of dawn revealed the bodies of their luckless herdsmen. The rest of the kine and the sheep had been driven off; nothing was left in the pens but death.

Who could have wrought such senseless woe? Some vengeful Trojans eluding the outposts in the dark? Perhaps. But many whispered in fear the name of Ajax. And a sentinel told Odysseus that he had seen a warrior, a giant with reeking sword and monstrous shield, charging across the plain that night. His brazen armor glistening in the moonlight had marked him for a Greek. And such was his size, unless it had grown with the sentry's fear, that the man could have been no other than Ajax, son of Telamon.

Yet Odysseus wondered. Ajax, his hated rival, still held his respect as a warrior of worth. For ever since Achilles' death, Ajax had been the greatest bulwark of the Greeks. He towered a head above other men, and his mighty shield, formed from the hides of seven bulls, repelled all spears. He alone had saved the Greeks from Hector's screaming men of Troy when they leaped the trench with fiery brands to set their ships ablaze.

Ajax feared no living man. He even spurned the gods. For when his father Telamon had said in farewell at Salamis, "Seek victory with your spear, my son, but always with the help of heaven," Ajax had answered, "Father, even a weakling could win with the help of the gods. But my might alone shall bring home glory." And once, when he saw Athene in battle by his side, he had shouted, "Go away, Goddess! Take your help to other Greeks who need it. Where I stand, the line will never break."

But only yesterday this proud and surly man had been humbled. He had been defeated, outwitted, disgraced, not by mighty men in arms, but by puny men of wit and words. The Greeks had gathered to give as a prize the golden arms of Achilles to the greatest warrior left alive. And all the talk was of Ajax until Odysseus, the weaver of words and wiles, stepped out before them and said:

"This should be more than a contest of strength, for brawny backs and fearless hearts alone have never won a war."

Agamemnon and Menelaos, the sons of Atreus, agreed. The lesser chiefs applauded, for there were few who liked the haughty Ajax. But then they divided in sharp debate over who had served them best. At last they turned to worthless men. They asked their Trojan captives to declare which of the Greeks had wreaked most havoc on them. And the prisoners said that the spear of Ajax was less to be feared by day than Odysseus' cunning by dark of night.

Their word prevailed. So the wily Odysseus carried home Achilles' armor as his prize, while the mightier Ajax bore naught to his tent but a baffled rage against the nimble-tongued Odysseus and the kings who had slighted him.

Could Ajax have taken such vengeance in the night? Surely he would have slain his rivals rather than helpless cattle. Odysseus set out to learn the truth. As he neared the tent of Ajax, the voice of Athene, unseen, came clearly to his ears:

"Your scent is as keen as a Spartan hound's, O crafty son of Laertes, for Ajax was the one."

"But why, O dearest of all the gods," Odysseus asked, "should he vent his rage on helpless beasts?"

"He thought he was bathing his sword in the blood of kings."

"What madness could have misled him so?"

"That was my doing. He stole out by night to slay you all, and reached the very tents of the sons of Atreus before I turned his purpose awry."

"I do not understand."

"He had an ungodly rage in his soul, but I turned its force aside. I cast a veil of delusion over his eyes so that in his madness he saw the poor dumb animals as his enemies. And after an ecstasy of slaughter he bound the rest of the beasts together and drove them like prisoners to his tent. Even now he slays and tortures them within." Then she called, "Ho, Ajax! Come out!"

Odysseus paled. "What are you doing, Athene?"

"Hush! Do not be taken for a coward. Ajax is only a man."

"Yes, but a madman who hates me."

"You never feared him before."

"I would not fear him now if he were sane."

"Would it not be sweet to mock your enemy?"

"No, let him stay in his tent."

"Fear not. His sickness will blind him from seeing you. Ajax! Come here!"

The flap of the tent was lifted and Ajax emerged. His huge body was gory with slaughter, a gleam of triumph in his eyes.

"Rejoice, Athene born of Zeus!" he hailed the unseen goddess. "You have come in good time to be crowned with golden spoils."

"Is that the blood of Greeks on your sword?" she asked.

He laughed. "Aye, the sons of Atreus will cheat me no more, nor all the rest, for I have slain them."

"And what of Odysseus, son of Laertes?"

"That slippery fox! I have no mind to let him die. Not yet. He is the sweetest prisoner in my tent. He is bound to a pole, and I mean to scourge him alive."

"Be not so cruel," said the voice.

"In some things, Goddess, I would obey you," Ajax replied, "but you cannot stop me from having my way with him." And he went back in and picked up a bronze-studded harness strap to flail without mercy the hapless, white-footed ram he thought was the son of Laertes.

"He was my enemy," said Odysseus, "yet now I pity him. And in his plight I pity all men. For we poor mortals are nothing. We live as phantoms and fleeting shadows."

"Be warned, then," Athene said, "never to scorn the gods nor boast of what you may chance to win merely by strength or wealth. One day can change the lot of any man. The gods love wisdom but smite the proud"

When her voice had melted away, Odysseus turned and sadly left.

Within the tent of Ajax, Tecmessa cowered in terror before the frenzy of her lord. She was his concubine, a princess, the captive of his spear. But she loved the mighty, passionate body that others feared; she admired the pride that others hated. Tecmessa pitied the wives of weaker men and though

Ajax was fierce and masterful, in his arms she had found exquisite tenderness.

Yet the day before, when he had returned from the council of kings without Achilles' arms, he had not had a word for her, and the thunderclouds were gathered on his brow. He sat for hours in fearful, brooding silence, seeming not to see or hear her, ignoring the food she set before him. Long after the evening's campfires flickered out, he remained in his tent alone, unreachable. Then close to midnight she heard him stirring in the dark, buckling on his clanking arms and groping for his two-edged sword and shield of seven hides.

"Ajax, what is wrong?" she asked. "The army is fast asleep. No messenger has been sent for you, and I heard no trumpet blast."

"Silence is a woman's fairest jewel," he told her brusquely and would say no more till he strode alone out into the night.

Where he went or what he wrought she did not know. But in time he came back, driving into the tent the frightened animals—sheep and sheep dogs and cattle all lashed together. She hid their child Eurysaces from his sight, then watched in frozen horror as he raged among the screaming beasts with his sword, beheading some and slitting the throats and spines of others. And, strangely, as he mocked and tortured them, he called them by the names of kings.

Then, shortly after he spoke with the voice outside, his frenzy seemed to abate. He looked around in sudden wonder at the slaughtered beasts, pounded his head and tore his hair, then uttered a cry of agony and fell in a faint among them. When he awoke he asked Tecmessa what had happened.

"Tell me, woman. What have I done? Tell me everything, or you will suffer the fate of these."

In terror she told him all she knew. And then this man, who

despised as cowards all men who weep, fell to the saddest wailing that she had ever heard. It was like the low moan of a wounded bull. Tecmessa longed to comfort him, but she knew not how. She feared what greater woes might be brewing in his tortured mind.

Rumors of the night's outrage had quickly spread to Ajax' warriors from Salamis, encamped by their twelve stout ships along the shore.

"Surely these are Odysseus' lies that strike with joy so many willing ears," one said. "Such is the jealousy of Ajax' might that the tales grow sweeter with every telling."

"Aye, no one would bandy such tidings of you or me," said another, "but a great, good man is always a target for scandal's arrows. Yet if creeping envy destroys our leader, we, too, may perish in the crash."

"We should go to Ajax ourselves," one of his crew suggested. "Only he can come forth and quash these stories. When he is out of sight the bird-brains will cackle. But let him once appear like an eagle soaring in the sky and they will all cower in silent fear."

So the men of Ajax' own ship set out for their leader's tent. If he had truly raged among the herds, they agreed, he must be afflicted by the gods. But they prayed to Zeus and Apollo it was not so. Outside the tent they called his name, but he did not appear. Tecmessa came out instead, weeping bitterly.

"Mighty Ajax lies sick," she told them. "His soul has been tossed by a fearful storm."

"But yesterday he was well," they said. "What terrible change has this one night wrought? Tell us, O daughter of Phrygian Teleutas. We love him, too."

"It is a tale as sad as death," she said. "Smitten with madness, he lies in the blood of animals slain. He drove them here for some ungodly sacrifice, with curses that only some fiend could have taught him."

"Then the tales were true," one of them cried in dismay. "If he was indeed the one who slew the herds and the herdsmen, he will surely die."

They, too, might be stoned to death, they feared, such was the fury of the Greeks. Perhaps they should steal away now and flee in their ship before it was too late. But even at home they might face death for treason.

"His madness has passed," Tecmessa said, "as the lightning and wind die down from a sudden storm. Yet now his plight is still more pitiable. For while he was mad, he was happy. Now he is racked by cruel remorse, and I dread what this newer mood may portend."

As she told them the tale of the night of horror, they heard him groaning and cursing within. At last he cried out, "My son, my son! Where is my son? And where is my brother Teucer? Too long has my brother been off on his raid; has he left me here to perish?"

Then they knew he was crushed indeed when he could plead for another's aid. And base-born Teucer was a lesser man; a bowman who was wont to shoot his arrows from the shelter of Ajax' shield.

"Perhaps it would soothe him to see us," one man said. They drew the flap aside and gasped in dismay at the scene of carnage within. As they entered, Ajax raised his head from his hands and greeted them:

"Ah, shipmates, stout and steady at the oar! Swiftly you brought me here. Now swiftly obey my last command—and slay me."

"Ajax, my master!" Tecmessa threw herself at his feet. "Never speak like this."

"Out, woman! Begone!" shouted Ajax.

"No—heed her," they begged. "Remember your love for her."

He moaned: "Just look at me—the mighty Ajax who feared no foe. And now behold my latest victory—over helpless beasts that feared no harm. How can I endure the mockery, the shame? Poor fool that I was to let my enemies escape my sword."

They begged him not to afflict himself with the past, beyond all cure. But he went on:

"And that son of Laertes, that son of trickery and deceit, how he must laugh. I would like to meet him even now. O Zeus, just let me slay that knave and those twin-sceptered kings. Then let me die."

"If this is your prayer," Tecmessa said, "then pray that I die, too. For how could I live without you?"

"Darkness is now my light," said Ajax. "The shades of death glow brighter than light of day. So, kill me! Kill me, no longer fit to look upon gods or men. Where can I turn? Where can I flee? My fame is as dead as these creatures here. All the army cries for my blood."

"How could so noble a man ever speak such words?" Tecmessa sobbed.

"Too long," moaned Ajax, "I have tarried here in Troy. But now these waves, these caves, these green-clad shores will see me no more—the bravest warrior ever to come from Greece, and now the most dishonored."

They tried to find words to comfort him, but the words would not come.

Ajax' thoughts went back to Salamis and to his father Telamon, who, years before in another war, had also won renown in Troy.

"Then I came here," he said, "Telamon's son, no less in might than he, to serve the Greeks with deeds of equal worth

—only to die dishonored at their hands. But this I know: If Achilles were yet alive to award his arms for valor, I would not be empty-handed."

He railed against the fierce-eyed goddess whose tricks had foiled his wrath.

"Now I am hated by heaven," he said, "hated by friend and foe, hated by the very soil of Troy on which I stand. What shall I do? Desert the Greeks, deprive the sons of Atreus of my aid, sail home across the Aegean Sea? But how could I face my father in disgrace? Or shall I take up arms and storm the battlements of Troy alone, and by some single-handed deed of glory win a hero's death? No, that would please the sons of Atreus too much.

"Yet only a coward would choose to live on, day in, day out, in endless misery; I must show my aged sire it was not a coward he begot. The valiant must live nobly . . . or nobly die. They have no other choice. And of these two, one course alone remains for me."

"These are brave words and bravely spoken," one of his men said. "But in your hour of darkness you should heed your friends."

"Yes, Ajax, master, pity us who need and love you," Tecmessa pleaded. "None can escape the toils of fate. I was the daughter of Phrygia's king, once rich in wealth and power. Now I am a slave. Yet so it was willed by the gods, I think, and your own right hand. I bowed to my fate and learned to love you. And now as I share your bed, so do I share all your joys and sorrows.

"Oh, do not die and let me be seized and ravished by another! Nor let men mock me and say, 'Look at her, once the mate of mighty Ajax; how she has fallen.' Hard enough that would be for me, but think how low it would bring your name. Pity your father, old and comfortless, and your mother who prays for your safe return. Pity your son who needs a father's care. Let him not suffer an orphan's fate in hands that are strange and cruel.

"Think what sorrow your death would bring to him and to me. For I have no one to look to but you. My lands are wasted, my father and mother dead. If ever I gave you joy in the past, be not ungrateful now."

"Then do as I say," said Ajax.

"O dear Ajax, whatever your wish, I will obey."

"Bring me my son. Where is he?"

"I kept him from sight lest you harm him."

"If I had killed him in my madness," Ajax said, "it would have been a fitting crown to my other woes. So you did well. But now I would look upon his face. If he is truly a son of mine he will not shrink from the sight of blood. He must early learn the ways of war."

Tecmessa had servants bring in the child from another tent. Then Ajax drew him into his arms. The little boy's eyes were wide with wonder but showed no tears.

"Never be a weakling, my son," said Ajax, "but grow in your father's likeness in every way—save one. Let another teach you to be more fortunate. I envy your ignorance now in those blissful years before you learn joy and sorrow. Feed while you may on the gentle breezes and gladden your mother's heart. For when you become a man you must prove to your father's foes whose son you are."

Then, giving the child Eurysaces into Tecmessa's arms, he said, "No Greek shall harm this son of mine, for my brother Teucer will be his steadfast guardian. And to you, my comrades of oars and spears, I give this charge: Bid Teucer take this child home to Telamon and my mother Eriboea to comfort their aging years. And let there be no contest over my arms; the Greeks must not divide them as spoils. To my son I bequeath my sevenfold, spear-proof shield. Let all the rest be buried with me.

"Now, woman," he said to Tecmessa, "stop your weeping and lead the child away."

"O Ajax, my lord," Tecmessa asked fearfully, "what is in your mind?"

"Question me not," he said with a frown.

"But I tremble. Do not forsake me, I pray by the gods . . ."

"Speak not of gods," he said, "for the gods have no claim on me."

"Oh, do not offend them," she pleaded.

"Then vex me not," he said. "Save your talk for those who have ears for it. Be not such a fool as to try to teach me now."

One of his shipmates gave her a sign. It would be better, he seemed to say, for her to leave Ajax now. She need not fear, for some would remain close by to keep him from harm. Tecmessa led the child away. Ajax buried his head in his hands. The others crept out of the reeking tent, though they left it open to keep him somewhat in their sight.

They whispered softly of yearnings for Salamis, of their weariness of the fields of Ida, their fears of death. They recalled all the conquests of mighty Ajax, the envy he stirred and the curse it had brought upon him. No wonder if such a man would prefer to die rather than live in madness, hatred, and ill esteem. Yet if he died, his mother would weep for him ever as the nightingale; his father would sink to the grave in sorrow.

Meanwhile, the torment was passing from Ajax' mind. With calmer resolve he knew what he must do. And no one would stop him. He would cease to fight against gods and men. But he would never surrender the helm of his fate. He laid aside his armor but took up his sword and came out of the tent.

They would long remember the words he spoke, and long would they ponder their meaning.

"Time in its endless course," he said, "is ever bringing the new to birth and sweeping the old away. Nothing forever can stand unchanged, not even the strongest will or the direst oath.

"Just now I was hard as tempered steel, yet this woman's words have unmanned me. I pity the widow and fatherless child I would leave to the vengeance of my foes were I to provoke them further. So, first I shall go to the meadows by the sea and wash the bloodstains from my hands to avert the goddess' wrath. Then I shall find some untrodden spot to bury this hated sword in the earth. Let night and hell be its keepers. It is accursed. From the day I received it from Hector, my fiercest enemy, I have known no favor from the Greeks. How true is the saying that an enemy's gifts are no gifts at all but profitless.

"We must come to know obedience to the gods, and school ourselves to respect the sons of Atreus. Why not? They rule us. All nature teaches that even the fiercest things must yield to law. Snow-driven winter storms give way to fruitful summer, the gloom of night to the steeds of shining day. The fiercest winds in time must grow gentle and lull to rest the groaning sea. Who are we to scorn all nature's laws?

"We must curb our moods to reason. We should hate an enemy only so much as we could love him some other day, remembering that hate and love alike must die. Even friendship itself is a treacherous harbor."

He turned to Tecmessa. "Now all will be well with me. So go to the gods, my woman, and pray for fulfillment of my desire. And you, my comrades, must honor her as you honor me. Tell Teucer, when he comes, to care for us and to treat you well. For I must go where I must go. Do as I bid you, and you in time may know how I saved myself from the depths of my woe."

Lulled by these words, they let him go—to cleanse himself and bury his hated sword for good. Might it never plague him more. And in their joy they sang to Apollo and Pan and Zeus, even to Ares, the god of war.

Meanwhile, the dust billowed up in the hills. The raiding party which Teucer led was coming home, driving its herds from the Mysian heights. Now Teucer lived, as it were, in Ajax' shadow. For, though he was also the son of Telamon, the queen Eriboea was not his mother. He had been born of a Trojan princess, the captive of his father's spear, a war-wife like Tecmessa. Old Telamon, his father, had cautioned him when he sailed from Salamis to guard with his life his nobler brother, and he had not failed, for he loved him well. But even more, he loved the child Eurysaces, whose shadowed birth was so like his own.

From a distance Teucer had heard much shouting in the camp. And as he drew near he realized that the angry jeers were directed at him.

"Bastard brother of that crazy wretch who works our ruin," they cried, "you, too, shall be stoned and mangled to death. Nothing can save you now."

He did not know what they meant nor why they drew their swords and rushed to seize him. But blood would have flowed had not the sons of Atreus appeared, and with them Calchas the priest. One word of command and they all fell back. Then Calchas, the aged seer, pressed forward to Teucer, clasped him by the hand and led him aside. Quickly he told him of Ajax' frenzied deeds in the night. Then he said:

"For this one day till the setting sun, you must keep bold Ajax within his tent. Let him not wander out of your sight if you ever wish to see him alive again."

Ajax' pride had worked his ruin, the old priest said. Even so, if for one whole day he could sit in penance and stir no further wrath, he might still win back the favor of the gods. So much, he said, had Athene revealed to him.

So Teucer rushed away to save his brother. Alas, when he reached the tent of Ajax he found him gone. And when Teucer told them of Calchas' prophecy they were all afraid.

"Oh, he has deceived me, and I am lost," Tecmessa cried. "Ajax, my lord, despises my love and is hastening to the arms of Death. Oh, help me, help me, my friends! Quick, search the shores and the hills to the east and the west. Follow his fatal tracks and find him. Find him before it is too late."

They hurried out, but in their haste they rushed right past his hiding place. For Ajax had gone to a nearby cove by the sea. He had washed the blood from the sword and whetted the blade on a stone. Then indeed he had buried it, yet only by half. The hilt of Hector's fatal gift lay buried in the hard-packed earth, but its point stood upright, gleaming in the morning sun. "My friend, you will help me now to a speedy death," he said.

For indeed this was a world where gods must rule and kings must be obeyed. But such a world was not for Ajax. He refused to be vanquished by any man save by himself alone. He had little claim on the gods, but he prayed to Zeus:

"Let Teucer be first to learn of my death and lift my body from this sword so that he may give me the honor due to crown my life. Let not my enemies find me to cast me forth to the dogs and birds."

The woman's plea had moved him only to spare his enemies lest harsher vengeance fall on his mate and child. But he did not forgive his foes. He prayed to the Erinyes, those swift, relentless Furies, to scourge them with woe:

"Avenging virgins, mark how the sons of Atreus have destroyed me. Swoop down upon them, glut your fill and spare them not. Afflict the host with utter ruin."

Then he prayed to Hermes: "O guide of ghosts to the world beyond, help me pass swiftly to my rest."

He checked all thoughts of his father's sorrow, and of the mother whose anguish would ring through the city.

"Farewell, O light of day," he cried. "Farewell to far-famed Athens and Salamis who gave me birth. Farewell, you streams and fields of Troy who nursed my fame. Henceforth will Ajax hail the dead alone."

Then with a cry, "Come, Death, embrace me!" he hurled his mighty body down on the sword. His blood gushed forth as it pierced his heart.

It was Tecmessa later who found him there while his comrades searched the shores in vain. Her desolate cry soon brought the others to the scene.

"Who did it?" they asked.

"Who could slay the mighty Ajax but himself?" she asked. "This sword of doom half buried in the ground convicts him."

They cursed their folly in letting him go.

"O mighty Ajax," Tecmessa wept. "You chose the path you had to choose. Now even your foes must mourn and honor you. But what a yoke you have left for your child and me to bear."

"It was the will of fate," said one. "Shame, if Odysseus exults in his treacherous heart or the sons of Atreus find joy in this man's agony."

"Let them have their day," Tecmessa said, "but they will mourn him sorely when they need his spear. Then his death will bring them far more grief than joy, and he will have his heart's desire."

Teucer came and groaned at the sight he saw. Only two days ago he had left his brother with a happy gibe that

Achilles' arms would scarcely fit his mighty frame. Now his heart was broken to see him lying by the waterside. Yet, little time was left for grief when danger lurked on every hand.

"Where is the child?" he asked Tecmessa.

"Alone, beside the tent," she said.

"Then swiftly go and bring him here," said Teucer, "before some enemy snatches him like a whelp from a lion slain. For cruel men become brave against the weak when their foes are dead."

Tecmessa fled in alarm to find the child.

"This is well," said one of Ajax' crew, "for the last charge he put upon us was that you should guard his son."

He must not betray that trust, Teucer thought. But Telamon, he feared, would surely be wroth that he had betrayed Ajax. He could see his old father now, bowed in sorrow and fretful with years, cursing him on his return to Salamis. "Bastard and coward," the old man would chide, "you let your nobler brother die so you could rob him of his kingdom." Then hated at Troy and hated at Salamis, he would doubtless end his years in friendless exile.

Still, he had his duty now. A hero's death must be marked by a hero's funeral.

He wept to think of that hated sword. How well he remembered that day when Ajax had stood alone and battled Hector, the mightiest champion of Troy. He remembered how fiercely they fought, then called a truce and, in a fit of ill-starred gallantry, had parted with an exchange of gifts. A belt for a sword. Surely both were the handiwork of the Furies, for it was by the belt of Ajax that Hector was later dragged to his death in the dust of Troy behind Achilles' chariot. And now the sword of Hector was lodged in his brother's heart.

He was about to lift the mighty body from that sword when he heard a voice.

"Stop! I forbid you to move that corpse. Leave it dishonored where it lies."

Teucer looked up to see the golden bearded Menelaos facing him in anger.

"Who forbids?" he asked, curling his lip in contempt.

"I and the ruler of this host," said Menelaos. "We brought this knave here to aid the Greeks and found him worse than our Trojan foes. Were it not for the gods, he would have slain us all. Let his body rot on the yellow sands and feed the seashore birds. We could not master this rebel in life, but at least we can rule him now. If the wicked were free to oppose their rulers as this man did, no ship could safely sail the seas, no city prosper, no army be secure. He must pay for his insolence. If you try to bury him, I warn you that the grave you dig will be your own."

Teucer flared up at these words.

"You never ruled this man and you never will," he said. "He came here, freely, in no man's service. He did not come like your Spartan slaves to win back your faithless wife, but only in reverence to his oath. Go rule your Spartans as you wish, but if you come here again you had better bring more heralds and your chief."

"Such boasting from a bowman," Menelaos sneered.

"I could stand and fight you without a shield," said Teucer, "for bravery lies with the man whose cause is just."

"You call it justice to honor a king's assassin?"

"Assassin? Pray tell me what king he slew."

"Thanks be to the gods he could slay us only in his mind."

"Then honor those gods by not denying a good man burial."

"He was my foe; he hated me."

"Only because you cheated him of Achilles' arms."

"I was not the only judge," said Menelaos.

"Aye, but you helped corrupt the rest."

And so they might have gone on in fruitless wrangling, but Menelaos, lacking the strength to prevail, turned on his heel, saying, "I should feel shame to be seen bandying words where I ought to chastise."

"And I more shame," said Teucer, "to heed such a blustering fool."

But when Menelaos left him, Teucer knew he must lose no time, for other Greeks might come in force to shame his brother's corpse and cheat it of its honors. It was just the three of them—the woman, the child, and himself—and a faithful few, standing against the world. And when Tecmessa returned with Eurysaces, Teucer cut a lock of hair from each head—the mother's, the child's, and his own. Then, placing the locks in the hands of Eurysaces, he said:

"Come, my child, and kneel as a suppliant at your father's side. Lay these threefold gifts on his body. Clasp it tightly and do not move from this place. If any Greek should tear you away, may he, too, die and be cast from the land unburied. May he be cut off from all his kindred as we have severed these locks of hair. And you, my comrades, stand around, not like idle women mourners but ready to fight and die like men, while some of us go to prepare a tomb."

They chose a spot on a green-clad hill looking out over the sky-blue sea that stretched back in memory to far-off Salamis. Ten weary years had passed since last they stood on that silvery, sea-rimmed island looking across at the bright marble temples studding the violet crown of Athens. Ten years of exile, toil, and grief had been spent by Scamander's streams beneath the slopes of Ida. Ten years of yearning for home. They cursed their lot as they dug his grave. One of them paused to wipe the sweat from his brow and sighed:

"Would that that man had vanished in air or been swallowed by hell who first taught the Greeks the arts of war. He was the father of our ills."

"Aye," said another, "what wretched gifts he gave, not cheering wine, sweet music of flutes, or blissful sleep . . ."

"Sleep!" said another. "For ten long years I have not known a woman. I have had no bedfellow save for the cold and the dew. Troy has been cruel indeed. And now that our shield, our mighty Ajax, is lost, what joy will we ever know?"

But Teucer, gazing down toward the little group below that guarded his brother's corpse, saw a larger band of bronze-clad warriors approach. And at their head he descried the black beard of Agamemnon, the king himself, the commander of all the Greeks. He ran down the hill to confront him.

"Stand aside, O King!" he said. "Do not try to stop us now, for Ajax belongs to the deathless gods."

"You base-born bastard," Agamemnon cried, "do you dare defy me? Who was this man you exalt in death? The only man among all the Greeks, forsooth! Where did he ever face or drive back an enemy where I stood not, too? Just because he was judged unworthy to bear Achilles' arms were we to be stabbed in the back or now bear the lash of your uncouth tongue?

"A sorry thing would our laws become if rightful men must be thrust aside to crown less worthy churls. We must honor the wise. But Ajax, for all of his strength, was an ox. He needed the whip to keep him straight, and I think you need one, too. For he was nothing and you are less. And do not offend me with the accents of your Phrygian mother. Find, if you must, some Greek of decent birth to plead your cause."

"How treacherous is gratitude," Teucer retorted. "Have you already forgotten how many times he saved your life? No doubt you would like to forget that blackest day when you all were squealing like rats as you fled in a panic toward the sea. Who then was the only man among the Greeks? Who was it that stood between Hector and death for you all? It was Ajax. And who stood beside him? Not you. It was I, the slave woman's son.

"But who, pray, are you to mock my parentage? Your own grandfather Pelops was not a Greek, but a Phrygian. And think of the impious crimes of your father Atreus. Or was he your father? Was not your Cretan mother once caught with a lover whose body was thrown to feed the fishes?

"My father was Telemon, foremost hero of Greece, my mother a Phrygian princess of noble birth, though captive to his spear. I have no shame on either side. And I have no shame to guard my brother. All three of us you must slay to take him, and I count it nobler in the sight of all to die for my brother's sake than be slain for *your* brother's worthless wife, the Helen he could not hold."

Agamemnon's face grew white with rage at Teucer's taunts and he clenched his staff. But before he could raise it in wrath or speak, Odysseus came up and laid a friendly hand upon him.

"Why, my friends," he asked, "should such bitterness mark a hero's funeral?"

"Did you not hear his shameless words?" Agamemnon asked.

"Aye, they were harsh and wild, but such words have some excuse when a man is sore provoked."

"He threatens to honor this corpse in spite of me."

"And why not?" Odysseus asked. "May I speak the truth as a friend whose heart has always beaten in time with yours?"

"You may speak indeed," said Agamemnon, "for of all the Greeks I count you my dearest friend."

"Then, by the gods," Odysseus said, "do not deny this hero an honored grave. Do not let your hate trample justice underfoot. This man was my direst foe from the moment I won Achilles' arms. Yet, save for Achilles, I cannot deny that no other man so valiant ever set foot in Troy. It would flout the laws of the gods themselves if you let the madness of one single night blot out the fame of a noble life."

"You, too, Odysseus? You side against me?"

"I hated him, too, so long as hate was right."

"But now?"

"Let us honor his valor and not our spite."

"It is hard," Agamemnon sighed, "for a king to yield."

"Yet it becomes a king to be generous," Odysseus said, "and to heed a friend who counsels well."

"I marvel that you could forgive him even in death."

"He was my foe, but a noble one. His greatness outweighs all enmity."

"And you bid me allow these funeral rites?"

"Yes, for I, too, some day will come to this. While we live our fame lies within our hands. When we die we entrust it to others to keep."

"Then," Agamemnon said, "let this seem your doing, not mine."

"No matter," Odysseus said. "To yield to reason is a kingly act."

"Nay, I yield to friendship," said Agamemnon. "For you, Odysseus, I would grant even more than this. But as for Ajax, in death as in life, he shall have my hate. So do as you please with him.

The king turned away. The others lingered. Odysseus offered his hand to Teucer.

"Know that from now on I am your friend," Odysseus said, "no less than I was your foe. I would share your rites and honor him, giving all that a good man owes to a great man dead."

Teucer was touched.

"Noble Odysseus," he said, "I praise your words. You of all the Greeks, his direst foe, were the only one who dared to defend his cause. May the Olympian god and the Furies of Justice take all the rest. But, son of Laertes, kind as you are, I cannot let you join these rites. Even in death my brother may not be so forgiving, and I would scruple to offend his spirit. But in all other things I would toil by your side, for you are a friend with a noble heart."

"I still would honor him," Odysseus said, "but if you wish it not, I obey your wish."

The two men clasped hands and parted.

So the grave was dug. Then Teucer called for water and cauldrons and fire that they might cleanse his brother's corpse in piety. And he sent to the tent to fetch Ajax' arms, all but the shield he had left to his son, that they might be buried with him."

And as the word spread, many thousands came. And they honored him as they laid him to rest, for no man knows what destiny awaits him.

This is the only one of Sophocles' seven surviving plays in which an Olympian god appears. It would have been hard to leave out the traditional guardian deity of the *Odyssey*. But Athene is so much the moral inferior to Odysseus that one conclusion seems inescapable. Sophocles had little more respect for the Olympian gods than Euripides had. However, he felt no need to belabor them.

Ajax is one of the most misunderstood Greek tragedies. Much of our Christian philosophy goes back to Socrates and his successors, but it is an error to see too much of it in Sophocles. To equate Antigone with a martyr for the faith does little harm, perhaps, except for obscuring the play's political message. The real meaning of *Oedipus* is badly distorted if it is read as an "example" of divine justice. But the theme of *Ajax* is garbled most of all by assuming it to be one of sin and punishment (*hybris* and *nemesis*).

By that false theory Ajax confesses his sin in the speech on page 226 and then commits suicide. Why not end the play there? No writer is more purposeful at all times or has a stronger sense of unity than Sophocles. The idea, that he would add a long coda when his theme was complete, is unthinkable. The theme of *Ajax* is the triumph of heroic honor regardless of men, or gods, or death. The triumph is complete only with the recognition of the hero's worth. And it is the wise Odysseus, who appears like one of Euripides' *dei ex machina* to make that meaning clear.

Read the lines of Odysseus in the final scene to see if that or punishment is the theme. Read what Ajax says before he takes his life to see if he repented his own actions one iota. Then why the supposed speech of resignation to a world of restraint and law? We must remember that Greek tragedy is shot through with irony. Words, purposes, and actions are often directly counter to their surface appearance. We soon discover the real meaning of Ajax' vow to bury his sword, for example. He accepts the world of kings and restraints only as a fact—never as a code for his behavior. While he seems to be renouncing his code, he is actually renouncing the world. Men may trick him, gods may delude him, but under the bludgeonings of fate he remains the captain of his soul. Only he can destroy himself—and he does.

In only one sense does he yield to the world of ordinary men. He realizes that if he follows the course of vengeance, he may also involve his wife and child unfairly in his doom. But far from renouncing his vengeance, he bequeaths it to the gods and the Furies.

Today this old heroic code is obsolete. We can applaud the hero who holds his own life so cheap as to risk losing it for an ideal. But if Ajax felt he had no right to involve Eurysaces and Tecmessa, what of the pseudo-hero of an atomic age who would blindly involve the lives of the whole human race?

AGAMEMNON

CHARACTERS

Agamemnon (Ag-a-MEM-non): The great king and leader of the Greeks at Troy, son of Atreus.

Clytemnestra (Kli-tem-NESS-tra): Agamemnon's queen, sister of Helen.

Aegisthus (Ee-JISS-thoos): Agamemnon's cousin and Clytemnestra's lover, son of Thyestes the brother of Atreus.

Cassandra (Ka-SAND-ra): A true prophetess doomed never to be believed, daughter of King Priam, enslaved to Agamemnon.

An old watchman.

A soldier of Agamemnon.

Elders of Argos.

When the Greeks ravished Troy they spared nothing—not even the shrines of its gods. So disaster struck them on the voyage home. Most of them drowned in a storm, or were driven far off course. Menelaos and Helen were carried to the coast of Egypt. Odysseus spent years of wandering, as related in Homer's *Odyssey*. But Agamemnon outrode the storm. He was being hurried home for another fate . . .

Aeschylus' play thunders with brilliant imagery and symbolism. He delves into the most grisly sins and soars to heights of mysticism. His staging must have been spectacular. As a dramatist's dramatist, he could inspire his rivals and even influence a later Eugene O'Neill or Tennessee Williams. Yet, he can be as frustrating as the most obscure avant-gardist, as evidenced in plays like *Prometheus Bound* which lack plot and passion. They defy treatment as stories.

Less static, however, was his last trilogy which won first prize in 458 B.C. and has come down to us intact. *Agamemnon*, its first play, or "act," is notable for its fierce portrait of Clytemnestra, its rich and symbolic scene in which Agamemnon is lured to tread the crimson path to his doom, and the struggle of the mad Cassandra to shake off the curse that blocks her visions of horror from being believed. Even so, only a small part of the play is dramatic in our sense.

The timeless nature of the old chorus is indicated by the fact that while it is on stage many days elapse between the signal of Troy's fall and Agamemnon's return. A main flashback recalls the story of Iphigenia, with some differences from Euripides' later account. Euripides says the Greek fleet mustered in Aulis and was becalmed there. Aeschylus says it was driven there by fierce winds that would not abate. Somehow each situation suits the mood of its own story. Certainly the raging winds best suit the stormy theme of *Agamemnon*.

AGAMEMNON

(AESCHYLUS)

The night was pierced by a thousand stars.

By now the old watchman had come to know them all. He knew their risings and settings—those that brought the summer and those that brought the season of storms, when every bone in his cold, wet body ached.

"Soon," he prayed, "may the gods relieve me of my toil."

Every night for a year, at Queen Clytemnestra's bidding, he had taken his post on the roof of Agamemnon's palace. Hour after hour he lay there, doglike, looking for the first sign of his master's return. Resting on elbows, head in hands, he kept scanning the north for the promised signal fire.

All around, the city of Argos slept. Women, children, and old men lay dreaming, yearning, perhaps, for their warriors far away in Troy.

Ten years ago a wayfaring prince from Troy had come this way. Alexandros he was called—or Paris. Few could say either name now without a curse. In the halls of Agamemnon's brother, King Menelaos, he had been welcomed with all the hospitality Zeus demands—and more. He had slept and dined and been beguiled by the singing and dancing of fair women. In repayment he stole the gold and silver from

Menelaos' board; and, more, he stole Menelaos' wife, Queen Helen, to warm his bed in Troy.

Then the brother kings, Agamemnon and Menelaos, like frenzied eagles over a plundered nest, called down the vengeance of Zeus on the robber. They mustered a thousand ships and manned them with the flower of Argive youth. The watchman himself saw them sail away to destroy the city of Priam, to slay King Priam's adulterous son, and to bring the wanton woman home.

That was ten years ago, and many a spear had been broken since, and many a knee bowed in the dust. But this was the year the oracles said the Greeks would win in Troy—and ravage Ilium's citadel in plunder, blood, and fire. On every mountaintop from Ilium to Argos, unlit beacon fires stood ready to signal the news of victory.

"Soon may I see the sign," the watchman prayed.

Night after night he had waited there with no companions but hope and fear to keep him awake. Sometimes he tried to hum or whistle a tune, but the sound would die in a groan as he thought of the evil that lurked in the halls below. For many a night from his post on the roof he had seen a shrouded figure steal across the courtyard from a secret gate. And once a sudden flash of lightning had revealed the man's face.

An ox, as they say, lay heavy on the watchman's tongue. He dared not tell a soul what he knew. All Argos thought Clytemnestra was as virtuous as she was bitter, and as true as her sister Helen was faithless. Only the watchman knew that Clytemnestra lay sleeping in the arms of a captain who had not gone to Troy—Aegisthus son of Thyestes, the hated cousin of Agamemnon.

Now suddenly a fire was seen in the distance. The watchman sprang up with a cry. There it was! The beacon, more welcome than the sun, was flaming on Mount Arachnae. For once, all his fears and forebodings were drowned in a surge of joy.

"Awake! Awake!" the watchman shouted. "I have a clear message for Agamemnon's queen. Let her rise and lead the songs of thanksgiving! For the beacon tells that Troy has been taken."

The dice of the gods have come up all sixes for me and my master, he thought. Soon I shall see his face once more and clasp his hand . . .

Again the shadow crossed his mind.

But why remember such things now? He was free! He would join the dancing in the streets.

The shouting had roused Clytemnestra from a fitful sleep. She shook Aegisthus at her side.

"The news has come at last," she whispered. "Wait here until you can join the crowd unnoticed. Then prepare to do as we have planned. I, too, shall do my part. And may the gods stand by us!"

She put on her robes and went out to light the altar fires in feigned joy. How different she was from her sister. Of Tyndareus' two daughters wed to the brother kings, Helen was fair—the fairest of women—soft, gentle, and all too yielding. Clytemnestra was dark, with dagger eyes and the mind and passion of a man. A butterfly the one; the other a spider. And the spider had begun to spin her net.

Throughout the city all was joy. The distant beacon soon multiplied a thousandfold. Every altar blazed with offerings to the gods of city, home, and marketplace—to the gods above and the gods below. The air grew rich with the scent of precious oils long stored to celebrate this happy day.

Up toward the palace the Argive elders came, the "three-legged ones," who leaned on their staffs and canes. They,

too, remembered, better than they did more recent things—
that day the fleet first sailed away. Alas for their feeble limbs
in the yellow leaf of age. Too old for Ares—weak as children
and frail as passing dreams—they had been left behind.

"The news seems good," said one.

"Aye, Troy has fallen," another said, "if rumors can be
trusted."

"But Agamemnon's men have many seas to cross."

"So many chances for jealous gods to strike," another
added. "Our sons are still not safe at home."

> *Sing of sorrows piled on sorrows,*
> *Yet may good prevail.*

"Zeus, the god of hosts and strangers, could not let the
defiler Paris escape," said one. This they believed. But while
Zeus had remained aloof on his throne of justice, lesser gods
had often been malignant.

"Surely Helen would never have left the bed of Menelaos,
had Aphrodite not cast her spells," said one.

"Aye," another agreed, "and I have heard that the Love
Goddess even joined fierce Ares in battle against our Argives."

"But the direst of the gods was Artemis the Huntress!"

They all shuddered. The Virgin Goddess of the moon had
demanded an abominable appeasement. Could any exploit, so
bathed in innocent blood at the beginning, ever come to any
good?

> *Sing of sorrows piled on sorrows,*
> *Yet may good prevail.*
> *When the scales of Justice balance,*
> *Wisdom comes through bitter pain.*

The very first omen had boded some evil. They all knew
the story well. Barely had the fleet set sail ten years ago when

Agamemnon and his crew beheld two eagles of Zeus on the lucky side of their ship. One was black like the hair and beard of Agamemnon. The other was tawny like Menelaos. Between them they were feasting gluttonously on the still-quivering flesh of a pregnant hare.

"What is the meaning?" asked Agamemnon of Calchas the seer.

"They are kings among birds as you are kings of men," the soothsayer Calchas replied. "Thus you will devour Troy and all within her." But he added this warning:

"Beware the wrath of Artemis who hates her Father's eagles. They are feeding on the unborn young, and the Virgin Goddess loves the young of all wild creatures, even the suckling cubs of lions. Pray that she send no contrary winds or, even worse, demand a cruel, unholy sacrifice that will stir vengeful evils in your home."

> *Sing of sorrows piled on sorrows,*
> *Yet may good prevail.*

None of the old men knew how Agamemnon had first offended the Virgin Huntress. But the anger of Artemis sorely plagued him on his way to Troy. Furious winds from the south drove the fleet off course and deep into the bay near Aulis. For days and weeks the winds raged on relentlessly. The fleet was trapped. Ships and cables began to molder. Food ran low. The men grew desperate.

All this was learned from the messenger who returned by land to summon Iphigenia to her father's side. She was his dearest child, and when he called she gladly went forth, little knowing the doom that awaited her. For at Aulis, Calchas the seer had revealed an awful truth.

"The winds will blow," he said, "your ships will rot and your men will waste in hunger until the wrath of Artemis is appeased. You must slay on her altar the thing you hold most dear. The Virgin Goddess demands a virgin's blood!"

Agamemnon had wept long and bitterly. What should he do? To disobey a god meant heavy doom; to slay his dearest daughter meant heavier grief. Yet could he desert his fleet and fail his allies? They clamored madly for him to make the sacrifice and calm the wind.

In the end he bowed his neck to the yoke of necessity and steeled his heart to pay with a sinless child for the war for a sinful woman. He sent for his daughter. Once bent on the awful course, his mind reeled. He prepared with fanatic eagerness to do the act—the impious, unholy, unspeakable thing—from which he had recoiled in horror before. He became its priest. He said the prayers. He gave the sign.

Her pleas, her helpless cries of "Father!", her virgin loveliness meant nothing to his eager ministers. He had them bind her lips against any ill-omened cry that might bring a curse on his house. As her saffron robes were torn from her unblemished body and fell at her feet, her fearful eyes stabbed them all with the piteous message she could not speak. They lifted her fainting body above the altar like a lamb.

The seercraft of Calchas did not fail. As the blood of the slain Iphigenia flowed over the altar the winds fell. The fleet sailed on to Troy.

> *Sing of sorrows piled on sorrows,*
> *Yet may good prevail.*
> *Zeus triumphant, teach the lesson:*
> *Wisdom comes through bitter pain.*

"Evils purge evils," an old man said, "but when will the chain of evils end?"

Clytemnestra came out into the palace courtyard, and the eldest among them greeted her:

"We have come in all obedience, Clytemnestra; with your lord away, his throne is yours. We would know if the tidings are true."

"Beyond our hopes," she assured them. "The Argives have taken Priam's city."

"Tears fill my eyes," the old man said.

"They prove your loyalty to be like mine," she replied.

"But might this not be just a dream—some rumor fed by hope?"

"Do you think I am a silly child?" Clytemnestra asked. "Troy has fallen this very night."

"This very night?" they exclaimed in disbelief. "What messenger could ever travel so fast?"

"Only the Fire God," said Clytemnestra. "High above Troy huge trees were felled and piled atop Mount Ida in an unlit pyre. Only the torch of victory was needed to blaze the message to the skies. Watchers on Lemnos, across the sea, beheld the sign and lit a second beacon. From there the word swept over the Thracian Gulf to Mount Athos and was passed like a torch in a race to Macistus where crackling pitch pines flashed it on to Messapius' peak. The fire of withered heather there was seen from Cithaeron. Almost before a breath could be drawn the tidings of victory were sped to Aegiplanctus to leap across the Gulf of Corinth and set the skies aglow from Mount Arachnae. On every peak I had watchers who would not play me false."

"Then I shall thank the gods forthwith," the old man said. "But tell us more, my lady."

"What more can I say than that the Greeks hold Troy? The Argives and Trojans will be intermingled, yet each, like oil and vinegar shaken in a bottle, will still be separate. The cries of victors and vanquished will blend, yet fortune will give them each a different note. Women will fling themselves on corpses of husbands and brothers, children on the bodies of their fathers. And the Argives will sleep on soft beds under the pillared roof of Priam, no longer forced to brave the frost and dews of open skies.

"Yet I pray they respect the conquered shrines of the gods and not let greed drive them on to forbidden plunder. Let there be no excess that might doom their safe return. Such are the prayers of a faithful wife."

"I shall join your prayers, my Queen," the old man said, "for yours is the wisdom of a man."

They prayed to Zeus the all-conquering, who had cast a net on Troy that none could escape. To Zeus the god of hospitality whose bow had found its mark in the faithless guest. To Zeus the god of vengeance—no careless god, as sinners say, but one who smites down the transgressor. Some prayed, too, never to be tempted by riches. For wealth that lures to pleasures and lust is a fragile fortress against the wrath of the gods.

There followed days of anxious waiting until the fleet should return. Since the future was veiled, the folk of Argos talked much of the past.

"Menelaos has won back his bride," said one, "but what a dowry she took to Troy in that false marriage of pleasure—avenging ships, the clash of spears, destruction, death!"

"Think not of her," another said, "but of the sorrow of Menelaos—his empty home, the bridal bed still warm, still bearing the imprint of her lovely limbs. He sat alone in his anguish; silent, dishonored, yet loving her still. And she, though speeding across the sea, remained as a ghost to haunt his thoughts. The beauty of her statues mocked him. At night she came to him in his dreams and he would try to seize her; but groping for her form in the dark, his hands would find only emptiness."

"Ah, but we ourselves have still greater sorrows," another broke in. "How dear to our hearts and familiar to our eyes was every lad who went to war! But how many will return? The war god Ares is a cruel money-changer. He takes the gold of our youth, and what does he give back? A sword, a spear perhaps—and a hero's dust in a funeral urn."

So the talk spread. Their men had conquered Troy. Ah, yes, some had. But how many others lay conquered beneath her soil? "How nobly they fell," many would say—adding under their breath, "for another's wife." Resentment against Menelaos and Agamemnon began to grow until many were daring to voice it openly:

"A plague on the sons of Atreus and their quarrels!"

And one man who heard of such mutterings laughed to himself. I shall yet be king, thought Aegisthus son of Thyestes who already possessed Agamemnon's queen. He had only a handful of followers, but they might be enough with the people's anger on his side.

Thus the people's talk grew bolder as spirits fell.

"Those beacons might be just some trick of the gods," said one old man to his cronies in the marketplace.

"Our minds dance too quickly to every rumor," another said.

"It is just like a woman to seize on good news before she learns the truth," a third remarked. And he spat in the dust.

"Aye, there are no bounds to a woman's belief, and the tales she spreads are quick to die."

"But, look over there!" cried another, pointing. "That is no beacon, but a man." They looked and saw a figure running toward them from the harbor—a soldier, indeed, though his tunic was old and torn and stained with blood, and dust, and sweat.

"Now we shall know," one said. "And better let there be no more idle talk against our rulers."

"Land of my fathers, Argos, I am here!" the soldier cried as he fell and kissed the earth. "Ten years—and I never thought I would see you again. Now I can die happy. Thank Zeus! Thank Apollo! Thank Hermes! Thank all the gods! Receive in kindness those few of us who return."

"Rejoice!" said the elders in greeting.

"And I do rejoice," the soldier cried. "I will gladly die on the spot if the gods wish it."

They plied him for news.

"Agamemnon our king has returned," he said, "bringing light to darkness. Make ready to greet him, for he has uprooted Troy with the spade of Zeus. He has destroyed her utterly—yes, even the shrines and altars of her gods. Paris has lost his prize and he, with the other sons of Priam, has paid the last full debt for his sins. But how are things here in Argos?"

"You have yearned for us no more than we have for you."

"Has anything been amiss?"

"Sometimes silence is best," one elder said. "But now our lord is returning, and we are as ready as you to die with joy."

"Aye, the war is well ended," said the soldier, "and in the years between, you might say some things went well and some were cursed. But only a god escapes all pain, I guess. If I were to tell you about the hell of those crowded ships and all our complaints—but it was even worse afterward on land. The dirt, the lice, the rain, the cold that even killed the birds! Well, it is all over now—all over, indeed, for too many. But why should the living stop to count the dead? At least a few are now home safe—thanks be to Zeus—and rich with loot from the temples of Ilium."

"I was wrong about those beacons," one of his hearers admitted. "An old man can still learn from a young one. But come with us now to tell the queen."

Clytemnestra's face was hard as she heard the gist of the soldier's tale but her eyes glowed fiercely. She jeered at the elders:

"So I was only a foolish woman to trust the signal fires! When I stirred the city to kindle incense on every altar, men scoffed at me." She turned to the soldier. "But tell me no more. I want to hear every sweet word from my king himself. I shall welcome him with joy. For what is more wonderful for a wife than unbarring the gate for her lord come back from war? Let him speed to the arms of his faithful wife, who has guarded his home well. The seal of his love has not been broken in scandal. For as surely as bronze can never be dyed, I have not known pleasure from any other man."

"True boast of a noble wife," said the soldier with a bow. Yet her words seemed strange. For in war men often say of a sword that the bronze has been dyed—with blood.

"And how fared Menelaos?" one of the old men asked. "Did he, like our dear master, come home with you?"

A shadow crossed the soldier's face.

"It is bad luck to mingle sad news with good," he said. "But I am a simple man. You asked me and I can tell only the truth. He and his ships were snatched from our sight in a storm."

"You mean he perished? Had you no reports?"

"Only the sun who sees all things can know for sure. In the night a cruel storm blew up from Thrace, shattering ship against ship in the driving rain. When the next day's sun arose we saw the Aegean Sea flowering with Argive corpses, planks, and spars. Some god or Fortune must have seized our helm to guide us safely through. We mourned the dead, yet doubtless some escaped. They may right now be safe somewhere and mourning us as lost; for if any man should have the care of Zeus, surely it would be Menelaos. There is hope he will soon return."

"Aye, the name of Helen has meant hell enough already," an old man grimly quipped.

"There must have been feasting and joy when Paris first brought her to Priam's palace," another said. "I am minded of a man who once brought home a lion's cub, a suckling taken from its mother's teats. At first it was playful and gentle, and the children loved it. So did the old men. It would curl in their arms, bright-eyed and fawning for its little belly's sake.

"But, alas, it grew—and then one day its lion nature seized it. Murderously it ravaged through the flocks and filled the home with blood. So too, I think, the pampered Helen brought death and devastation to the halls of Priam. For sin and pride dwell in the halls of the mighty. Justice, it seems, prefers the humble, smoke-stained cottage."

He might have gone on, but now loud cheering in the city told them that Agamemnon was drawing near the palace gate. Then in he rode, resplendent in his bright though battered armor, his raven beard now streaked with gray—still unmistakably a king. Behind him, seated in another chariot, rode a tall, spare woman, proud, yet frightened and wild of eye. And they saw she bore the symbols of a seer, for in her hand was a divining wand and on her black, disheveled hair she wore the wreath of prophecy. In their wake came captured women slaves and bearers laden with silks and gold and jewels—rich spoils of fallen Troy.

Brief but malevolent was the glance that Clytemnestra gave the wild-eyed woman before she turned back to smile on her king.

"Wait here, my lord," she said, "and do not set your foot on the ground until we prepare a fitting path." Then she went within to bid her maidens strew his way with the richest of silks and velvets and brocades that he might enter like a god. As Agamemnon stood before them in his chariot, one, who was eldest among them, greeted him:

"All hail, O son of Atreus—sacker of Troy! How shall I name you? How give you all the honor due, yet kindle no anger in the gods by my excess? Even here among us there may be some whose smiles are false. That day you left for Troy I was one who doubted the wisdom of your rule. But you have won and I rejoice. You will not be deceived by those who merely feign a loyalty. Good shepherds know their flocks. In time you will ask and learn who have been true and who have failed your trust."

"First," said Agamemnon, "it is meet that I should hail Argos and my country's gods who granted me justice and a safe return. The gods in conclave voted at last that Ilium should fall. Into the urn of vengeance every ballot was cast; in the urn of mercy nothing but unanswered prayers."

Then he told how Greek deceit had won. How the Argives had feigned to sail away in despair and left on the shore a monstrous wooden horse as though it were a votive offering to the gods for their safe return. In blindness of joy the Trojans hauled it within their walls and danced around the strange device to celebrate the end of all their woes. But late that night the fleet came back. And silently, out of the horse's belly the wily Odysseus and other hidden Greeks descended to overpower the guards and open the gates for all the rest.

Then for the rape of one woman the city was ravished, the folk and all its princes slain.

"Nothing is left," said Agamemnon, "but ashes that may be smoldering still. Now, here at home in Argos, you hint of other ills. That some may be disloyal, I can well believe. Few men are born that can revere the great and fortunate without envy. The man who is already sick with misfortune finds not medicine but a poison in another's happiness. Too many times have I myself encountered false images of friendship and counterfeits of praise. Of all who went with me, only Odysseus—and he sailed against his will—proved ever true in harness. And this I will say though I do not know whether he is now alive or dead.

"But soon," said Agamemnon, "we shall call a council and debate such things as touch the gods or the welfare of our state. We shall strengthen all things we find good. And if there is anything diseased or rotten, we shall apply the red-hot iron or the surgeon's knife.

"Now let me enter my home and pray that this victory of mine will abide with me till the end of my days."

But Clytemnestra, whose maids were now spreading a carpet of priceless fabrics, stayed him with her hand as she addressed them:

"Citizens and elders of Argos, I am no maiden who would blush to confess her hot desires or to admit how she suffers without her lord. And, oh, how many dire rumors were brought to me! Indeed, my husband would have been a fish net, full of holes, had he sustained each wound they told me of. And he would have needed more bodies than the threefold monster, Geryon, to have ever died so many deaths. So distressed was I that often others had to tear from my neck the rope with which I tried to hang myself."

Turning to Agamemnon, she said: "Our child Orestes, the fruit of your love and mine, is not here to greet you as he should be. But I feared if anything dread should happen to you in Ilium the people might rise in revolt and slay him too. So I sent him to the home of Strophius, our friend in Phocis."

So she said, but in truth it was the violent hands of her lover Aegisthus she feared.

"My eyes are dry," she said, "for they have drained the well of tears. They are sore from ever watching for beacon lights and weary from loss of sleep. For any sleep that came would quickly end with but the faintest buzzing of a gnat. O my lord," she cried, "you are everything to me—like a faithful watchdog to a flock—a stout mast to a ship—the pillar that supports a roof—an only son to a father past begetting —land to a shipwrecked sailor—clear dawn after a storm— water to a desert traveler . . ."

"Enough, enough, O daughter of Leda!" Agamemnon broke in. "Your protests, like my absence, have run to too great length. And grovel not before me as to some barbarian king. Respect me as a man, but do not revere me as a god. And do not ask me to tread on all these costly tapestries. To show such folly and presumption would surely draw the envy of the gods and well might I be smitten by the hand of vengeance. How blest I am will truly not be known till I am dead. Yet, if I always act with such humbleness as I feel today, I shall never fear the wrath of heaven."

"Oh, do not deny me," Clytemnestra pleaded. "The foot that trampled Troy is far too mighty to tread the common earth."

"No, I must not," Agamemnon said.

"Must not? Are you afraid? Did you make some vow to the gods to come home like a common peasant?"

"No, I made no vow. It is only what any man of sense would approve."

"What would King Priam have done had the triumph been his?"

"Doubtless he would have set his foot on all this finery."

"Then care not for what the envious people think."

"You are indeed determined," Agamemnon said.

"O my lord," Clytemnestra pleaded, "will you who have

won so many victories begrudge your wife this very little one?"

"Then, woman, have your way," Agamemnon muttered. "But even if the gods care less, this is a shameful waste of wealth, to grind such precious handiwork into the dust."

"We have a sea of costly purple and none can drain it dry," said Clytemnestra. "This house is rooted deep in riches and ever puts forth leaves. Ten times these costly tapestries I would have trodden underfoot a thousand times to ransom your life and buy your safe return from Troy."

Yet, to remain as humble as he could, Agamemnon bade his servants take his sandals off that he might tread the crimson pathway barefoot. A moan from the woman in the other chariot brought her to his mind.

"Receive this woman kindly," he urged his wife, "for God looks down with favor on a gentle master. No one wears the yoke of slavery willingly. But she, the choicest flower of Troy's rich treasures, was my army's gift to me and never since has left my side."

The woman wild of eye and bearing the signs of prophecy was Cassandra, famed daughter of King Priam. Apollo had given her the gift of prophecy, yet cursed his gift so that her words should never be believed or understood. In vain she had cried in Troy against receiving Helen in her father's halls. In vain she had inveighed against the treacherous horse, laden with its cargo of death. Now she sat in speechless horror, appalled by some new vision.

His concubine! The knife of jealousy still could pierce the breast of Clytemnestra, but she smiled at her husband. "She is most welcome to our hearth and altars, and gladly will I minister to you both. But come, my lord. Your bath awaits."

Her black eyes shone with triumph as Agamemnon set his cautious foot down on her path and made his way within.

The old men dimly sensed some lurking evil, like the unseen rocks beneath a glassy sea that suddenly tear a ship asunder. Clytemnestra turned to Cassandra.

"Come within," she said, "and join our slaves in sacrifices to our bounteous gods. Leave your chariot, and be not proud. Even mighty Heracles once ate the bread of slavery. And be not afraid. The newly rich are often cruel, but in our halls of ancient wealth you will receive such treatment as you merit."

Cassandra gave no sign, but stared as in a trance.

"She speaks to you," an old man told her. "You should answer her."

"My words were plain enough," said Clytemnestra, "unless she knows only some barbaric tongue. Even so she could not mistake my gestures."

"Go with her," the old man bade Cassandra kindly. "You have no better choice." But the prophetess did not move.

"I have no time to dally with this woman," Clytemnestra exclaimed. "Already the victim stands ready at the altar for the sacrifice within—O joy unexpected that is mine!"

"The woman may be frightened like a wild thing newly captured," the old man said softly.

"No, she is mad from brooding on her fate," said Clytemnestra. "I will waste no more words nor heed her insults any longer." She turned and went inside.

Then suddenly Cassandra sprang up in her chariot with an anguished cry:

"Oh, my god! Apollo! Apollo!"

"Here, here!" an old man admonished her. "You must not call upon Apollo with a voice of wailing."

"O Apollo! Apollo!" she sobbed.

"This is ill-omened," the old man protested. "It ill befits the god of the golden sun to go where there is lamentation."

"O Apollo, my destroyer," she cried, "I see him!"

Her eyes were on a marble statue, but her terror seemed to make it live.

"Is she gripped in some prophetic spell?" one asked.

"O Apollo, my destroyer, what house is this you have brought me to?"

"Surely you know it is the house of Agamemnon son of Atreus," they assured her.

"No," she cried. "It is a house hated by heaven, a human slaughterhouse, a house of slain kin. Its floors are running with blood."

"Like a hound she is tracking down old evils," one whispered in horror.

"I see them, I see them!" Cassandra screamed. "Babes crying, babes who were slain and roasted for their father's meal."

"No! No!" But the old men's cries came too late to stop the ominous words. The Trojan woman had brought to light the darkest rumor ever to haunt these halls. Murder, lust, deceit, and greed long had raged in the bitter struggle for the throne of Pelops, and some of the tales had seeped beyond the palace walls. That Aegisthus' father, Thyestes, had seduced his brother Atreus' wife was one of them. But who could believe that in revenge Atreus had butchered Thyestes' children—all except Aegisthus who escaped—and in a palace banquet served the children's flesh to their hapless father.

Who could believe it? Who would dare speak of it? Still who could doubt it now when this woman from an alien land, a stranger to Argos and its whispers, had seen it all again with a seer's sure eyes?

"Oh, woe! woe!" Cassandra cried. "What monstrous horror is she now planning within—for him—for me?"

Before they had understood her all too well. But now the curse of Apollo lay on her words of things to come. They understood her not.

"O monstrous creature," Cassandra shrieked, "is this your

plan—for your own bed-partner while you bathe him? I see her evil hands reaching this way and that."

They stood bewildered at this woman who seemed to see through liquid time and walls of stone.

"Ha! I see them," she cried on, "the overhanging tapestries—enfolding nets of death—the hounds of vengeance."

These nets? This vengeance? They paled as the blood shrank back in their veins. Yet what did she mean?

"O gods, keep the bull from his mate," she cried. "Furiously she will gore him with her horn. He falls in the water. Oh, the guile of that murderous bath! Why did you bring me here to look on death—and die?"

"What god afflicts you?" they asked. "What is this clouded prophecy?"

Still she chanted at length, moaning over Paris and his fatal bride . . . the River Scamander of her unhappy youth . . . Hell's Rivers of Hate and Wailing that lay ahead . . . her father's city on whose altars hundreds of kine had been slaughtered in vain.

"We know of these woes and pity you," one said, "but the end you tell we cannot see."

"I shall speak plainly," she said as she tried to shake off the spell. "Above these halls a discordant choir chants endlessly of evil. Furies, drunk with human blood, revel in hatred for the defiler of a brother's bed. Now am I a false peddler of tales in the streets or do I speak the truth?"

"What god has given you—bred beyond the sea—such knowledge of old evils here?"

"It was Apollo, who burned with desire for me, enfolding my body in a wrestler's arms and panting eager love."

"And did he spend his lust in you as common mortals do?" they asked eagerly.

"Alas, no! I promised him, I led him on, but in the end I cheated him."

"And still he gave you his prophetic gift?"

"What he had given already he would not take back. But since I had played him false, he added a curse to his gift so that none should ever believe me."

"We believe you," they said. But in truth they grasped only those words that spoke of the past which none could change.

"It is for those slaughtered children," she said—"I see them sitting on the roof holding their entrails in their hands—that the cowardly lion has wallowed in my master's lair. Little does the conqueror of Ilium know the evil plans of that hateful bitch who fawned and licked his hand. But what will be, will be. And soon in pity you will find my words too true." Then struggling against the curse of the god, she forced the words out plainly: "You shall see the doom of Agamemnon."

"May the gods forbid!" they cried, thinking she spoke of some distant day.

"Are you only going to pray," she asked, "while murder brews?"

"What man would dare?" they asked.

"Man?" she cried in despair. "Then my words still miss the mark."

O the curse of Apollo! In vain she struggled against her coming doom. In vain she sought help. In vain she tried to use the speech of common men and make them understand. But the god ruled her tongue and forced her into such dark sayings as only oracles and poets use.

"Woe! Woe! The fire comes over me," she told them. "That two-footed lioness, who beds with the wolf when the noble lion is away, will slay me, too. My doom is mingled in her poison brew. Already she is whetting the sword. Why then do I bear these trappings of the god that only mock me?"

Cassandra broke in two the seer's wand. She tore the prophetic wreath from her hair. She threw them on the ground and trampled on them, shouting:

"These at least I will destroy before I am destroyed. Damn these symbols of Apollo! Because of them my friends became foes, and I was taunted as 'beggar' and 'wretch,' like some starved fortuneteller in a wandering carnival.

"I shall kneel at a butcher's block rather than at my father's altar. But my death shall not go unavenged. Far away a man-child is being reared, the rightful heir of this line. And he shall come back a wanderer to slay the mother and avenge the father, to put the capstone on this house of hate." Her voice grew calmer. "But why do I lament? This has been my fate since first I saw the light in Ilium. I greet these portals of death, and all that I pray for is one swift stroke to end my agony."

"If death indeed awaits you," one asked, "how can you go calmly, like some well-omened ox, to the altar?"

"There is no escape and no more time, my friends."

"You have a brave spirit."

"Ah, those are words a happy person never hears."

At the very door, however, she leaped back with a cry, like a heifer that catches the first scent of the butchery ahead.

"Ugh! This house reeks of blood."

"It is only the victims of sacrifice at the altar," one tried to reassure her.

"No, it is the stench of the tomb," she said, "but I must go on. Remember me in the day when the avenger comes to slay another woman and her sinful consort." She turned her eyes to the sun she would never look upon again and prayed that those who slew would be as easily slain.

"Alas, for the life of man," she said. "Whether his life be blessed or cursed, his little story is quickly wiped off the slate by one stroke of a wet sponge. For this I weep."

They pitied her. But the spell of disbelief was still upon them until they heard a cry of mortal pain within.

"Help! Help! I have been struck a deadly blow!"

Whose voice was that? A man's.

"Oh, help me! Save me from this sword!"

The mist was swept away. There was no doubt. The cries were Agamemnon's. But who were the slayers? Was this some plot to seize the throne?

They heard a woman's shriek and trembled. Dared they face these armed assassins?

"Come! Death is better than tyranny," an old man cried.

They burst through the palace doors and beheld an awful sight.

In the silver bath, its waters red with blood, lay the corpse of Agamemnon, tangled in the draperies like a beast that is caught in a net. Nearby on the marble floor lay the body of Cassandra, her wild eyes still staring at the vaulted ceiling. Above them Clytemnestra towered, sword in hand, her robes all spattered with blood, mad triumph shining in her eyes.

"Yes, I lied to you before," she said, "and I have no shame to say it now. How else could I have achieved this glorious end? Right here I did the deed; I will not deny it. In these draperies I entangled him, then struck him twice—and twice he cried out, then his limbs fell slack. When he had fallen I gave him one last stroke of grace to commend him to the God of Death. And as he gasped his life away his blood showered over me like the dew of heaven. Elders, rejoice! The cup of sorrows he filled in this house he has drunk to the very dregs."

"Brazen-tongued woman," one cried, "how can you glory so over this man?"

"You treat me still as a witless child," she said, exulting, "but I care no more for your praise or blame. Here lies my husband Agamemnon dead, the skilful handiwork of my just right hand. What is done, is done."

"Woman, on what poisons have you fed," one cried, "to do

this unholy deed and win a people's curse? You shall be driven from this land."

"So now you would decree my exile," she said in scorn, "though never against him were your voices raised. Caring no more than if she had been an animal—and he had sheep aplenty in his folds to sacrifice—he slew his own daughter, my dearest child, to stop the Thracian winds. That was the pollution you should have purged. Well, now you may work your will with me—if you can find the power."

"Proud words!" said one. "But stripped of friends and honor you will pay for this, blow for blow."

"The debt is already paid," she said. "It was in justice for my child that I sacrificed this man to Vengeance and the Furies. Nor will I have any fear so long as the fire on my hearth burns for my protector Aegisthus. There in the bath is the faithless husband who lay with Chryseis and all the captive women at Troy. And there she lies—his latest slave, his prophetess, his shipboard harlot. Both met their proper fate. And she, like the swan, has sung her last lament. The memory will add relish to my new bed of delight."

"Oh, what fiends you sisters were to bring disaster to so many lives," one exclaimed. "Helen blinded by love and you by hate. Alas, my King, my King! How shall I weep for you, caught in the web of this fateful spider, slain in treachery by your own wife?"

"Call me not his wife," said Clytemnestra, "but a Fury who put on the guise of a wife to purge the sins of the house of Atreus."

"These old evils do not make you guiltless of this present murder."

"He capped those evils by his own," Clytemnestra said. "And with this sword I have avenged my tears for that child of his and mine."

"Would to the gods I had never lived to see this day," an old man cried. "Now who will bury him or weep? Will you, cruel woman, crown your handiwork with a widow's tears?"

"We shall bury him ourselves and no concern of yours," said Clytemnestra. "But I promise you no tears will be shed for him within this house. No, let Iphigenia greet her loving father at the river's brink in Hades and embrace him with a loving kiss."

Thus did one reproach lead to another.

"True justice is hard to find," said the eldest among them. "Crime begets crime and slayers are slain. So long as Zeus abides on his throne, this law abides: As ye sow, so shall ye reap. Who then can ever cleanse this race of the very seeds of its curse? For it is rooted in mad lust for ruin."

"Ah, there you have hit on the bitter truth," said Clytemnestra. "So let this deed be the end of it all. Gladly will I make a bargain with the fiends that haunt this house. All that is past I will endure, hard though it be, if they will carry away this carnage of kin to plague the halls of others. For if I can rid this house of murder, I shall be content with only a little of its wealth."

Before they could ponder her plea, Aegisthus and his men at arms moved in among them.

"O happy dawn of vengeance!" Aegisthus son of Thyestes cried. "Now I can say the gods of retribution do look down upon us. Behold how this man, enmeshed in a robe spun by the Furies, has paid for the evil deeds of his father."

He reminded them once more of the ghastly banquet.

"And when my father learned the truth," he said, "he vomited forth his children's flesh. He smashed the table with a mighty curse—that all the race of Atreus should perish. Atreus he slew with his own hands, and now my wits have slain his son. That is why this man has fallen here. It was I who justly contrived his death. A babe in swaddling clothes when exiled with my father, now grown to manhood, I was brought back by Justice. For years I schemed for his death, and now its taste is sweet."

"Shame, Aegisthus, to sully sorrow with such insults," an old man rebuked him. "If this plan was yours you will not escape the stones and curses of the people."

"Is this a fit way for a slave at the oar to talk to the master of the ship?" retorted Aegisthus. "You may have to learn a bitter lesson. Hunger and chains are good teachers even for the very old. The ass that kicks against the goad will only hurt its heels."

"You are really the woman," the old man said scornfully, "staying at home while men were fighting—and soiling the bed of a warrior's wife."

"These are words to bring tears to the eye," Aegisthus scoffed, "but the tears will be yours."

"How can you lord it over Argive men, you who could plan a murder but had no stomach for doing it?"

"The trickery was rightly woman's work," Aegisthus explained. "I, as an ancient enemy, would have been suspected. But now with this man's wealth I shall control the people. And hard it will go with those who are unruly."

"Your cowardly soul," the old man persisted, "left this slaying to a woman—a pestilence to her country and her country's gods. But if Agamemnon's son Orestes is alive, then, the gods willing, some day he will return to slay you both in triumph."

"So you want your lesson now," Aegisthus cried. "My guards, here is work for you."

"Let every man seize his sword," the old man shouted impotently.

Aegisthus drew his own, but Clytemnestra stepped before him.

"No, my dear one, let us put an end to strife," she said.

"Blood enough has flowed already. Old men, go home and yield to the needs of the hour before you suffer harm. We did what we had to do. Beyond that, let fate take its course."

"But these men have insulted me," said Aegisthus.

"No Argive cringes before a coward," the old man said.

"You will suffer for that."

"And be avenged if God guides Orestes home."

"Exiles can only feed on hopes," said Aegisthus.

"Go ahead, soil justice; grow fat while you may," the old man cried. "But some day Orestes will return."

Clytemnestra took Aegisthus by the arm.

"Come with me, my love," she said. "Pay no heed to their idle yelpings. You and I are masters now. We two shall set this house in order."

But would it ever be in order?

Evils purge evils, the old men thought as they slowly went away. But when would the chain of evils end?

Does man possess a rational will or only a complex set of responses to stimuli? Agamemnon, Clytemnestra, and Aegisthus all act under compulsions but rationalize their deeds as just. There are close ties between Aeschylus and modern Freudian literature, for each assumes some deep, consistent patterns beneath our tangled deeds and feelings.

Sin or crime has a chain reaction in Aeschylus. Evil begets evil with almost the same inevitability as Newton's Third Law of Motion, that "for every action there is an equal and opposite reaction." Aeschylus was concerned with how the chain of evil could be ended, but it is not surprising that he saw it as a sort of divine or "natural" law in operation.

In discovering the difference between *nature* with its immutable laws and *custom* with its capricious beliefs, the Greeks touched off a great debate about the gods. Were they realities of nature or figments of belief? The Sophists, who influenced Euripides, assigned the gods to custom as pure inventions of human minds; there were man-made laws but no divine ones. Crimes were crimes only if you were caught. Fears and guilt feelings were inside you and not something inflicted on you by the gods or their Furies.

The opposite view was that the gods—in some form—were real. That is, they were a part of nature, or nature itself, and operated by fixed and eternal laws. So Aeschylus believed. And since natural laws do not conflict, he did not believe the moral law could be found in such conflicting deities as Artemis or Aphrodite. There must be some higher power whose name he did not know. He thought it might well be called Zeus. Hence his essential monotheism.

The Greek principle of the golden mean or "nothing in excess" was supposedly all-pervading. Defying nature's limits, as we know too well, leads to injury, disease, or death. Similarly under moral law, going beyond the limits (*hybris*) must be followed by punishment (*nemesis*). However, the gods do not always operate this moral law directly. The guilty are not always immediately maimed, blinded, or slain by bolts from the blue. The gods usually act through men claiming blood for blood. Often, one member of a family suffers for another.

We forget, today, what must have been very evident before the establishment of criminal justice —that punishment itself is akin to crime. Our law slays—and it used to beat and torture—it kidnaps, it imprisons, or it commits "robbery" by fining a man. These sanctioned "crimes" are committed in the name of "the People" or "the Queen," as they were once committed in the name of the gods.

Clytemnestra and Aegisthus both assert they are mere instruments of divine justice, but the Athenians, like ourselves, tended to take a dim view of self-appointed enforcers of moral law.

The problem is first stated in *Agamemnon* with its refrain of "Evils purge evils, but when will the chain of evils end?" For casual readers, *Agamemnon* is the most interesting story of the trilogy because it presents a case history of lurid crime. We can read of its sex, blood, and gold and not worry about its deeper meanings. In the end, Clytemnestra, like all aggressors, calls for peace, which means only that she wants to be left in peace now that she has gained what she wanted.

But a new theme begins. The pendulum of evil has not stopped swinging. Orestes lives, with a sacred duty to avenge his father.

The second play of Aeschylus' trilogy, then, will set up a perfect test case for the third. As Aeschylus relates it, there will be no question that moral law demands Orestes slay his father's slayers; there will be no question that this act of justice will in turn be a horrible sin—that is unless gods and men can devise some means of stopping the pendulum in its fearful swing.

ELECTRA

CHARACTERS

Electra (Ee-LEK-tra): Daughter of the murdered King Agamemnon and of Clytemnestra.

Chrysothemis (Kris-SAW-them-is): Sister of Electra.

Clytemnestra (Kli-tem-NESS-tra): Slayer of her husband Agamemnon, now living with Aegisthus.

Orestes (O-REST-eez): Long-absent brother of Electra, awaited as the avenger of his father's murder.

Aegisthus (Ee-JISS-thoos): The usurper-king of Argos, Clytemnestra's consort, who abetted the murder.

Pylades (PILL-a-deez): Son of Strophius of Phocis, Orestes' cousin and constant companion.

An old tutor of Orestes.

An old nurse of Orestes, called "the Cilician woman" or Cilissa (Sil-LISS-a).

Servants of the palace at Argos.

All three dramatists wrote of Electra and Orestes, and by luck, all three plays have been preserved. They are gold mines of comparative evidence on how each poet carried out his creative task. Sophocles focused on Electra as an unyielding hero, Aeschylus on Orestes and the great moral dilemma, Euripides (with much free invention) on psychological studies of all his characters.

To create a single story, I have risked the ire of purists by blending two of the three plays. In essence, I have taken the more dramatic story of Sophocles and blended with it some of the elements of *The Libation Bearers,* as Aeschylus calls this play of his trilogy. Neither dramatist alone would have written precisely this story. Aeschylus would not have ducked the moral issue, and Sophocles never would have presented a conflict-torn hero.

Hamlet to the contrary, drama is not the best medium for presenting inner conflict. A novelist can go into a mind to see what is churning there, but the dramatist has to externalize conflict in some way. Instead of a soliloquizing Hamlet, Sophocles would probably have created two brothers. Thus he avoids any conflict in Antigone by splitting her, as it were, into her self and the more yielding Ismene.

The same technique is used in this story. Electra does not debate the issue with herself but with a sister, Chrysothemis, who does not appear in either of the other two versions.

ELECTRA

(SOPHOCLES AND AESCHYLUS)

Dawn's bright beams had set the birds to twittering, but not a soul was abroad in Argos as three travelers, an old man and two youths in Phocian dress, plodded through the empty streets.

The old man was lean and leathery, with a grizzled beard, yet agile enough as he led the way. One youth was fair, of sturdy build and pleasant countenance. The other was taller and dark, with a somber, restless look. He seemed to be in deep thought, little heeding the old man's tales of the city's founder, Inachus, and his daughter Io, beloved by Zeus and changed to a gadfly-driven heifer by the jealous wife of the god.

At last the three came out into an open square.

"This is our marketplace, named for Apollo, the Wolf-slayer," the old man said. "Over there on the left is the far-famed Temple of Hera." They cut across the still-shuttered agora and came to some steps and a short, broad mall leading up to a massive marble structure.

"There it stands," the old man said—"the palace, rich in treasure, lust and blood; the ancient home of Pelops, Atreus, and Agamemnon. Today, please the gods, it will be yours, Orestes."

The brooding youth came to with a start. His dark eyes surveyed the lofty walls, the brazen gates, and the stone-carved lions overhead. The palace of his father Agamemnon! It was just as the old man had often described it to him, but he had little memory of it. Somewhere within was his mother, Clytemnestra. He could not really remember her either. Yet she haunted his thoughts like some fabled creature too awful to be believed—that monster in blood-spattered robes who, sword in hand, had stood over his father's corpse and laughed at the people's curses.

And now, as he knew from Electra's secret letters, this mother was keeping his sisters in hateful virginity for fear of their breeding avengers while she lay with her lover Aegisthus, begetting children to cheat him of his birthright.

"It was here," he heard the old man saying, "that I received you from Electra and Cilissa, your nurse, to carry you off to the halls of Strophius far beyond the murderous reach of Aegisthus. A mother's love may have flickered still in Clytemnestra's breast, for she failed to stop us then. But since the day she slew your father she has often tried to lure you back, for only your death could let her rest."

Through childhood and youth this old tutor had served Orestes well. He had taught the boy all the arts of statecraft, and molded his body and mind for this very day when he should return to avenge his father and claim his own.

By all the laws of earth and heaven, the defiler of his father's bed and usurper of his throne must die. But what of the faithless wife who slew his father with her own hand? Dimly Orestes knew what that word "mother" meant to other men. To him it meant nothing but evil. And when he had gone to Delphi to seek advice from the oracle of Phoebus Apollo, the answer had been clear: He must slay the slayers or bear forever the torments that come from a father's spirit unavenged.

"The hour has come," the old man said. "And before the people fill the streets, we must lay our plans, then swiftly act. What say you, Pylades?"

The fair youth smiled at the older man—so loyal, he thought, to his cousin Orestes, so like a well-bred charger that never grows too old to prick up its ears for battle. Yet, as he looked at those massive walls, Pylades hesitated.

"Should we not return to Phocis and beg my father Strophius for an army?" he asked.

"No," said Orestes. "The Pythian oracle commanded otherwise. I was not to bring shields or arms, it said. My vengeance was just, but I was to steal it by hand and wit alone." He turned to the older man. "You know the city well. So stay for a time in the marketplace and glean all the news you can. Then watch your chance to enter the palace and note all that happens there. I shall need your report. Have no fear of being known or suspected, for age with its frosted foliage should be your best disguise. And you can feign a Phocian accent.

"Tell them their friends in Phocis have sent you here to report my death, and confirm it with an oath. Let us say I was killed in a chariot race at Delphi. Oh, you can tell it well, for I still remember your wonderful stories when I was a lad."

"I shall tell a tale that will make me weep myself," the old man promised.

"Meanwhile," Orestes said, "I shall go with Pylades to my father's tomb, as the oracle bade, to pour libations and leave, with my prayers, a lock of hair. Then, when the sun is halfway up in the sky, I will bring this brazen funeral urn to the palace to confirm your tale, I shall show them that I am dead and harmless as dust and ashes. Our enemies will rejoice and welcome us to their evil hearts. Then shall I rise from the dead to blaze like a meteor on their sight. Enough! Take care, old man. Time will be master of our task."

By now a sleepy peasant had prodded his laden donkey into the marketplace. A merchant was opening his little shop. The day had begun in Argos. Orestes embraced the old man in silence, then went his way with Pylades, seeking his father's tomb. He knew from Electra's letters that he should find it beyond the palace, down by the river. Beneath the walls he paused for a moment. Was it only his fancy or did he hear a groan from within? No matter now. With the help of the gods he would soon be purging this palace of evil. His enemies would be slain, the ancient wealth all his, and his banishment ended forever.

Within the walls, Electra arose from her bed of straw in the dark and musty servants' quarters to greet another day with hate and lamentation. Like Niobe, who was turned to stone but still shed tears for her slaughtered children, Electra had never ceased to mourn her father. Even her friends had chided her unrelenting grief. And Aegisthus and Clytemnestra, irked by the endless reproach of her eyes and tongue, had banished her from their hall and banquet table to feed on servants' scraps and flaunt her rags of mourning beyond their sight.

This day, since Aegisthus had taken his henchmen down to the harbor to guard the unloading of a rich, new cargo from Asia, Electra knew she could wander out and not have to see his leering face. In the courtyard she found her sister, Chrysothemis. Chrysothemis, she reflected once again, was beautiful, gentle and fair, like their long lost sister, Iphigenia. Electra's own features were stern and dark, more like her hated mother's. And while Electra proclaimed her martyrdom with unkempt hair, a ragged dress and tear-stained cheeks, her well-groomed sister wore shimmering, sea-blue silks and the costliest of finery. For Chrysothemis had long since yielded to evils she could not change. Though guarded against all men, she was otherwise free to share the luxuries of the palace and live as a pampered princess.

Electra despised her sister. The gentle Chrysothemis could feel only pity in return.

"Poor sister," Chrysothemis said, "all your prayers and moaning can never bring back our father from Hades' shore. Eight years he is gone, and you only destroy yourself with your hate and grief."

"I can never forget—nor forgive his foes," Electra said.

"But mighty Zeus, who sees and rules all things, is still in his heaven. Leave your cares to him and to Time, the healing god."

"How can a woman so nobly born fawn on her father's slayers?" Electra demanded. "How can you endure the evils that flourish around us? Our mother becomes more hateful day by day. She laughs and glories in her sins. And every month she awaits the return of that day she trapped and slew our father to mark it with dances and sacrifices of sheep.

"How can you bear to see Aegisthus sitting smugly on our father's throne, wearing the very robes he wore, spilling wine at the hearth where he was slain? And most monstrous of all, how can you bear to hear them reveling in our father's bed; that assassin locked in the embrace of our shameless mother, if a harlot deserves that name?"

"Do you think that I never weep from shame?" Chrysothemis asked. "But against their might I have no strength. One cannot always be brooding to no avail. You weep too much."

"I do not have tears enough to weep as my heart desires," said Electra. "But do not berate me the way our mother does. She calls me a spiteful, godforsaken wretch and jeers, 'Are you the only one who has ever lost a father, the only mortal touched by grief?' Then, if she hears of Orestes' threats, she comes shrieking in my ear: 'This is your doing. You stole him from my hands and you will pay for it.' And he eggs her on that mightless mate of hers, that bed-sheet warrior. Oh, if only Orestes would come and end these evils!"

"Surely the people would welcome him," Chrysothemis agreed.

"He says he yearns for us," Electra complained, "but he lingers far away. He says he will come, but he does not come."

"On the brink of great deeds a man must be cautious."

"I was not cautious when I saved him."

"Surely one so nobly born could never fail us utterly."

"I hope not," Electra said, "or I would not have lived so long."

"But meanwhile," Chrysothemis said, "you must learn to curb your idle raging. I, too, chafe at all these wrongs. Were it any use, I would even decry them from the housetops. But in a storm one must reef his sails. Threats that we cannot carry out are useless. I grant that right lies more on your side than on mine. But I remain free by keeping a silent tongue. What have *you* gained but misery?"

"For shame to forget our father and plead your mother's cause," said Electra. "These are her words, not yours. What could I gain by yielding as you have done? I still have my life—a wretched one, I admit, but enough. For while I live I can vex them. In that poor way, at least, I can honor the dead. You deny any love for our father's slayers, yet you dwell with them in comfort. Never will I thus sell my soul to sup at their table. You could have won praise as the daughter of the noblest man that ever lived. Instead, you choose to proclaim yourself as your mother's child."

"I understand you too well to be offended," Chrysothemis said, "but still I must warn you of danger."

"Tell me what worse I could suffer," Electra scoffed, "and I *will* be silent."

"If your plaints do not end," Chrysothemis said, "they plan to shut you away in a dungeon to mourn alone. Never chide me for failing to warn you. There still is time to repent."

"And when will this be?" Electra asked.

"As soon as Aegisthus returns."

"Then let him hurry. At least that will take me farther away from you."

"Why will you never heed me?"

"And learn to betray my friends?"

"No. Learn to submit to the strong."

"I would sooner suffer for my father's sake."

"Surely our father forgives my weakness," Chrysothemis said.

"A noble thought—for a coward," Electra sneered.

Chrysothemis gave up, sadly.

"Well, I must go," she said, "for my mother has bidden me take some offerings to our father's tomb."

"What is that—offerings to her direst enemy?"

"Yes. Why not say it—to the man she murdered?"

"What caused this whim?"

"Some terrible dream she had, I think."

"Gods of my father, help me!" Electra exclaimed. "What was the omen? Tell me all."

"She dreamed she gave birth to a serpent."

"I am not surprised. What else?"

"She wrapped it in swaddling clothes like a babe, then offered her breast to it."

"And the creature sank its fangs in her nipple, I hope," said Electra.

"No, she suckled it, but the milk it drew was mixed with

clots of blood. She woke up screaming. So much I overheard from her frightened prayer at dawn to the Sun-god. I know no more, except for these offerings. It all means little, I think. But, Sister, listen to me. Do not destroy yourself by your folly."

"I think the dream means much," said Electra. "But never let these offerings touch our father's tomb. It would be sinful to soil his grave with gifts from such a wife. Cast them to the winds, or bury them in the ground. Let her find them there when she dies herself. Our father would not receive them kindly, nor could they purge her guilt. But take this lock of hair instead and give him one of your own as well. Take also my maiden sash and lay it upon the tomb. Then kneel and pray that Orestes will come to avenge the dead so that soon we may crown his grave with costlier gifts. This dream was surely a sign from him."

"I will do as you bid," Chrysothemis agreed, "for it is good and within my power. Still, if you love me, never let my mother know of my boldness, or I shall suffer."

As Chrysothemis left, Electra pondered the dream. What could it mean but that Orestes, born and suckled by Clytemnestra, soon would return to quench his vengeance with blood?

Suddenly her thoughts were broken as Clytemnestra loomed before her, an awesome figure in robes of scarlet and Tyrian purple, her harsh, gaunt features unrelieved by the clusters of jewels that dangled from her ears and the heavy circles of gold that jangled about her arms and ankles.

"So! Out-of-doors again to peddle your grief and scandal," she exclaimed. Then, disturbed by her dream, perhaps, she changed her tone to one of defense. "If I ever abuse you," she said, "it is only because I am stung by your insults. Your father's death does not excuse them. I killed him, yes, but not I alone, for Justice guided my hand. You, too, would side with Justice if you were wise. For that father you mourn was the only one of all the Greeks brutal enough to slay his daughter. And Iphigenia was your sister."

"What he did was not by choice," said Electra.

"Then why did he sacrifice her?" demanded Clytemnestra. "For the Greeks, you say? They had no right to kill my child. For Menelaos? He had two children himself—more fitting victims for his and Helen's war. Why was your father so tender to them, so cruel to the child I bore in pain? He was no father at heart. If my own dead girl could speak, she would say the same. So be not blinded by passion or hate if you wish to be my judge."

"I did not begin this argument," Electra said, "but by your leave I would answer you."

"You have my leave," Clytemnestra said. "Had you always shown as much respect, you might have vexed my ears much less."

"Then listen. You admit that you killed my father. Could any deed be blacker than that, whatever its cause? A faithful wife, indeed! You hoped Agamemnon would never come back.

"But consider this, too. Why did the Huntress Artemis have her way with the winds at Aulis? She was angry at my father and no one else. Only *his* daughter could appease her. Nothing else would let the suffering Argive host sail either for Troy or home. It was under such dire necessity and sore against his will that my father gave the goddess his daughter.

"But even if your words were true and he did it for Menelaos' sake, should you have slain him? If blood for blood is your law, then by that same law you yourself would be the first to die. Nor do your words excuse your shaming yourself in the bed of your partner in murder, bearing bastards to cheat your lawful children. Do you call this justice for a daughter's life?"

"Shameless girl, how can you say such vicious things about your mother?"

"It is not my words, but your deeds that are vicious. I merely clothe them in speech. But if motherhood is your only plea, I waste my breath. You are no mother—only a tyrant. And if there is anything shameless in me, it surely must come from you."

"You will rue those words when Aegisthus returns."

"Ha! First you give me leave to speak, then you threaten."

"You have had your say. Now hush your mad raving while I make the sacrifice for which I came."

"Go, make your sacrifice, if any god will heed you. I will say no more."

Clytemnestra called on her maids to lay offerings of fruit on the altar of Phoebus Apollo. Then she prayed in cryptic words:

"O Phoebus, protector, heal the dread that is haunting my soul. I cannot tell everything here among my enemies. For this girl would spread it all through the town with a poisonous tongue. But thou knowest all. Fulfill the meaning of this vision if it bodes me well; if not, protect me and turn it against my enemies. If any are plotting to steal my wealth and power, smite them down. Let me rule the house of Atreus in peace and wealth with those who love me and those of my children whose hearts are not warped with hate. Grant, I pray, what my heart desires, for nothing is hidden from thee."

"Grant her deserts and not her desires," Electra muttered beneath her breath. Then she and her mother both turned as they heard a voice at the gate.

"Excuse me, ladies, is this the home of the ruler Aegisthus?" The old man who spoke seemed a Phocian by his voice and dress.

"Your surmise is right," a handmaid said.

"Then I surmise this must be his mistress," the old man said with a bow to Clytemnestra, "for she looks like a queen. Rejoice, my lady, for I bring fair tidings from one of your friends."

"You are welcome," Clytemnestra said, "but who has sent you?"

"Phanoteus of Phocis with a weighty message."

"He is a friend, indeed. And what is your news?"

"To be brief, Orestes, your son, is dead."

Electra screamed in anguish.

"What—what did you say?" Clytemnestra asked, her black eyes gleaming. "Pay no attention to her."

"I say it again. Orestes is dead."

"O gods, this is the end of everything," Electra moaned.

"Be off about your business," Clytemnestra snapped at her, then turned to the stranger. "Tell me all of it."

The old man sighed and began:

"He went to that glorious festival famed through all Greece to compete in the games at Delphi. And what a handsome figure he was! When the heralds announced the first foot race, he stepped out on the track and everyone marveled at his body—so lithe and gleaming. And swift as an arrow he sped from the starting post to the finish line, winning their plaudits and the wreath of victory."

"And then?"

"O lady, I cannot begin to tell you of every contest that day. I must be brief. Suffice it to say he won them all. And a glad cheer rose from the crowd each time the judges proclaimed, 'Again the Argive wins—Orestes, son of Agamemnon, conqueror of Troy.' But anon my tale grows sad, for some god smote him for all his strength."

"Yes, yes?" Clytemnestra was leaning forward, as though she were trying to seize his words in her hands.

"It was toward sunset of another day when the chariot race was held. Many charioteers were entered, and the judges lined them up as each was assigned his place by lot. First was a driver from Sparta, then an Achaean, and one—no, two—from Libya. Yes, I remember Orestes' place was fifth with his mares from Thessaly. An Aetolian was sixth with a pair of golden fillies. A Magnesian was seventh, an Aenian eighth, with white horses as I recall. The ninth was from Athens and the tenth from Boeotia.

"Then the brass trumpet sounded and they were off, each shaking the reins and shouting at his steeds. The dust billowed up in clouds and the whole Crisaean plain echoed with thudding hoofs and rattling wheels. At first they were crowded together, none sparing the goad as each tried to pull away from the other's whirring wheels and snorting horses. The foam flew back on the chariots, and any driver who pulled ahead could feel the hot breath of other horses on his back.

"And what a race Orestes drove! You should have seen how closely and cleverly he grazed each pillar by checking his inside horse and urging on the outer one."

"And so his daring cost him his life?" asked Clytemnestra impatiently, but the old man was not to be hurried.

"Ah, lady, the race had only begun. All went well for many a round. Then, just past the turn for the seventh lap, the Aenian's hard-mouthed colts, the white ones, bolted headlong into the chariot from Barca. And that mishap sent them all careening and crashing into each other till the whole course was strewn with chariot wrecks. The shrewd Athenian driver saw the danger and pulled his team to one side."

"But my son . . ."

"He, too, steered clear, for he was running last just then, saving his mares for a burst of speed in the final stretch. But when he saw only the Athenian to beat, he shouted to his team and took out after him. So they plunged on yoke to yoke; now the one, now the other straining ahead by half a length.

"So far Orestes had driven a shrewd and steady race. But, just as he was rounding the very last pillar, he cut the turn too fine and his axle struck the pillar's edge. His axle-box was shattered, and he was hurled over the front of his chariot and caught in the reins, as his team dashed wildly on in panic. A wail of pity rose from the crowd to see him, the greatest champion of all till now, being dragged along, his body tossed heels over head in the air one moment and smashed to the ground the next. Finally, the other drivers stopped the mad dash of his frightened mares and cut him loose. But it was too late. His corpse was covered with dust and blood and mangled beyond the recognition of his dearest friends."

Electra buried her head in her hands as the old man went on:

"They burned his body on a pyre, and Phocian envoys will soon be bringing it here—shrunk to the measure of one small urn—so that his ashes may rest in the land of his birth. O it is sad enough to tell about, but to those of us who were there, it was the most piteous sight we had ever beheld."

He wiped the tears from his eyes.

"O Zeus, what can I say?" said Clytemnestra. "Shall I call these happy tidings or terrible for all their gain? Life is hard to bear when only such evils can save it."

"Why do you feel thus?" the old man asked.

"It is a strange thing to be a mother," said Clytemnestra. "No matter how she is abused she cannot wholly hate her child."

"Perhaps I should not have come."

"Oh, yes, you should. And let them hasten here with the proof. Orestes was born of my flesh, but he spurned the breast that nurtured him. He was stolen from my home and sight and grew up to breathe vile slanders and threats against my life. So long as he lived I never knew a single hour of sweet, untroubled sleep. Now, despite this vampire's thirst for my blood, I think I shall live in peace."

"O poor Orestes," Electra cried, "even in death you feel your mother's insults. Is there no justice?"

"Justice enough for him, though you have escaped," said Clytemnestra.

"How you gloat in your victory."

"A victory, indeed," said Clytemnestra, "and you cannot cheat me of it now."

"Alas it is we who are cheated," Electra said bitterly.

Clytemnestra turned to the old man and said, "Your tidings deserve a rich reward if only for stopping her endless yelping."

"Then I may go if all is well?"

"No, you must not go," said Clytemnestra. "Such hospitality would be unworthy of me and the master who sent you. You must come inside. Let us leave this wretched girl to her wailing."

Never before had Electra felt so desolate. Even the gods had deserted her now. She went in to her heap of straw and lay down, resolved to die. Let them kill me if they wish, she thought. That is the one kind deed they could do.

How long she lay there she did not know. But at last she felt a gentle hand on her brow. She looked up to see her sister's radiant face.

"I have come with words of hope," Chrysothemis said.

"Oh, do not afflict me more," Electra moaned.

"O Sister, I ran all the way to tell you; you will soon be free of your suffering and woe."

"I will—if you leave me to die."

"No, no," Chrysothemis said, "for Orestes has come, just as surely as I am standing here."

"My poor, witless sister," Electra said, "have you gone so mad that you laugh at our misery?"

"I am not mad. I swear I saw with my own eyes . . ."

"His ghost?"

"No, the proof he is here. When I went to our father's grave, I found it wet with fresh-poured milk and wreathed in flowers. I looked around in fear, then crept nearer. On the ledge of the tomb I found this lock of hair. Whose could it be but Orestes'? It is not our mother's, and you cannot leave these grounds. I took it in my hands and would have shouted aloud if I dared. Oh, it must be his, and destiny smiles at last."

"How I pity you in your dreaming," Electra sighed.

"Why do you not also rejoice?"

"Because Orestes is dead. And the dead cannot save us."

"It cannot be. Who told you this?"

"Alas, the very man who saw him perish. Even now you will find him in the palace—our mother's most cherished guest."

"Then who could have made the offerings?"

"Someone mourning Orestes, perhaps. They are bringing his ashes home in an urn."

"Oh, I was a fool," Chrysothemis wept, "running here with happy tidings the while he was dead. O what will become of us?"

Electra wondered. Orestes was her last hope, or was he? What right had she to die while her father was still unavenged? She sprang up with a surge of hate-fed strength. She led Chrysothemis out to the courtyard where no one could hear them without being seen.

"There still is hope," she said. "Will you help me?"
"To raise the dead?"
"That is silly. No, something within your power."
"I would help if I could," Chrysothemis said.
"Death has robbed us of our allies, but not of our lives," Electra said. "We must act ourselves. No, do not shrink back! If our mother alone could slay a far better man, surely two of us can be her equal. *We must kill Aegisthus!*"

Chrysothemis recoiled with a gasp.

"What else is left?" Electra urged. "Just look at yourself, ripe but unloved, unwooed, and unwed. Aegisthus is not such a fool as to let any man beget children by you. Only in dreams will you ever know any man so long as Aegisthus lives. Are you going to wait while your beauty withers, when one bold stroke could win you honor and freedom—yes, and the kind of man who would cherish a woman of spirit? Think how people will exclaim, 'Look at those sisters who risked their lives to avenge their father.' In life or death we will win men's praise. The choice is yours. Which shall it be: one deed of glory or a life of endless shame?"

"It is too late now," Chrysothemis said. "The time to strike was when our father died."

"I would have then if I had had my wits."

"You have lost them now," Chrysothemis said. "What frenzy drives you to rush to arms and seek my aid? We are women, not men. Our enemies' hands are strong while ours are weak. Their star rides high, but ours has set. Why, if your threats were even heard we would surely die. Forget your madness, and I will forget you breathed it."

"I might have known," said Electra. "Then I must do it alone."

"And I must try to stop you."

"Then go to your mother and tell her everything."

"I do not hate you," Chrysothemis protested. "I only tremble for us both."

"I envy your prudence," Electra said, "but I hate your fear."

"O heed me," Chrysothemis begged, "and when your words are wiser, then I will listen to you."

"I cannot heed words of shame and fear," said Electra, "so do not waste them on me. Just leave me to my fate."

It was useless, for neither would yield to the other. Too late, Chrysothemis felt, would Electra learn the wisdom born of necessity. But as she was turning away, two young men came in through the gate. Evidently mistaking the drab Electra for a servant, the taller and darker of the two addressed her:

"If this is the home of Aegisthus, will you tell your master two Phocians are waiting to see him?"

Electra could recognize neither youth. But, her eye fell on the urn in Pylades' hands, and she gave a cry:

"O strangers, have you come to confirm our woes?"

"I know naught of your joys or woes," Orestes answered warily. "I only know old Strophius sent us here to bear what little is left of Orestes."

"By the gods I beg you, strangers," Electra said, "let me hold his ashes in my hands that I may mourn for myself and all our race."

"Give her the urn," Orestes said, "for she seems a friend who will do us no harm."

As Electra clasped the urn, she wept:

"O dearest of mortals, have all of my hopes now turned to these ashes that lie so light in my hands, so heavy in my heart? A radiant child I sent you forth to meet your death in an alien land. And to think that strangers tended you at the last, so far from the sister who should have washed your dear dead body and gathered these remnants from the smoldering pyre. Would I had died instead. You were always my child and never your mother's; but all my loving care, though toil it never was, has been in vain. Your father perished, and now in your death I, too, am dead—and our enemies laugh. That mother, who is no mother, rages with joy to escape the vengeance you promised.

"Was this destined to be the return I was praying for, to clasp only lifeless dust instead of your vibrant body in my arms? O take me with you. For I am nothing and would share your nothingness. We shared our hopes among the living. Now let us share our lot among the dead who have ceased to mourn."

As Orestes realized this was Electra, this pitiable, wasted, unwed woman, tears welled in his eyes. Even the traces of lingering beauty made her plight seem sadder still.

"Stranger, why do you look at me so?" Electra asked.

"My woes are greater than I had thought," he said. "You must be Electra, and my heart is smitten to see your sad estate."

"There is far more that you cannot see," Electra said. "For I dwell with my father's murderers and feel the blows of a cruel mother."

"Can no one stay her hand?" Orestes asked.

"There was one—once," Electra said, "but now I hold his dust in my hands."

"Poor lady, I pity you."

"No one has ever pitied me before," Electra sighed. "Who are you, stranger? Some distant kin, perhaps?"

Pylades gave a warning glance toward Chrysothemis.

"If this fair maiden with you is a friend . . ." Orestes said.

"She is my sister Chrysothemis," Electra replied, "a friend in heart if not bold deeds."

"Then give me the urn, for you have no need of it."

"Oh, no!" Electra clasped it more tightly. "Do not rob me of the dearest thing left on earth. At least let me give Orestes burial."

"You shall not bury him," Orestes said, "for these ashes are only a sham."

"Then where is my poor brother's grave?"

"The living need no grave."

"He is alive?"

"As surely as I am," Orestes said.

"You mean you are . . ."

"Look!" Orestes held up his hand. "Is this not the token you sent me—our father's signet ring?"

With a cry of joy Electra threw herself in his arms, while tears of happiness shone in Chrysothemis' eyes. But as Electra began to pour out her joy and relief, Orestes kept trying to warn her. This was reckless. Someone within might overhear.

"There are only women within," Electra said. "What do I need to fear from women?"

"But one at least has the might of a man," Orestes said.

"Oh, do not remind me of what I can never forget," Electra said. Orestes' return had released her from such a weight of care that she would have talked on and on in her joy had not the palace door opened. She checked herself and they all fell back to their pose as strangers. The old nurse Cilissa came out.

"Oh, the troubles I have seen," she muttered to herself, "but never the like of this. Poor little Orestes! How lovingly I tended him all in vain. The dear helpless thing he was. For a child has no words to spell its needs, and its little body must work its own relief. A prophet I had to be, and a poor one at that. For I would no sooner change him than he would deceive me again. A busy laundress he kept me. And now to think he is dead!"

Time had grown vague in her mind, and she wept for Orestes still as a child.

When her dim eyes revealed the sisters she told them, "My mistress has sent me to fetch Aegisthus to hearken to the stranger's tale."

"How does she take the news?" Chrysothemis asked.

"To deceive her servants she drew a veil of gloom across her face," Cilissa said, "but she could not hide the light in her eyes from me. Then, to give full range to her joy she dismissed them all and bade me fetch Aegisthus to share it with her. And as I left she was showing the stranger Aegisthus' sword, the very one by which she slew my master."

"Tell Aegisthus she bids him speak to no one but to hasten here alone," Electra said.

The old nurse eyed her curiously. "You seem almost happy," she said.

"Why not if our fortunes change?" said Chrysothemis.

"Is there something I do not know?"

"No, of course not," Electra broke in with a warning look at her sister. She trusted Cilissa's heart but not her mind. "Just bid Aegisthus come swiftly—alone."

The old woman promised and went off, still moaning, "Poor little Orestes."

"Now there is no more time or need," Orestes said, "to tell me how evil our mother is or how Aegisthus is wasting our wealth. But let not your radiant face betray our secret."

"No fear, my brother, for I have suffered such evils at their hands that I can never smile when I look upon them." They went to the palace door, where the old man met them impatiently.

"Why have you tarried so long?" he whispered. "What

folly is this, these outbursts of joy and careless talk? Had I not been watching here, your secret would have been in this palace ahead of you. Only thanks to me, she still does not suspect."

"Brother, who is this man?" Electra whispered.

"Know you not the one to whom you entrusted me?"

"Oh, my faithful friend, my savior!" said Electra seizing and kissing his hand. "To think just now I was hating you, not knowing the joy you were really bringing. Hereafter let me call you 'Father,' the dearest name I know."

"Hush, daughter," he said. "Time enough for this in the days and nights to come." He told the two youths to follow him.

"Gods of my father, help me now," Orestes prayed.

And then he was facing her, the cruel, crafty, sinful creature of his dreams. Yet to his sight she seemed only a stranger; a woman, harsh-featured, aging, but much more frail than his dreams had pictured her. At the thought of his task he felt faint and ill, as on that day when first he had had to steel himself to sacrifice a trembling animal on the altar.

Remember your father, the bath, the net, the sword, he told himself. Remember all she has done. Into the reality of the woman before him he must fuse the monstrous image of his dreams. Like a priest in a trance he let the avenging god take possession of his mind and body.

She was speaking now in words of welcome, but he did not hear. Then she grew impatient. "The urn! The urn!" she cried. "Where are the ashes of my hated son?"

Slowly Orestes thrust his hand in his tunic and clasped the handle of his hidden dagger. Then he saw the sword of Aegisthus lying on the table—the sword that must have slain his father. He picked it up instead. Clytemnestra screamed as he moved toward her.

"You killed my father," he said, slowly, as one trying to recall a lesson.

"No, no," she cried. "It was not I but Justice."

The voice of the god seemed to speak through his lips as he said, "I am justice."

"Where is Aegisthus?" she asked wildly.

"Your lover will soon be here, and you will sleep by his side forever."

"Can you slay your mother, my child?" Her voice was reaching him in a dream and in that dream he was answering her.

"With this sword you slew yourself long ago."

"Do you not fear a mother's avenging Furies?"

"I must heed the wrath of my father's gods."

Then desperately Clytemnestra clenched her scarlet dress at the neck with both her hands. She wrenched it apart, tearing it down to the waist, to bare her sagging breasts to his gaze.

"Oh, my son, my baby," she pleaded, "have you no love, no reverence for these breasts that suckled you?"

Orestes stood paralyzed. Then he asked:

"Can I slay my mother, Pylades?"

"Remember the oracle of Apollo," said Pylades. "Choose, if you must, the reproach of all men, but never the anger of the gods."

The wild-eyed figure before him blurred. The room seemed to reel around him. But through the dark hallway came Electra's shrill voice:

"In the name of the gods, brother, do not let her talk. Strike! Strike! *Strike!*"

Clytemnestra heard it and paled. She stood transfixed as he came toward her, his eyes glazed. She could not reach him now.

O Apollo, she thought, this is the serpent I bore and suckled. . . .

When Orestes came out of his dream, she lay dead at his feet. Blood was dripping from the sword of Aegisthus in his hand.

He groped his way out to the daylight and found Chrysothemis weeping softly, but Electra's eyes shone with a fiery brightness.

"Justice dwells in the house," he said, then added, "if justice dwelt in Apollo's command."

"Is the wretched woman dead?" Electra asked.

"Yes, you no longer need fear the lash of her tyranny."

For a time they were silent. Chrysothemis all sadness, Electra all triumph, while triumph, sadness, and guilt all surged together in Orestes' mind.

The old man went now to the servants' quarters to make himself known to the serving women. Most of them, he knew, had been loyal to Agamemnon of old and should be ready to serve Orestes. They could hold any others in check. With Clytemnestra gone, he doubted if any would try to aid the usurper Aegisthus. Only let them keep silent and out of sight.

"Here he comes!" Electra cried as she caught sight of Aegisthus hurrying up from the marketplace. "Back, brother, back!"

Orestes' mind cleared. He had no doubts about Aegisthus. He returned to Pylades to prepare his welcome.

Aegisthus was all but out of breath when he came. "Where are the Phocian strangers?" he demanded. "I hear they have news of Orestes' death, yet I could draw little from the old dame's addled mind." He turned to Electra. "Come, you should know, you bold and thankless wretch."

"I know too well," Electra said, "for what has happened to my brother touches me most of all."

"Then, tell me first—where are the strangers?"

"Within—they have won their way to the heart of the queen."

"And they say for sure he is dead?"

"More than that. They have brought his body. But you will not find it a pleasant sight."

"For the first time," said Aegisthus, "your words bring me joy. I will show that body throughout Argos. It will teach all of those too stubborn to bow to my yoke that they have been feeding on empty hopes. Let them learn their lesson in time. Out of my way, girl! I must see for myself."

As he thrust her aside and rushed in, Electra said, "You were right, my sister. I yield to the strong."

Aegisthus paid little heed to the strangers as his eye fell on the shrouded form that lay by the altar.

"So—if the gods forgive me—may all my enemies feel the wrath of heaven," he cried. "Draw the cloth aside, strangers, that I may feast my eyes and mourn as a kinsman should."

"No, you should lift it yourself," Orestes said, "for one so dear to you."

"So I will," Aegisthus agreed. "But where is the queen? She should be here to share this moment."

"She is not far off," Orestes said.

Aegisthus could not wait. He jerked back the coverlet. His face paled and his eyes leaped out as he saw the ashen features of Clytemnestra.

"Why do you tremble so?" Orestes asked. "Do you not know her?"

"Who set this fiendish trap?" Aegisthus cried.

"Has the dead not revealed the living?'

"Orestes!" Aegisthus gasped.

"A late-come soothsayer!" jeered Orestes.

"I am destroyed," Aegisthus groaned. "But let me speak."

"Your deeds have spoken," Orestes said. "So take your last look on this sword that slew my father and judge how well it served you."

As Orestes advanced toward him, Aegisthus desperately drew from its sheath the sword he was wearing. Pylades was about to seize him, but Orestes waved him back. Then, for a time, there was a clash of blades as the two men thrust and parried. But soon the older man, weighed down with weariness and guilt, began to falter. Orestes lunged forward and Aegisthus sank to his knees. Another thrust and he lay dead beside the body of Clytemnestra.

"Father, I give you back your enemies," Orestes cried. Then he turned to Pylades, "Let the people be summoned that I may declare myself before them."

He felt no pang in Aegisthus' death. Justice, honor, ambition, love, and hate had all alike been satisfied. He had taken only the law's just price for adultery, treason, and tyranny.

But the corpse of Clytemnestra mocked his reason.

Her crime had been greater. For she had betrayed the sanctities of home and wedlock; her hands were red with a husband's blood. Yet she was still his mother. The deed was right but its doer accursed. He had plunged a sword in the breast that had nursed him, violated his own flesh, doomed, perhaps, his own soul. She had broken the laws of gods and men. And men were weak against tyrants. But surely the gods were strong. Why had they not smitten her down in their wrath? Why did he, a son honor-bound to avenge his father, have to serve as their instrument?

Why? Why? Madness was already closing in upon him when the people assembled to hear his story—the story he had to tell them before all his reason fled. They gazed in awe and horror as he stood, with reddened sword and garments, amid the proofs of crime and retribution—the tapestry that had trapped his father, the corpses of the slayers slain. Chrysothemis had fled to her chamber, but Electra stood nearby, leaning on the strong arm of Pylades.

Pointing to the bodies, Orestes began:

"Behold this pair of tyrants—the murderers of your king, my father, and the wasters of my home. You know how high they rode in majesty. Now you see how low they have sunk in love. They swore a compact to kill my father or die together. Now I have helped them keep that oath in double measure."

Though his mind was reeling, he struggled on:

"Look, too, at this deadly device that shackled my father hand and foot—the murderous shroud." He bade the servants hold it up that all might see how the hues and patterns of its embroidery were blurred by the long-dried stains of Agamemnon's blood. "Let the Father—not my sire who is dead, but the all-seeing sun—behold the impious handiwork of my mother. Let it be witness that justly I wrought her doom.

"Of the adulterous Aegisthus I need not speak. He has paid the lawful penalty. But it was she who devised this abomination against the husband whose children she bore in love, though later in hate she spurned them. What think you of her, this fangless eel of the sea whose touch alone can rot its victim? And what shall I call this thing—a curtain for a bath, a shroud, or a snare to delight the heart of a highway assassin?"

And now, he said, it would be fitting to praise his father—to pronounce the eulogy so long denied in his shameful death. But they all knew his worth, and there was little need or time.

"Instead," he said, "I shall speak of his victory, his and

mine. For it is a victory. And it is just—though I abhor it, for it sears my very soul."

Fierce terrors were beginning to sing and dance in his mind, but he fought against them, crying out, "I tell you it was just that I slew my mother. Apollo is my witness. He said I would be free of stain if I slew her, tormented if I let these evils lie. I call on him, on you, on all of Greece to speak for me, for I can no longer plead my case. My mind is overpowered. Like a blinded driver in a shattered chariot I can no longer hold the track; my wits are hurled about by frenzied steeds."

"Come, all is well," one elder told him. "Do not harness your mind to ill-omened words, for by one swift stroke you have lopped off the heads of two serpents who ravaged this land."

"The handmaids of wrath are upon me," Orestes cried, seeing visions of Gorgon forms, clothed in night, with writhing serpents in their hair.

"Come, you must not let your fears conjure such fancies," his old tutor told him.

"These are no fancies," Orestes cried, "but the hounds of my mother's wrath."

"Her blood is still wet on your hands," the old man said, "but these fears will pass."

"O Lord Apollo," Orestes cried, "they are coming upon me more and more. Their eyes are dripping with blood."

"Apollo's touch will heal you."

"You cannot see them," Orestes cried, "but I am pursued. I can stay no longer."

Wild-eyed, he plunged madly through their midst, down the steps, across the marketplace, through the streets of Argos and beyond its gates. On and on he went, the Furies howling in his wake. On and on toward Delphi, to the shrine of

Pythian Apollo, to the altar of the undying fire, to the stone that was called the navel of the earth.

Perhaps there the god would give him peace.

This Sophocles-based version of *Electra* does not hew strictly to the theme of the second play of Aeschylus' trilogy. In Aeschylus, Orestes is not so much an answer to Electra's prayers as a tortured man driven by the gods to commit an abhorrent crime in the name of justice. Aeschylus is gruesomely explicit on the point. Zeus, through Apollo, commands Orestes to slay his mother or suffer madness, exile, and a lingering death while his flesh rots away in leprous ulcers.

Several elements from Aeschylus were incorporated in our story, however. These include his version of Clytemnestra's dream, the character of the nurse, the confrontation of Orestes and his mother, and the closing scenes where Orestes tries to justify himself to the people before the Furies rob him of all reason.

The chain of evil is ultimately brought to an end in Aeschylus' third play, *Eumenides* (*The Furies*). The story of this play is a difficult, implausible one for modern readers. But in outline it goes like this:

Orestes, pursued by the Furies, who take shape as a foul and fiendish chorus, reaches Delphi and throws himself on the mercy of Apollo who commanded his crime. Apollo puts the Furies to sleep and tells Orestes to flee to the goddess Athene in Athens. As the Furies wake up muttering, the ghost of Clytemnestra goads them into taking up the pursuit again.

At Athens a trial is arranged on Ares' Hill, the Areopagus. There, Athene summons the leading elders of the city to inaugurate what historically became Athens' highest court of morals and criminal justice. Before this jury, the Furies prosecute Orestes, and Apollo defends him, each side citing some curious arguments.

The Furies say, for example, that they did not plague Clytemnestra because the husband she slew was not of her own kin.

By a still more curious argument Apollo insists that a son is no kin of his mother, that he is solely the child of his father and resides before birth as a stranger in his mother's body.

In the end, the Athenian elders are split in their verdict, and Orestes is mercifully acquitted by the tie-breaking vote of Athene. Thus, symbolically, the divine burden of vengeance is lifted from the individual to be assumed by the courts of men blessed with wisdom from the gods. Thus, too, did Aeschylus use his art as propaganda for the high court of the Areopagus which was under fire at the time as an undemocratic institution.

The play does not end here but continues as a cult pageant. The Furies are angry at the verdict and are appeased only when Athene promises that they will be given a shrine and worshiped forever by the Athenians under the new name of *Eumenides*—"the Kindly Ones." The play ends with a torchlight procession as they are led away to their sacred grotto.

We need not worry that Sophocles represented Oedipus as arriving in Colonus many years before to find the Furies already worshiped as the *Eumenides*. No one could ever harmonize all the wealth of Greek legend. And the creative inventiveness of the Greek drama only added to the inconsistency.

APPENDIX

APPENDIX
THE THEATER OF THE GREEKS

Despite the realism of many of its stories, Greek drama was highly conventional in its presentation. It was a fusion of all the arts into a form that no longer exists. Grand opera began as an attempt to recreate that form, but developed along very different lines. The form might be said to include even the architecture of the Greek theater itself.

Just as the drama developed out of the more ancient chorus, so the physical theater grew up around the place where that chorus danced. This dancing place, or *orchestra* (or-KEES-tra) as it was called, was a paved circle, 60 to 90 feet across, with an altar of Dionysus at its center. More than halfway around the outside of this circle, the spectators' seats rose in many tiers, as they do in a modern football stadium, sometimes seating as many as 30,000 or more.

STAGE AND SCENERY

Across the dancing circle from the spectators was some sort of stage, for the principal actors seldom came in direct contact with the chorus. The stage had movable painted scenery, though this scenery was rarely, if ever, changed in the course of a single play. Many of the most important actions did not take place on that stage, however, for murder and violence were never portrayed before the eyes of the audience.

Such actions supposedly occurred offstage but were vividly described soon afterward by a wild-eyed messenger who rushed in with the news. An example of this is the servant of Medea who describes the deaths in the palace. In story form, however, the traditional tragic messenger can usually be eliminated by taking the readers directly to the scene of the crime. In a story one is also free to let some other actions happen in more appropriate places than the single stage setting.

The setting of most Greek plays was a palace courtyard. The audience often heard threats and screams from within the palace, but never saw the murder take place. Immediately afterward, however, the doors would open wide to show the room inside, corpse, assassins, and all. Then the whole room itself would roll forward into the sunlight for a clearer view, for it was built on a smaller stage with concealed wheels.

DEUS EX MACHINA

The strangest devices of the Greek theater were the "machines" which were used to make the gods fly through the air. The picture of a god dangling by ropes from a derrick certainly must have taxed even the facile imagination of the Greek audiences. It has been suggested that the machines might have been some sort of elevator located behind the scenery. Such a device would give the illusion of the god mysteriously floating up and stepping forth on the palace roof.

Euripides used the gods rather freely in his plays. He was accused, a bit unfairly, of always bringing in a machine-borne god whenever his plot became too tangled to manage any other way. The term *deus ex machina* is now used by critics to label any kind of trick an author uses to make something happen for no good reason except that he wants it to happen.

THE CHORUS

The chorus, numbering twelve or fifteen, was the oldest part of the drama. In early times the story and action of the dramas emerged only as little bits of realism set in the midst of choral dance and song. Eventually, however, the play became the thing, and the choral parts dwindled to interludes. As actors contended among themselves, the chorus became little more than passive observers and commentators on the action taking place—a sort of intermediate audience which the playwright could use to guide the real one.

Once it appeared, the chorus remained on stage for the rest of the play. Hence, its presence could be awkward when scenes of intrigue developed. Somewhat artificially, the members of the chorus would have to be sworn to secrecy. If one wonders why the women of Corinth did so little to stop Medea, the technical answer is that they were a chorus, and by convention were almost as helpless as the audience. Often, where the conventional chorus becomes psychologically irrelevant and unrealistic I leave it out. Thus, in *Hippolytus*, for example, the story spares Phaedra the embarrassment of disclosing her love life to the gossipy women of Troezen.

Some choral odes, however, are so justly famous, that they are retained, complete or in substance, even though they delay the story. On the other hand, some of the "That reminds me" odes, which are full of obscure allusions to other legends are dropped for the sake of the general reader. Where a chorus seems to be the playwright's voice, its sentiments are incorporated in the narration. The reader may assume that all unspecified characters are, in the original play, part of the chorus.

POETRY, DANCE, AND SONG

The actors spoke all their lines in iambic trimeter—much like the blank verse so common to Shakespeare. The chorus, however, sang its lines, in a variety of lyric meters, while dancing in appropriate measures. Often the chorus was divided into two groups, responding to each other in equal stanzas. Sometimes the chorus leader entered into spoken dialog with the actors, and in some highly emotional passages, an actor and the chorus responded to each other in song.

The lyric poetry of the Greeks, with its subtly interwoven patterns of sounds and contexts, can never be translated exactly. There have been poetic translations of Greek tragedy, it is true, but these are translations that have been reworked into some kind of English poetry.

MASKS AND ACTORS

The mask seems common to primitive ritual almost everywhere. In Greek drama it served the practical purpose of letting one actor play several different roles. Apart from the chorus, most Greek dramas were presented by only three actors—all men. We even hear of an ancient "method" actor who played Electra. In the famous urn scene he is supposed to have carried the ashes of his own dead son to induce the right emotions.

Nevertheless, the masks must have greatly hampered emotional expression. Between scenes an actor could change masks to denote a change from serenity to anguish, for example, but throughout a scene he could wear only one expression. Hence actors were often forced to talk of their feelings. However, the strict conventions about the form and color of wigs and costumes let the audience immediately identify what sort of character it was seeing.

The actors faced still another handicap in later times. As theaters grew, so did the actors—with "elevator" boots, extensive body padding, and masks that exaggerated the height of their foreheads. Thus, any vigorous bodily action must have been ruled out.

PROLOGUES

A Greek chorus never came on stage until the play was well under way; all that happened before its appearance was termed the prologue. There were no programs to guide the audience and no curtain. One or more characters came out on the stage. Their opening lines would usually reveal their names, the place, and enough about the situation for the audience to know what it was all about. This knowledge was easy to grasp, for the tight, unified stories of Greek tragedy have been likened to fifth acts of Shakespeare for audiences who did not need to be told the other four.

The basic facts of the old legends were seldom altered, except by Euripides. So the audience, already knowing the chief characters and complications, was ready to be plunged *in medias res*—into the middle of an action already approaching its denouement when problems created by earlier events would be untangled. Since modern readers need more background, some of our stories have to start differently, though elsewhere they depart very little from the original dialog or structure.

Sophocles' prologues usually begin dramatically with two or more actors—perhaps in an argument as in *Antigone* or laying plans as in *Electra*. Less realistic is the soliloquy of the lone watchman on the rooftop in *Agamemnon*. Still less so is an audience-briefing by a *deus ex machina*.

Euripides, especially, is guilty of many flat prologues. In *Hippolytus*, for example, Aphrodite appears to tell the audience not only what has happened but also to reveal the whole plot in advance. She was eliminated in my story because, fortunately, authors like gods can be omniscient revealers. Whoever rewrote Euripides' *Iphigenia in Aulis* used the more modern technique of having Agamemnon explain his troubles to a servant while the audience listened in. We see both techniques in *Medea*—first a flat prologue by the nurse, then a more dramatic explication in her argument with the old servant.

SET SPEECHES

In addition to masks, choruses, messengers, gods, and flat prologues, a modern theatergoer might be disturbed by the long, unnatural set speeches. These I have sometimes tried to shorten or break up with interruptions. Like Hamlet's soliloquy, they are a lure and a challenge to great actors. Some of the set speeches are marvelous articulations of thought that few people could or would put into words in real life. Others are almost show-piece declamations. But the Greeks loved oratory and subtle debate. They might demand encores for particularly good renditions, and they were not likely to mind —any more than we object to songs in opera—if these things were stretched far beyond the bounds of realism.

THE THREE UNITIES

Some might add to this list of conventions the three unities of plot, time, and place. But the latter two were occasionally "violated," and their usual observance was more from habit or convenience of staging than from any canon of artistry. Contrary to popular belief, Aristotle, the great critic of Greek drama, demanded only one unity—the unity of action or story. He merely remarked that most plays did occur within one day "or a little more." Of unity of place he said nothing.

Down through the ages many have tried to achieve the greatness of Aeschylus, Sophocles, and Euripides, by aping conventions suitable only to their own time and place. What made these dramatists great was not the "rules" they followed but their search for truth, their insight into the souls and minds of men, their artistic discipline, and above all, their creative genius.

As a student of the classics, a teacher, and a newsman, H.R. JOLLIFFE was particularly suited to presenting modern readers with a vivid account of the great plays of ancient Greece. Jolliffe first learned these marvelous tales from his father, a professor of classics in Canada. He labored through their grammar and syntax while pursuing his Ph.D. in Latin and Greek at the University of Chicago, then taught them in translation to his students.

Prior to 1945, Dr. Jolliffe taught primarily classical languages at Albert, Brandon and Victoria Colleges in Canada, and at Tulane and Ohio State Universities in the United States. His increasing interest in journalism – dating back to a 1929-32 stint in the editorial department of the *Toronto Star* – prompted him to change his focus to journalism which he taught for two years at Ohio State and for twenty years at Michigan State.

In 1960 Jolliffe became an exchange professor in Afghanistan at the invitation of the government. He established a school of journalism there and wrote the textbook for it. He made national headlines in 1963 by participating in efforts to circumvent a segregation law barring white instructors from teaching at the all-Black campus of Mississippi's Jackson State College. He lectured Jackson State students on Greek drama via telephone from his Michigan home.

Greek Drama in Translation by Robert Emmet Meagher

Euripides: Iphigenia at Aulis and Iphigenia in Tauris
176 pp. (1993) Hardbound, ISBN 0-86516-266-2

Euripides: Bakkhai
vi + 97 pp. (1995) Paperback, ISBN 0-86516-285-9

Euripides: Hekabe
viii + 55 pp. (1995) Paperback, ISBN 0-86516-330-8

Aeschylus: Seven Against Thebes
x + 44 pp. (1996) Paperback, ISBN 0-86516-337-5

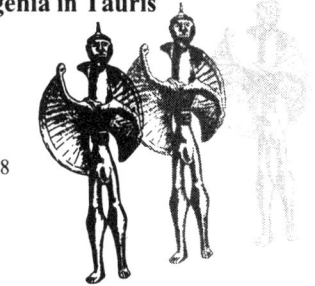

I feel a very strong admiration for Robert Meagher. He has a talent for making a classical text spring to life...certainly knows how to write for actors.
—**Irene Papas**
Actress

Robert Meagher is the finest living translator of ancient Greek drama.
—**Michael Joyce**
Samuel Beckett Centre, Dublin
and the Royal National Theatre of Great Britain

In Robert Emmet Meagher's translations, Greek drama springs to life with poetic immediacy, elevating the past into a timeless present.
—**Michael Cacoyannis**
Director, *Iphigenia* and *Zorba the Greek*

Greek Drama in Translation by Paul Roche

Three Plays by Plautus
288 pp. (1968, Reprint 1984) Paperback, ISBN 0-86516-035-X

Aeschylus Prometheus Bound
128 pp. (1962, Reprint 1998) Paperback, ISBN 0-86516-238-7
Illustrated by Thom Kapheim

Plautus made comedy what it is today.
—**Paul Roche**

His translations of Aeschylus are the best I have ever read.
—**Edith Hamilton**

A triumph in directness and dramatic force. Those incredible choruses come thorugh as exciting and beautiful poetry.
—**Bernard Knox**